THE BODY, SELF-CULTIVATION, AND KI-ENERGY

SUNY Series, The Body in Culture, History, and Religion
Howard Eilberg-Schwartz, Editor

THE BODY, SELF-CULTIVATION, AND KI-ENERGY

YUASA Yasuo

Translated by

Shigenori Nagatomo and
Monte S. Hull

State University
of New York
Press

Published by
State University of New York Press, Albany

Printed in the United States of America

For information, address State University of New York Press,
State University Plaza, Albany, N.Y. 12246

Production by M. R. Mulholland
Marketing by Dana E. Yanulavich

Library of Congress Cataloging-in-Publication Data

Yuasa, Yasuo.
[Ki, shugyō, shintai. English]
The body, self-cultivation, and ki-energy / Yasuo Yuasa ;
translated by Shigenori Nagatomo and Monte S. Hull.
p. cm.—(SUNY series, the body in culture, history, and
religion)
Includes bibliographical references and index.
ISBN 0-7914-1623-2 (alk. paper).—ISBN 0-7914-1624-0 (pbk. :
alk. paper)
1. Ch'i (Chinese philosophy) 2. Body, Human (Philosophy) 3. Self
-actualization (Psychology) 4. Philosophy and science.
5. Philosophy, Comparative. I. Nagatomo, Shigenori. II. Hull,
Monte S. III. Title. IV. Series.
B127.C49Y83 1993
128—dc20 92-36569
CIP
Rev

10 9 8 7 6 5 4 3

CONTENTS

Translator's Introduction ix

Author's Preface to the English Version 1

PART I: EASTERN MIND-BODY THEORY AND THE CONTEMPORARY PERIOD

Chapter 1 Eastern Mind-Body Theory

I. Introduction 7
II. The Eastern Tradition of Self-Cultivation and Western Mind-Body Dualism 7
III. Meditation in Stillness and in Motion 10
IV. Meditation and Psychotherapy 14
V. Meditation and Mind-Body Oneness 20
VI. Self-Cultivation and Artistry 23
VII. Characteristics of the Japanese Martial Arts 28

Chapter 2 Beyond the Contemporary Period

I. From Disjunctive Mind-Body Dualism to Correlative Mind-Body Dualism 37
II. Three Information Systems in the Body 42
III. Conditioned Reflex and Control of the Autonomic Nerves 55
IV. A Methodological Reflection 61

PART II: *KI* AND THE BODY: MARTIAL ARTS, MEDITATION METHODS, AND EASTERN MEDICINE

Chapter 3 *Ki* and the Body in the Martial Arts and Meditation Methods

I. Introduction 69
II. Unifying Mind and *Ki*-Energy 70
III. Meditation Training Transforms *Ki* 76

IV. The Transformation of *Ki* 82
V. Aspects of Inner Image Experiences Accompanying the Transformation of *Ki* 90
VI. The Meaning of Knowledge in Eastern Thought: An Intermediary Methodological Investigation 97

Chapter 4 *Ki* and the Body in Eastern Medicine

I. Introduction 99
II. Fundamental Characteristics of Eastern Medicine's Theory of the Body 100
III. The Relationship Between *Ki* and Emotion in the Meridians 109
IV. The Unconscious Quasi-Body's Function Directed Toward the External World 118
V. Memory and the Lived Body 122

PART III: THE PRESENT AND FUTURE OF THE SCIENCE OF *KI*

Chapter 5 The Science of *Ki* and Its View of Human Being

I. Introduction 131
II. *Ki*-Energy and Its Relation to the External World 133
III. Transpersonal Synchronization of *Ki* and the Problem of Teleology 142

Chapter 6 *Ki* and the Problem of Paranormal Phenomena

I. Introduction 149
II. Problematics of the Dispute 152
III. An Assessment of Parapsychology 157
IV. The Need for an Epistemological Critique of Modern Science 163
V. Beyond Causality 169

Chapter 7 Toward an East-West Dialogue

I. Teleology and Science 175
II. Objectivistic Science and Subjectivistic Science 178

III. Concluding Remarks: Mind, Life, and Matter 182

Postscript *189*

Notes *193*

Glossary *215*

Index *225*

TRANSLATOR'S INTRODUCTION

> The progress of science and technology in modern times shows for the destiny of the human species two faces, like the two-headed god Janus. One face revealed by science and technology is that of the God of Light brightly illuminating the future for humanity and guaranteeing an affluent and pleasant happiness. The other face is the God of Darkness, who betrays a power that could bring terrifying destruction to the world and humankind. Today we are confronting the God with these two faces.
>
> —YUASA Yasuo, from the preface to *New Age Science and the Science of Ki-Energy*

I. INTRODUCTION

We are approaching the end of this century and preparing to welcome the dawn of a new century, which we hope will be mindful of a global perspective on everything human and yet will also acknowledge the traditional cultural differences that each nation and ethnic group has long cherished. In this transitional period we may expect the hitherto accepted intellectual paradigm to be questioned in an effort to erect a new one most appropriate for the coming generations, so that they can enjoy a maximum sense of *eudaimonia* while dwelling on this beautiful planet, Earth.[1] A change in the paradigm of thinking is called for now especially, considering the adverse, shadow effects which science and technology, along with their shining marvels, have brought to us on a global scale ranging from environmental issues to dehumanization in every aspect of our life.[2]

When the rise of a new theory suggests a change of direction in scholarship, history attests to a common pattern of reaction among the established intellectual community. There is often flat dismissal or at best vehement attack in order to kill and bury the theory, especially if it signals an imminent as well as immanent possibility of shaking the secure and comfortable foundation upon which the existing paradigm of thinking rests. While such an attitude is understandable, since human beings including intellectuals are often chained to their habits[3] through their fragile, incarnate nature,[4] there is equally another tendency observed in history. If a theory accords with and reflects the *Zeitgeist* of a given period, the latter allows the theory to permeate it, though unknowingly, through the inner chamber of its intellectual life.

Although it is not the task of a translator to predict the future course of Yuasa's *The Body, Self-Cultivation, and Ki-Energy* in the English-speaking world, Yuasa does attempt a thoughtful and provocative project, addressing to the reader several broad and significant questions: (1) Is it not time now to articulate the essential philosophical reason for the current global situation? (2) Can we not trace it to views of human nature and the world espoused by the modern Western paradigm of scientific thinking?[5] (3) Can East Asia make any significant contribution to tackling this issue? In responding to these questions[6] Yuasa draws on his scholarship that covers, just to mention the relevant fields of Western and Eastern scholarship, philosophy, depth psychology, medical science, modern sports, and parapsychology; and, their approximate Eastern counterparts, Buddhism, Daoism, Eastern medicine, the martial arts, and *qìgōng* (Chin.; Jap. *kikō*).[7] Yuasa is probably unique as a philosopher in his ability to bring these diverse fields into a unified thematic inquiry—a very rare interdisciplinary feast. Yuasa moves with admirable freedom through these diverse fields of scholarship, and his inquiry in *The Body, Self-Cultivation, and Ki-Energy* has an uncompromising lucidity that also makes it accessible to the non-specialist.

With these intellectual tools in full operation, Yuasa questions the philosophical assumptions of the scientific paradigm of thinking based on the Cartesian *disjunctive* mind-body dualism, and evaluates it from an Eastern (or East Asian) perspective of mind-body oneness achieved through the practice of self-cultivation. In so doing, he offers a corrective to the paradigm by examining a unique, psychophysical energy phenomenon, called *ki,* which cannot properly be accommodated by the ontological and methodological foundation of mind-body dualism. Yuasa invites the reader to a thought-experiment that calls for an epistemological critique of the existing scientific paradigm of thinking.

In this introduction to *The Body, Self-Cultivation, and Ki-Energy* I will (1) outline an overview of Yuasa's project, and (2) sketch a synoptic summary of each chapter.

II. AN OVERVIEW OF YUASA'S PROJECT

I would like to sketch briefly the overall organization of *The Body, Self-Cultivation, and Ki-Energy* to show the strategy of Yuasa's bold and provocative project. In part I he examines the Eastern mind-body theory from an historical perspective, clarifying its ideal embodiment of achieved mind-body oneness (chapter 1), and he reinterprets and reevaluates the significance of this theory from a contemporary perspective, incorporating research especially from depth psychology, medical science, and physiological psychology (chapter 2). These chapters establish the relevance of the Eastern mind-body theory for the contemporary period while pointing out a direction whereby future scholarship may be guided, as Yuasa envisions, into the intermediary domain between science and religion.[8] Accordingly, these two chapters prepare Yuasa to pave the way beyond the contemporary period, although this larger task is deferred until part III.

In part II Yuasa examines the concept of the body and its relationship with *ki*-energy as the latter bears on martial arts, meditation methods, and Eastern medicine. Since "*ki*-energy"[9] is an unfamiliar concept to most Western readers, it may be helpful to offer a preliminary understanding. In the Japanese language, the phrase translated as "*ki*-energy" is simply "*ki*," without specifically suggesting that it is a type of energy. The translators have added the term "energy" to suggest that it can be approached as energy phenomena, and also because Yuasa maintains that it is detectable as energy phenomena. The scope which this concept covers is very comprehensive; it can include, for example, a climatic condition, an arising social condition, a psychological and pathological condition. It also extends to cover a power expressed in fine arts, martial arts, and literature.[10] To give some idea of how this term is used in Japanese, we may cite a few examples. In referring to the weather, when "heaven's *ki* is bad," it means bad weather. Or when two persons are congenial to each other, it is expressed as "*ki ga au*," literally meaning "*ki* accords with each other [in these persons]." Or when a person encounters a situation, person, or place which gives off a strange, eerie, and perhaps suspicious sensation, Japanese uses the expression "*ki mi ga warui,*" that is, "the taste of *ki* is bad."

Yuasa, while confining his use of the term "*ki*" to human beings and their living environment, defines *ki*-energy as a third term with a *psychophysical* character that cannot be properly accommodated within the dualistic paradigm of thinking. The important point to keep in mind about this concept now is that it is not arrived at merely through intellectual abstraction, but is derived also from the observation of empirical phenomena detectable both experientially and experimentally in and around the human body (chapter 3).

Yuasa goes on to articulate the fundamental characteristics of Eastern medicine, particularly acupuncture medicine, while making comparisons with Western medical science. According to acupuncture medicine, an invisible psychophysical *ki*-energy circulates within the interior of the body, while at the same time intermingling with the *ki*-energy pervasively present in the environment including that of other persons.[11] Through his analysis of *ki*-energy, Yuasa provides the empirical basis for the old wisdom that human being *qua* microcosm is correlative with the physical universe *qua* macrocosm (chapter 4).

In part III Yuasa introduces recent results of experimental research on *ki*-energy in China and Japan, and through its careful analysis he proposes the need for an epistemological critique of the existing scientific paradigm of thinking. To accomplish this bold and provocative task Yuasa introduces scientific measurements of the external emission and "transpersonal synchronization" of *ki*-energy, and draws the conclusion that these phenomena admit of explanation by teleological synchronicity rather than causality. Behind Yuasa's discussion of the "science of *ki*" is his concern to articulate the view of human being characteristic of the East (chapter 5). Yuasa then examines the methodological problems of parapsychological research and attempts to overcome them from the standpoint of *ki* research. In so doing he contends that *ki* research offers an ontological and methodological perspective that will squarely question the scientific paradigm of thinking, particularly its principles of causality and the repeatability of experiments. In this manner Yuasa attempts to go "beyond causality" (chapter 6). This issue leads him to examine the meaning of teleology, for he believes that teleology is at work in parapsychological phenomena which occur, according to Yuasa, due to the synchronistic principle. For this purpose he interprets Jung's hypothesis of synchronicity while relating it to the salient characteristics of paranormal phenomena, a new movement in physics toward the indistinguishability of mind and matter at the micro level, and the worldview espoused by the ancient Chinese text *Yìjīng*. In so doing Yuasa criticizes the scientific attitude that excludes the investigation of meaning, value, and purpose, and affirms that science is not the final judge on everything. Behind his criticism is the Eastern worldview in which nature is a stage upon which its original activity expresses itself vis-à-vis *ki*-energy through a vessel that is the human being. The concluding chapter, designed as "an East-West Dialogue," brings out the importance of human being as a life phenomenon resonating with the invigorating activity of nature. Let us now examine a little more closely the content of each chapter.

III. SYNOPSIS OF CHAPTERS 1 AND 2 (PART I)

In chapter 1, "Eastern Mind-Body Theory," Yuasa's main concern is to explicate, from an historical perspective, the Eastern mind-body theory uniquely inherited in the various Eastern religious-philosophical system such as Yoga, Buddhism, and Daoism. The focus of his analysis, however, is on the methods of self-cultivation (*shugyōhō*) in the Japanese cultural and historical tradition. His analysis begins first with Buddhist meditation methods, since these have played an important role in Japanese cultural and intellectual history. For example, Japanese Buddhism is unthinkable without meditative self-cultivation, particularly the method of "meditation in motion," at its experiential foundation. Yuasa succinctly traces its influence through Nō theater, the theory of *waka* composition, the way of the samurai warrior, and the martial arts.

All forms of self-cultivation utilize in one way or another the body, or more precisely "one's own body," as a vehicle for cultivating one's self. Yuasa's philosophical quest begins here. How is the body understood within the tradition of self-cultivation methods? According to Yuasa's study, the philosophy of self-cultivation stipulates the goal of "enhancing the mind (or spirit) by training the body." In order to correct the distortions of the mind, one must first correct the modality of the body such as in desire, emotion, and instinct, and suspend the theoretical question of what *is* the relationship between the mind and body. It is foremost a practical project of enhancing the spirit by training the body. Yuasa thinks that this understanding presupposes an inseparable oneness of mind and body. For if the modality of the mind can be corrected by correcting the modality of the body, it presupposes a correlative relationship between the functions of the mind and the body. Otherwise, the practical project of self-cultivation is a futile attempt. But Yuasa convincingly demonstrates that this presupposition is in fact verified by many Buddhists' accounts of their meditational experience. For instance, Myōe (1173–1232) characterizes his deep meditative experience as "crystallization of mind and body" and Dōgen (1200–1253) as "casting off mind and body." Both of these examples describe, according to Yuasa, an experience in which the distinction between mind and body has disappeared.

Accordingly, self-cultivation methods have the following philosophical scheme: they presuppose an initial correlative or provisional dualism between mind and body. This characterizes our everyday "natural attitude." But once the project is completed, it holds the position of inseparable mind-body oneness, which culminates in Buddhism as *satori* and in Daoism as Dao. In short, the philosophy of self-cultivation within the Japanese intellectual tradition recognizes an existential transformation from provisional dualism to non-dualism.[12]

In meditational self-cultivation, then, the meditator learns to correct the various distortions of his or her psyche and balances the competing forces of consciousness and the unconscious. Yuasa describes this experiential process of meditation while relating it to the structure of various kinds of altered states of consciousness (ASC) including dream experience and sensory deprivation.

Yuasa's study shows that the goal of self-cultivation parallels in a certain respect that of the depth-psychological method, especially its idea of synthesizing unconscious complexes within consciousness as, for example, in Jung's transcendent function. Yuasa points out, however, that the Eastern concept of meditative self-cultivation differs from depth psychology in that the latter aims at bringing the subnormal to the normal, while the former focuses on elevating the normal to the supernormal. Furthermore, he demonstrates that the goal of modern sports also differs from Eastern self-cultivation because it aims only at enhancing the motor capacities of the muscles in the limbs without attempting to enhance the spirit or personality. This shortcoming also applies to the methodological assumption accepted by medical science, which mainly investigates the anatomical organization of the body and its physiological function, ignoring the problem of mind. In short, Yuasa contends that both modern sports and medical science have inherited the Christian spirit-flesh dualism via its secularization in the Cartesian mind-body dualism, which goes back still further to the Greek distinction between *eidos* and *hylé*. Guided by the Aristotelian either-or logic, they have emphasized only one aspect of the whole person. Can we be satisfied with becoming only half of a person?

The practical consequence of Eastern self-cultivation, as for example embodied in the martial arts, is perfection of one's personality vis-à-vis achieving mind-body oneness, or alternatively the state of "no-mind." According to Yuasa this is the ethical as well as spiritual significance of self-cultivation. Through the achieved ideal of self-cultivation he implies that humans can relate to each other through accommodation while harmonizing the *ki*-energy shared between "I" and "the other." This consequence differs radically from the Western concept of the individual wherein one feels from within a split between rationality and irrationality, as well as the anxiety of an ex-istence facing alienation; these are the unfortunate and unnecessary consequences of accepting the dualism.

Chapter 2 is entitled "Beyond the Contemporary Period," which signals Yuasa's implicit agenda for the whole book: to go beyond the existential situation of ethical and spiritual crisis for the contemporary person, by offering an Eastern view of human nature. Explicitly, however, Yuasa analyzes in this chapter contemporary mind-body theories as developed in depth psychology (starting with Freud), in Selyé's stress theory, and in neurophysiology, and shows that these fields are moving toward a *correlative* dualism which recognizes the intimate functional interrelationship between mind and body—a change gradually taking place within the Western world. This correlative dualism differs from the Cartesian *disjunctive* dualism accepted, for example, in modern organ-oriented medicine. Yuasa explains that the above fields do not accept a reductionism of the mind, either by reducing it to the mechanism of matter or by reducing the whole to its parts. Nor do they presuppose a one-to-one causal relationship between the mind and the body (e.g., stress theory), which is a rejection of one of the cardinal pillars of science.

Given this new development of correlative mind-body theory, Yuasa wonders if he might not be able to articulate the meaning and mechanism of meditational self-cultivation from the standpoint of contemporary physiological psychology. Behind this question the reader may sense Yuasa's efforts to resurrect the value of the traditional wisdom nurtured in the East. In responding to this question, he devises his innovative and comprehensive concept of the body-scheme, taking the lived body as an information system.[13] He conceives the body-scheme as consisting of three layered circuits.[14] This is a further conceptual refinement of the dual structure Yuasa proposed in his earlier book, *Body: Toward an Eastern Mind-Body Theory.*[15] A brief explanation of these three circuits may be in order here.

Yuasa calls the first circuit the "external sensory-motor circuit," following the models of Bergson, Merleau-Ponty, and Penfield. It designates the activity of sensory nerves passively receiving stimulus from the external world and the activity of motor nerves actively responding to it. The second circuit concerns an information apparatus which enables us to become aware of internal conditions in the body. It is termed the "circuit of coenesthesis" and is comprised of two further circuits, "kinesthesis" and "somesthesis."

According to Yuasa, the circuit of "kinesthesis" designates the activity of sensory motor nerves attached to the motor organs. We become aware of this circuit through motor sensation. He points out that this motor sensation is found in the *periphery* of the Cartesian *ego cogito* represented by such mental activities as thinking, willing, feeling, emotion, and imagination. The second circuit within the circuit of coenesthesis is called the "circuit of somesthesis" which is comprised, among other things, of splanchnic nerves that inform our brain of the condition of the visceral organs, though our awareness of it may be dim due to the small area on the neoencephalon receptive to this condition. It is a dark and vague (protopathic) sensation found further back at the periphery of motor sensation. This circuit is compared to a biofeedback mechanism, although Yuasa admits that we do not have sufficient understanding of this mechanism, since there is insufficient knowledge connecting the psychological function of memory with its corresponding physiological function. At any rate, the circuit of coenesthesis consists of these two circuits of kinesthesis and somesthesis, and experientially, as Yuasa informs us, it is felt as an awareness of one's body.

Yuasa calls the third information circuit the "emotion-instinct circuit," which is governed by the autonomic nerves. Noting its close ties to emotion and instinct, he considers this circuit essential for maintaining the life of a body, for without its functioning life ceases. A main characteristic of this information system is that it does not reach the neoencephalon. In other words, the activity of the visceral organs are not, under normal circumstances, brought to our awareness. This circuit converts the stimulus received through a sensory organ into an emotional response (pleasure or pain) or information about stress, which affect the activity of the visceral organs. Because of this conversion, Yuasa points out that this circuit holistically affects the whole person.

A major characteristic of Yuasa's foregoing concept of the body scheme is that, epistemologically speaking, one's awareness decreases as one moves from the first to the third circuit, but this increases the chance of being controlled by them. In incorporating the second and third circuits within his inquiry, Yuasa has broadened the scope of the concept of the body-scheme, and thus brought out a deeper dimension of our experience. The majority of Western philosophers interested in mind-body theory have been concerned solely with the first external sensory motor circuit and rarely with the circuit of kinesthesis.[16] As Yuasa makes clear, it was through depth psychologists and psychiatrists interested in Eastern self-cultivation methods that the importance of the second and third circuits became evident for the health of an individual.

In examining the Eastern meditational self-cultivation method in light of the foregoing psychophysiological standpoint, Yuasa makes the important observation that meditational training has the effect of correcting distortions in the emotion-instinct circuit, that is, of dissolving unconscious emotional complexes which cannot otherwise be fully controlled by conscious will. In other words, meditation has a practical goal of enhancing the intimate *correlativity* between the psychological functions of the mind and the physiological functions of the body. Philosophically interpreted this means that meditational self-cultivation is to achieve an intimate oneness of mind and body. Here the reader will find a further refinement as well as confirmation of the thesis developed in chapter 1.

In this connection, Yuasa analyzes the meaning of controlling the emotion-instinct circuit, that is, of controlling the autonomic nerves in the contemporary theory of conditioned reflex, to substantiate his earlier claim that meditation corrects distortions in the emotion-instinct circuit. Pavlov's theory of conditioned reflex established that a connection can be made between a stimulus to the sensory organ and the autonomic nerves through the function of emotion rooted in instinct. (This is seen in Pavlov's experiment where a dog's salivation is aroused via its appetite and the ringing of a bell.) The emotion-instinct in this case is responsible for creating a temporary connection between the otherwise uncontrollable function of the autonomic nerves and sensory stimulus. Together with this analysis, Yuasa shows that the working of conditioned reflex parallels the theory of depth psychology in that the emotional complex suppressed beneath consciousness distorts the balance kept in the autonomic nervous system, creating a dysfunction in the visceral organ.

Applying this knowledge to the Eastern meditational self-cultivation method, Yuasa advances an interpretation that meditation is a practical way of developing the functions of both the autonomic nervous system and the emotions to a higher degree of correlativity. His interpretation is based on the mechanism evident in breathing exercises, which all forms of self-cultivation methods emphasize as an integral part of training. Neurophysiologically speaking, breathing has an ambiguous function: it is most of the time unconsciously performed, because it is controlled by the muscles attached to the autonomic nerves, and yet it can also be consciously controlled. Taking advantage of the latter fact, breathing exercise in meditational self-cultivation consciously works on the autonomic nerves so as to correct or eliminate the emotional distortion in the unconscious. Through this Yuasa demonstrates that the theory of conditioned reflex supports the significance of meditative self-cultivation from a neurophysiological standpoint.

At the end of chapter 2 is a brief methodological reflection that is helpful for understanding the Eastern pattern of thinking, particularly Yuasa's foregoing analysis of meditational self-cultivation. Yuasa emphasizes that the Eastern standard for analysis is those who have achieved, after long training, a high degree of mind-body capacity, and this standard remains simply an ideal possibility for the average person. In contrast, the West has focused on the average, ordinary person for analysis in formulating hypotheses. Empirical laws thus formulated have a general validity. Yuasa's analysis shows, however, that this methodological procedure tends to ignore exceptional cases. A case in point is the concept of being "normal" and "healthy." According to this model, anyone who falls outside of the average mean is labeled either "abnormal" or "unhealthy." Yet, Yuasa asks, shouldn't we recognize that there are two kinds of "abnormality"? One is subnormal and the other supernormal. Eastern mind-body theory, focusing on the supernormal, has attempted to understand a deeper, potential mechanism which remains opaque and incomprehensible when one studies only the average person's mind-body capacity. This is, for example, evident in Yuasa's own schematization of the second and third information circuits within his concept of body-scheme.

IV. SYNOPSIS OF CHAPTERS 3 AND 4 (PART II)

Yuasa's general plan for part II is to delve into the concept of the lived body as it is understood in the martial arts, Daoist meditation methods, and Eastern (acupuncture) medicine, while using the concept and phenomenon of *ki*-energy as a key, pivotal concept. He does this with a view to articulating Eastern views of human nature and the world.

In chapter 3, "*Ki* and the Body in the Martial Arts and Meditation Methods," Yuasa begins with the analysis of an ultimate technical secret sought in Japanese martial arts, that of "unifying mind with *ki*-energy." This secret lies in developing the area a couple of inches below the navel, called *seika tanden,* which is believed to store an abundance of *ki*-energy. The martial artist learns to control this energy center within one's own body as well as in that of an opponent, that is, one learns to detect the flow of *ki*-energy in oneself and in others. In doing this one faces one's surrounding external environment, the world of matter. In this situation, Yuasa interprets "unifying the mind with *ki*-energy" to mean that "the mind comes to feel the flow of *ki*" between the inner world (mind) and the outer world (matter) by using the intermediary being of "one's own body," which is distinguished from the world of matter by virtue of its feeling of being "alive." Here, the concept of "one's own body" functions as an indispensable mediator. Yuasa contends that the Eastern mind-body theory has attempted to understand "one's own body" *qua* life phenomenon, which would remain incomprehensible within the Cartesian dichotomy.

Ki in this context is understood more specifically as "a function intuitively apprehended as a sensation of power arising from the base of coenesthesis." By the phrase, "the base of coenesthesis," Yuasa means that this function belongs to the unconscious, indicating that its access is denied to everyday consciousness. However, through mind-body training in meditation and breathing exercises, Yuasa states that the mind gradually becomes capable of detecting its flow. He illustrates this process through experiences recounted in Eugen Herrigel's *Zen and the Art of Archery* in which *ki* is explained as "a spiritual power" flowing throughout the body.

In order to conceptually refine the process whereby the mind comes to detect the flow of *ki*-energy, Yuasa turns to an analysis of the meditational process that brings about the transformation of *ki*-energy. His task here is to conceptually differentiate *ki*-energy into its materially based energy and its subtle spiritual energy. Following a Daoist interpretation, Yuasa shows that meditation transforms the materially based *ki*-energy (or sexual libido) into a subtle spiritual energy, which Yuasa interprets to be an awakening and activation of original human nature, or Dao, a fount of creativity. In the Daoist meditational method, this process of transformation is understood as reversing the predominance of *yīn* over *yáng ki*-energy that characterizes our everyday mode of existence. Yuasa also supplements his explanation by approximating this Daoist scheme to Freudian and Jungian psychoanalysis.

Yuasa next examines the meaning of reversing the predominance of *yīn* over *yáng ki*-energy in more concrete detail, focusing on a Daoist text, *The Secret of the Golden Flower.*[17] This text claims that original human nature, or Dao, lies dormant between the eyes and is symbolically expressed as "heavenly light." However, this "heavenly light" is inactive in our everyday existence because conscious activity suppresses it, or in other words because *yīn* predominates over *yáng*. To awaken this dormant original light, the text states that the meditator must "circulate the light" in a reverse direction by adjusting the breath so as to enter the state of true or pure *yáng*. Reversing is understood as a way to restore original human nature or Dao, and to change the relative dominance of *yīn* over *yáng*. Specifically, the meditator must learn to concentrate on a thought-image while synchronizing it with the rhythm of breathing. This is required for establishing a correlative relationship between the movement of the mind and the rhythm of breathing. This point confirms Yuasa's earlier discussion of breathing in connection with conditioning the autonomic nerves. Yuasa's textual interpretation explains the relationship between the mind and *ki* as follows: "*ki* is originally a transformation of the activities of the original nature of mind."

In learning to restore the original light by adjusting the breath, the text warns of the danger of falling into two unfavorable states, a "depressed twilight state" and a "dispersed, distracted state." However, when the meditator succeeds in overcoming these unfavorable states, he or she will start "experiencing something that is not a being in the midst of all that exists." At this stage, the spiritually subtle energy becomes active and yet the meditator does not clearly understand its experiential meaning. However, if the meditator continues, he or she will start "experiencing something which should not be existing when there is nothing." This is a definite sign revealing to the meditator that the reversal of predominance of *yīn* over *yáng* is clearly advanced. Yuasa's foregoing analysis is suggestive of how a cultivator comes to detect the flow of *ki*-energy.

What becomes of interest at this point then is to understand "inner image experiences accompanying the transformation of *ki*" to which Yuasa now turns. Yuasa's textual interpretation informs us that deepening meditation brings about the experience of "a subtle spiritual fire" within which, after a further deepening, the meditator recognizes the development of "one point of true *yáng*," accompanied by a sudden realization that "the seed of yellow pearl" is generated in the lower abdomen. This is compared to the blossoming of the golden flower.

The process leading to the blossoming of the golden flower is not always smooth, and in fact the meditator often encounters "mistakes in the circulation of light." "Mistakes" specifically refer to pathological and hallucinatory states, or what Zen Buddhism calls "Zen sickness" and Tendai Buddhism calls "demonic states." Yuasa's explanation also draws on Jung's concepts of compensatory image and shadow, which may aid readers unfamiliar with meditative experience. The images accompanying hallucinatory states may be those of buddhas and bodhisattvas, luring the meditator into captive fascination, while at the same time preventing him or her from making further progress.

After dealing with the warning of the projective character of images appearing in the deepening process of meditation, Yuasa goes into a textual interpretation of the "subtle signs in the circulation of light" in which he examines, and correlates with depth psychology, three confirmatory experiences that verify the blossoming of the golden flower. This is followed by the discussion of an ideal way of everyday life, in which the model of the Daoist sage is described as manifesting a hidden power to help people without their realizing it.

At the end of chapter 3 is another brief methodological reflection, which may be especially valuable and appropriate after having gone through Yuasa's textual interpretation of *The Secret of the Golden Flower.* To those readers who expect from Eastern texts on self-cultivation an intellectual knowledge or proof, Yuasa warns that the philosophical-religious knowledge in the Eastern tradition is *practical* in nature. On this point Yuasa echoes Jung's observation that the East has sought "religious cognition" or "cognitive religion," in contrast to religious faith.

In chapter 4 Yuasa approaches *ki* from the perspective of acupuncture medicine to articulate its characteristics as they pertain to the concept of the human body, while providing, where appropriate, comparisons with Western medicine. The result is a radically new concept of the human body. Yuasa sees that the fundamental characteristic of acupuncture medicine is its *holographic* view of the internal organs. Unlike organ-oriented medicine, which focuses on the localized function of each viscus, acupuncture medicine takes each viscus to be functionally connected with other viscera through the physiologically invisible network of "meridians" through which *ki*-energy flows. The second noteworthy point Yuasa observes as essential to acupuncture medicine is its contention that *ki*-energy, while circulating within the interior of the body, intermingles with that of the external world.[18] This idea presupposes that the body is an open system, again differing from organ-oriented medicine which takes the human body as a closed system. A third characteristic point which Yuasa singles out is that acupuncture medicine is a medicine of the somatic surface. That is, the skin is understood as a boundary wall, as it were, between interior and exterior where there is an interfusion of *ki*-energy. This idea reinstantiates the macrocosmic-microcosmic correlativity between the human body and the physical universe as also found in some thinkers of the Western philosophical tradition, such as in the early Greeks and Leibniz.

With these characteristics in mind Yuasa makes a comparison with modern science. Yuasa writes critically:

> [T]he logic of modern science started with a methodology disregarding the fact of mind-body union that common sense recognizes in our everyday experience. This suggests that the logic of science is divorced from our human life, and proceeds independent of us.[19]

Science, walking independent of human life, according to Yuasa, situates the contemporary person ethically and spiritually in a desolate field of dehumanization. Here Yuasa sees the need for a theory which unifies the logic of modern science with common sense operating in our daily life. Methodologically, Yuasa finds the concept and phenomenon of *ki* to be a supreme candidate for envisioning such a possibility, because *ki* is *psychophysiological* in nature. More concretely, the meditation process verifies the activation of *ki*-energy in the *psychological* function vis-à-vis the experience of images while acupuncture medicine attests to the activation of *ki*-energy in the *physiological* function vis-à-vis its therapeutic effect.

In this connection, Yuasa discusses the "relationship between *ki* and emotion" in acupuncture medicine as this was also important in meditation. Noting that acupuncture medicine considers emotion a major etiological factor, Yuasa offers the interpretation that acupuncture medicine is psychosomatic in character. Since psychosomatic medicine regards disease as correlative with the distortion of emotion, to cure is to correct this distortion. Acupuncture medicine accomplishes this by inserting an acu-needle into the surface of the skin to restore the balance and harmony of *ki* flowing in the body. If a disease is correlated with the distortion of emotion, the method of acupuncture cure suggests that it understands emotion as a flow of *ki*-energy since the insertion of an acu-needle activates its flow at the physiological level.

Having established that acupuncture medicine understands emotion to be a flow of *ki*-energy, Yuasa's next concern is to verify both experientially and experimentally that there is indeed *ki* flowing in the body. To do this, Yuasa introduces the case of the "meridian sensitive person" who can feel, upon the insertion of an acu-needle, the direction and speed of "vibration," that is, a dermal sensation of something dispersing in specific directions with a speed considerably slower than the nerve impulse. Yuasa reports an experiment in which this felt sensation coincides with the chart of meridians recorded since ancient times. Together with this experiential correlate, Yuasa presents various electrophysiological experiments which measured and verified the existence of meridians and energy running through them. In this regard, he deems MOTOYAMA Hiroshi's experiment to be decisive. Motoyama conducted an experiment by applying the principle of galvanic skin response (i.e., viscero-cutaneous reflex) on the circuited surface of the skin along a traditionally recognized meridian path, and obtained a result which would not be obtained if it were only the usual viscero-cutaneous reflex. This suggested to Motoyama that a circuit of energy response exists which is different from the galvanic skin response. Motoyama identified it as *ki*-energy flowing in the meridians.

Bringing the foregoing analyses together, Yuasa summarizes the concept and phenomenon of *ki*-energy as follows:

> [T]he substance of the unknown energy, *ki,* is not yet known. It is the flow of a certain energy circulating in the living body, unique to living organisms. . . . [T]he flow of *ki,* when it is seen psychologically, is perceived in the circuit of coenesthesis as an abnormal sensation, as a self-apprehending sensation of one's own body under special circumstances. . . . When it is viewed physiologically, it is detected on the skin. . . . Therefore, the *ki*-energy is both psychological and physiological. . . . [I]ts substance lies in the region of the psychologically unconscious and the physiologically invisible.[20]

According to Yuasa, the system of meridians has an effect on both mind and body; it is, in fact, a middle system that mediates them.

From this observation Yuasa concludes that it is a *third* term which cannot be understood in terms of the Cartesian mind-matter dichotomy. This conclusion convinces Yausa that the study of *ki*-energy serves as a "breakthrough" point capable of transforming the existing scientific paradigm of thinking based on the Cartesian mind-body dualism.

Yuasa now incorporates his findings about the meridian system into his concept of body-scheme, which in the previous chapter he conceived as a three-layered information system. He calls the meridian system the "circuit of unconscious quasi-body" and characterizes it as a pathway of emotional energy flowing in the unconscious which activates physiological functions. It is a potential circuit in the unconscious and is anatomically invisible. The circuit of the unconscious quasi-body forms the fourth circuit in Yuasa's body-scheme.

In view of the fact that *ki*-energy is said to intermingle with that of the external world, Yausa's investigation turns to the question of how the unconscious quasi-body's function is directed toward the external world, that is, how *ki* interacts between the lived body and external world. In this instance, Yuasa examines the hypotheses of the body-scheme proposed by both Bergson and Merleau-Ponty. They both speculated that there is an invisible system of the body, distinct from the object-body, that prepares in advance one's own body (i.e., the first external sensory-motor circuit) for action. Merleau-Ponty in particular thought that this invisible body-scheme, while directing and preparing the object-body to act, casts an intentional arc toward the goal of action. His hypothesis, Yuasa thinks, is commensurate with the idea of *ki*-energy intermingling with the external world.

Yuasa sees that Merleau-Ponty's hypothesis of the invisible body-scheme is related to the habitualization of the body (i.e., the circuit of coenesthesis). The habitualization of the body presupposes memory. But since Merleau-Ponty ignored this issue, Yuasa turns to the analysis of Bergson's "motor-scheme," particularly in connection with the function of "automatic memory." Bergson's "motor-scheme," like that of Merleau-Ponty, prepares and directs the body in advance for action. Yuasa demonstrates that Bergson's motor-scheme is designed to explain the unconscious capacity to "store" the learned memory, and in the habitualized body, when perception takes place, the meaning of such a perception is automatically re-cognized from this memory bank in the unconscious. Yuasa interprets this to mean that:

> Bergson's "motor-scheme" of the body is an integrative system which unconsciously directs the mind-body whole to an external action, while connecting and mediating the *mind's function* of recollecting memory (psychological function) with the *body's function* which receives information from the thing-events of the external world through the sensory organs (perceptual function *qua* the physiological function).[21]

This characterization of Bergson's motor-scheme parallels the characteristics enumerated for the function of *ki*-energy accepted in acupuncture medicine, particularly the fact that it is a middle system mediating between the mind and body. Nevertheless, Yuasa points out that neither Merleau-Ponty's hypothesis nor Bergson's hypothesis can be positivistically verified on its own. If, however, we examine these two hypotheses in light of Yuasa's concept of body-scheme, particularly in reference to the fourth circuit of the unconscious quasi-body, they can receive empirical support.

V. SYNOPSIS OF CHAPTERS 5, 6, AND 7 (PART III)

Had Yuasa's *The Body, Self-Cultivation, and Ki-Energy* stopped at part II, its general merit would be confined to the significance Yuasa brings out for the Eastern mind-body theory. This would have had a limited, regional relevance to areas such as philosophy, religion, East Asian Studies, and perhaps depth psychology, medicine, and physical education. However, from these regional confines of his study, Yuasa brings out issues that have a *global* relevance. Although already anticipated in the previous chapters, in part III he questions the very foundation upon which modern Western science, along with its view of human nature and the world, is erected. Yuasa approaches this task by examining "the present and future of the science of *ki*."

In chapter 5, "The Science of *Ki* and its View of Human Being," Yuasa introduces the research findings on *qìgōng* (Chin.; Jap. *kikō*), or *ki* training, which is based on recently conducted scientific investigation by Chinese researchers who examined the relationship between the unconscious quasi-body and the environment. The point to keep in mind regarding *ki* research is that its scientific detection and measurement of energy activities is focused on externally emitted energy from the human body. Noting that this kind of research had previously been confined to the interior of the human body, such as EEG, electric activity, and biofeedback, Yuasa remarks that the Chinese researchers' project is an important step forward in extending the scope of investigation on the phenomena of *ki* by opening up the possibility of studying in positivistic terms the relationship between the human body and its surrounding environment. This translates into the study of the three fields of psychology, physiology, and physics (or mind, life, and matter), that is, the study of a psychological and physiological condition along with its physical effect when the emission of energy activity is detected.

Various energy activities such as infrared rays and magnetic fields are reported to be detected from trained *ki*-therapists who demonstrate a *curative* effect on patients. Yuasa interprets this to mean that what is traditionally conceived to be the activity of *ki* has in some form a correlative relationship with the activity of *physical* energies, although *ki* itself may not be reducible to the latter. The significance of the emission and detection of energy activities lies, as Yuasa points out, in the fact that the generation of these energy activities is most strongly found in the meridians (acu-points) and in the fact that it is closely correlated with a function of human awareness capable of detecting the flow of *ki* in the unconscious (quasi-body). This leads Yuasa to postulate that there also exists a correlative relationship between the function of awareness and physical energy, that is, between psychological phenomena and physical phenomena, wherein *ki*-energy is understood to flow in the unconscious quasi-body, and is emitted outside the body as physically detectable energy activities with a definite effect on the environment. Based on this finding, Yuasa refines the definition of the concept of *ki*-energy as "an energy unique to the living human body that becomes manifest, while being transformed, at psychological, physiological, and physical levels."

Having established a definition of *ki*-energy, Yuasa moves on to discuss "transpersonal synchronization of *ki* and the problem of teleology." He reports the phenomenon of "transpersonal synchronization" of *ki* which emerged when Japanese researchers conducted an experiment to measure the electroencephalograph

(EEG) of *ki*-therapists emitting *ki*-energy to their recipients. "Transpersonal synchronization" may be understood as the occurrence of the same phenomenon between individuals in disregard of spatial distance. When measurements were taken on *ki*-therapists at the time *ki* was emitted, researchers detected a brain wave similar to the "flat" wave that is associated with brain death as well as the spike wave observed in the paroxysms of epileptics. These findings are surprising for they defy contemporary medical standards, but equally surprising was the finding that a transpersonal synchronization of α and β brain waves occurred between sender and recipient. This is, for example, suggestive of verifying empirically the ethical and spiritual goal of meditational self-cultivation studied in chapter 1. Rejecting the explanation of this phenomenon vis-à-vis causality, Yuasa interprets this fact to be an instance of Jung's concept of synchronicity, which is a "meaningful coincidence" between psychological and physiological (or physical) phenomena. He identifies this meaningful coincidence as philosophically rooted in teleology, claiming that the human body *qua* life phenomena is latently endowed with a teleological order.

Since these findings were obtained from master *ki*-therapists, ordinary people's consciousness and perception are incapable of generating transpersonal synchronization, or at least they are not aware of it. The teleological order, in other words, remains for most people concealed in the unconscious quasi-body. Nevertheless, Yuasa believes, following the methodological standpoint of taking the exceptional as the standard in the Eastern method of scholarship, that the above findings will open up a new perspective on the relationship between teleology and science. He defers his provocative analysis and discussion of this point to the concluding chapter.

In chapter 6, Yuasa discusses "*Ki* and the Problem of Paranormal Phenomena," which is a natural development from the previous chapter's concern for the external emission of *ki*-energy. Yuasa introduces a summary of a symposium held in Shanghai in 1979 which explored "the mystery of life science." The impetus for this symposium came from the discovery of a boy who demonstrated an ability to "read with his ears" which in parapsychological terminology translates into psi-ability, particularly clairvoyance. Yuasa points out three salient features concerning this symposium, two of which may be mentioned here: (1) The symposium approached paranormal phenomena from the standpoint of life science, while recognizing the necessity of cooperation with physics. When compared with paranormal research conducted in the West, this is a novel approach in that Western research has ignored, in principle, correlations with the human body and life science. (2) Paranormal research is related to the traditional view of the human body held by Eastern medicine.

Yuasa takes the latter point to be the major problematic issue, that is, how to relate Eastern medicine to parapsychology. Because parapsychology should study the relationship between the human body (including its mind/heart) and the environment, Yuasa reasons that it can be reappraised by means of the study of *ki* for the latter clarifies the function of *ki* as it flows in the interior as well as outside the body. In other words, *ki* research enables us to study the relationship between the human body and the environment from the combined standpoints of psychology, physiology, and physics.

While probing into the social and psychological responses for and against paranormal phenomena and its research, Yuasa assesses the academic status of parapsychology and traces its history back to psychic research through J. B. Rhine's establishment of the discipline. Rhine's research distinguished itself from psychic research in his restriction to psychokinesis (PK) and extra sensory perception (ESP), and by his subjecting them to statistical, experimental measurement. Although the American Association for Mathematics and Statistics found no flaw in Rhine's methodology, his research met with objections. In this regard, Yuasa pinpoints two positions that the scientific attitude may take toward parapsychological research: (1) scientific rationalism, which doubts the existence of paranormal phenomena, and (2) scientific liberalism, which recognizes paranormal phenomena as factual. Yuasa sides with the second option claiming that if one assumes scientific rationalism, it will not open up a *new* way of thinking. Yuasa's reason here is based on a philosophical concern: what meaning do paranormal phenomena have for understanding human nature?

When he asks the above question, he is also stating "the need for an epistemological critique of modern science," much the same as Kant did for the then existing paradigm of thinking. One reason for this critique is that not all physical phenomena are explained through the existing laws of physics, and thus many physicists have shown an interest in parapsychological research. While taking into account psychological conditions for parapsychological phenomena, they can search for the unknown relationship existing between spirit and matter. This suggests to Yuasa that they are questioning the dualistic paradigm of thinking that dominates science, while calling for a new paradigm different from scientific rationalism.

It is this very point on which *ki* research, Yuasa believes, has an epoch-making role to play. *Ki* research demonstrates that there is a methodological as well as an ontological perspective which goes beyond scientific rationalism and the dualistic paradigm of thinking, because according to this study, an invisible psychophysical energy, which is not reducible to either the mind or the body, flows in the interior of "one's own body" while intermingling with that of the environment.

In this connection, Yuasa offers the criticism that parapsychological research as it has been conducted in the West cannot satisfy the fundamental criteria of science. These include (1) the establishment of paranormal phenomena as facts through description, and (2) the repeatability of parapsychological experiments. As to the first condition, Yuasa maintains that it is difficult to come to a definite, conclusive position through scholarly debate, because at the foundation of the pros and cons surrounding this issue lie the social and psychological conditions of people, which are different from the surface exchange of scholarly opinion. For the second point, Yuasa contends that

> insofar as human being itself is an historical being with only the "onceness" of life, the repeatability of a person's experience is incompatible with the fundamental principle of modern science.[22]

Therefore, Yuasa concludes that as long as these criteria are applied to parapsychological research, the latter cannot qualify as "science." It is, in fact, a fundamental mistake of parapsychological research to use the hitherto established scientific criteria as the *absolute* standard. What differentiates parapsychological research from *ki* research, according to Yuasa, is that the latter takes note of "one's own body" as an intermediary to both the psychological and the physical, while the former has not paid sufficient consideration to this point.

Yuasa argues that the introduction of the psychological into the study of paranormal research will question the cardinal principle of the hitherto accepted science, that is, causality, for human experience has a character of onceness, and its psychological state cannot be perfectly reproduced. Yuasa takes this to imply that the principle of causality is incapable of explaining the psychological, and therefore the paranormal. More importantly, paranormal phenomena occur disregarding temporal limitation. If the temporal is disregarded, the principle of causality cannot serve as a genuine explanation for paranormal phenomena. In this way Yuasa argues that the epistemological critique of modern science must be sought in a direction that "goes beyond causality."

Yuasa advocates this position while drawing on Jung's hypothesis of synchronicity, which is a meaningful coincidence between a psychological and a physical event, as a natural position implied by mind-body oneness. Philosophically, it suggests to Yuasa that this position approximates Spinoza's idea that productive nature (*natura naturans*) and produced nature (*natura naturata*) are linked in "God as Nature." It also resonates with Leibniz's theory of pre-established harmony wherein the "windowless" monads are connected in the potential dimension of beings.

However, Yuasa's position differs from those of Leibniz and Spinoza, though it echoes their philosophical sentiment. For Spinoza, the intelligibility of the world hinged upon the understanding of causality vis-à-vis the "intellectual love of God," while for Leibniz God was postulated as a grand clock keeper of the world, wherein he saw a teleological mechanism at work. Yuasa discerns behind these philosophers' ideas the issue of teleology, but he formulates it differently than Leibniz. He examines this issue in the concluding chapter, "Toward an East-West Dialogue." Teleology stipulates that there is a purpose, for example, in a living organism: the lungs have the purpose of breathing air. That it has a purpose implies that it is endowed with value and meaning. Teleology in this respect is opposed to scientific causality in terms of which, for example, "human life and death are nothing but scientific facts." In this regard Yuasa charges that modern science has ignored the meaning, value, and purpose of facts, since it has modeled itself after the success of physics and astronomy, which are investigations based on the observation of external nature. This charge resonates with the earlier claim that science has walked a path independent of human life.

Guided by Jung's hypothesis of "synchronicity," Yuasa argues that a teleological function is latent in the unconscious (quasi-body), wherein a primal reservoir of "meanings" is found for human life. Noting that meaningful coincidences (i.e., synchronistic phenomena) spring forth from the unconscious, Yuasa interprets "meaning" here as having a certain ethical bearing on a person's practical way of living. While concurring with the contention of physicists such as Wolfgang Pauli that natural science should investigate the teleological intentionality in the unconscious that is expressed in life phenomena (the objects of study in medical science and biology), Yuasa explains that at the foundation of the theory of *ki* is a teleological intentionality which manifests itself in the natural healing power evidenced in acupuncture medicine as well as in meditational experience.

Having criticized hitherto accepted science, particularly its cardinal principle of causality, Yuasa introduces an important distinction between "objectivistic science" and "subjectivistic science." According to Yuasa, in "objectivistic science" the subjective factor is eliminated as much as possible in the observation of facts, while life phenomena are reduced to the mechanism of matter. This methodological attitude is based on the monism of matter, while presupposing the disjunctive mind-body dualism. In contrast, "subjectivistic science" is represented by depth psychology and psychosomatic medicine, in which mind-body correlativity is accepted as clinical fact. It investigates the mechanism of experiential phenomena while taking into its purview the problem of mind. Yuasa contends that the study of *ki* goes one step further than the subjectivistic science of depth psychology and psychosomatic medicine in that it recognizes a third function between the psychological and the physiological. His contention is based on the existence of *ki,* which he believes positivistically supports the idea of a third function. Yuasa notes that epistemologically speaking, cognition is an energy phenomenon, and as such it should be detected empirically as well as in the cognitive subject's participation in the phenomenon. *Ki* research satisfies this condition. In this regard, Yuasa believes that the philosophical mind-body problem and its empirical scientific research will be joined together after their long separation following Kant's demarcation of *a priori* from *a posteriori* cognition.[23]

In the concluding section, Yuasa delves into the interrelationship among "mind, life, and matter," by returning his reflection to Jung's hypothesis of synchronicity. As is well known, Jung divided the unconscious into personal and transpersonal contents, designating the latter as the collective unconscious. He advanced this idea, based on his many years of clinical observation, by temporally tracing the personal unconscious back into the past. Yuasa sees Jung's hypothesis of synchronicity as a reiteration of the collective unconscious in light of a *spatial* axis. This interpretation enables Yuasa to understand the collective unconscious also as a common domain spatially spread through the depths of many individuals. Here he believes we can find a potential experiential domain beyond the opposition between "I" and "other." This move is natural for Yuasa who has already dealt with both achieved mind-body oneness and external *ki* emission and its relationship with the environment.

In envisioning this possibility, Yuasa spells out three domains of scholarship which have bearing on Jung's hypothesis of synchronicity: (1) parapsychology, (2) a new movement in contemporary physics, and (3) the worldview espoused by the *Yìjīng*. According to Yuasa's interpretation, Jung maintains that the essence of parapsychological phenomena disregards spatial and temporal determination through a coincidence in meaning between the psychological and the physical. As such, it defies the principle of causality. Behind the order of causality observed under spatial and temporal determination there exists, Yuasa contends, a *teleological* synchronicity, wherein the psychological condition of the experiencer plays a crucial role. In this regard, Yuasa sees a possible connection between parapsychological research and *ki* research. That is, if we can take some of the parapsychological phenomena as energy phenomena, it is necessary to study the functional process of this unknown energy in the living body, in both its psychological and physiological function. This is where *ki* research can play a decisive role.

The second pillar which according to Yuasa supports Jung's hypothesis is concerned with a new movement in contemporary physics. Owing to the problem of measurement (observation) and its related non-localized function, some physicists such as Eugene Wigner and David Bohm, maintain that the essence of matter and spirit are ultimately identical at the micro level. However, Yuasa criticizes these physicists as concerned only with the *ultimate* relationship, and as ignoring the existence of life phenomena mediated vis-à-vis "one's own body." Yuasa's contention is that in order to erect a new paradigm of thinking (through *ki* research), it is necessary to have an *integrative* understanding of "mind, life, and matter," that is, psychology, physiology, and physics.

The third pillar supporting Jung's hypothesis of synchronicity, as Yuasa interprets it, is the worldview espoused in the ancient Chinese text, the *Yìjīng*. Yuasa states that according to this text there is an invisible pre-established harmony between the being of a human *qua* a microcosm and the movements in the physical universe *qua* the macrocosm. The *Yìjīng* teaches how to bring this latent harmony into possible human cognition. He concludes this last section of the book with the following remark:

> The human being is not a *homo faber* who conquers nature, but is an *ecological*, receptive being made to be alive by the invisible power working from beyond nature, for the human being is originally a being born out of nature.[24]

The Eastern concept of nature, the environmental world in which humans live, is not that which exists for the purpose of human control, but is understood as a field upon which its teleological meaning become manifests. Yuasa says that this becomes self-evident only when a human being becomes a vessel through which the original activity of nature expresses itself vis-à-vis the activity of *ki*-energy. Seen in this light, paranormal phenomena are natural expressions of the original activity of nature.

The proposal Yuasa has made in *The Body, Self-Cultivation, and Ki-Energy* may be slightly ahead of our time. He has shown, however, a direction for overcoming the contemporary period vis-à-vis using the analysis of *ki* and parapsychological research as a springboard for philosophically questioning the meaning, value, and purpose of human life, which modern science has ignored. His thought-provoking proposal to change the dominant scientific paradigm of thinking carries the seed for its epistemological critique. Who in the West will pick up this seed to nurture it into a flower?

VI. NOTES ON THE TRANSLATION AND ACKNOWLEDGMENTS

What is translated here as *The Body, Self-Cultivation, and Ki-Energy* is based on YUASA Yasuo's Japanese book, *Ki, Shugyō, Shintai* (Tokyo: Hirakawa Shuppan, 1986), which would be literally read as *Ki-Energy, Self-Cultivation, and the Body.* The English version reversed the order of the terms in the title primarily because *ki*-energy is a foreign concept unfamiliar to the majority of the English-speaking audience. The content of the present translation covers the first two parts of the original work, *Ki, Shugyō, Shintai,* and leaves out the last two parts in which Yuasa deals with the philosophical and depth-psychological meanings of meditation methods utilized, respectively, in Shingon (Esoteric) Buddhism and Pure Land Buddhism. The translators followed Professor Yuasa's suggestion for this omission. In lieu of this omission, he suggested an addition to the English version to form part III. The material incorporated in this part is taken mostly from part III of his recent book, *Ki towa nanika* [What is *Ki*?] (Tokyo: NHK Books, 1991). Professor Yuasa edited part III of this book before having it rendered into English.

The process of translating *The Body, Self-Cultivation, and Ki-Energy* was a cooperative endeavor between Shigenori Nagatomo and Monte Hull. Initially Nagatomo prepared a rough draft from the original, which Professor Yuasa read, adding and deleting phrases and sentences wherever he felt appropriate, creating thereby a text slightly different from the original. Hull then went through the first draft and modified it into more appropriate English syntax and expressions. Nagatomo rechecked Hull's revisions against the original, after which Professor Yuasa kindly checked it for a second time and made many useful and helpful suggestions for improvement. Although the translators took the utmost care to avoid errors, it is their responsibility if there are any.

We have usually adhered to standard Japanese name order, which is surname first followed by personal name. To indicate this and to minimize confusion we have used small capitals with Japanese surnames where in the full name the surname is written first. Chinese names also follow their standard order of surname first.

The translators would like to acknowledge the service rendered by Mr. Lu Junjie and Mr. Wang Youru, friends at Temple University, who kindly provided the transliteration of Chinese terms into the Pinyin system. They would like to express their appreciation to Mr. Gereon Kopf of Temple University for his assistance in finalizing the glossary, to Tom Downey (of University of Southern Maine) and to John Thomas (of Temple University) for skillfully proofreading the manuscript. Monte Hull would like to thank his wife Janet for her constant loving support. Shigenori Nagatomo would like to extend his heartfelt appreciation to Emiko Takahashi, Samuel and Evelyn Laeuchli, and Thomas Dean for their moral support. He also would like to acknowledge Mr. HYŪGA Hidemi of Nippon Hōsō Kyōkai (Japan Broadcasting Company) for his longstanding friendship, and for providing a video copy of a documentary program dealing with the external emission of *ki*-energy. In this regard, he would like to extend his gratitude also to Dr. MARUYAMA Toshiaki who kindly gave him a video copy of *tōate* technique performed by the martial art master, AOKI Hiroyuki and his colleagues for a martial art demonstration of external *ki* emission. He would like to express his deep gratitude to Yuasa *sensei* for his constant and unfailing guidance.

Toward the end of this project, the translators greatly benefited from the services rendered by the following persons. They would like to express their gratitude to the competent and meticulous copy-editor, and to the staff members of SUNY press, Ms. Lois Patton and Ms. Megeen R. Mulholland for bringing this translation to completion. Last but not least, the translators thank the series editor, Professor Howard Eilberg-Schwarts, for overseeing the project from beginning to end.

Shigenori NAGATOMO
Winter, 1991

AUTHOR'S PREFACE TO THE ENGLISH VERSION

Over the years I have studied the experience of self-cultivation commonly found at the foundation of various religions in the East. Found within it are many problems needing investigation, not only from the perspectives of philosophy and religion, but also from that of medicine, physiology, and biophysics. Viewed from the standpoint of psychology, the experience of self-cultivation bears on the region below consciousness. Here we must grasp afresh the relationship between a human being and the world from a perspective different than that of modern philosophy, which has been constructed with ego-consciousness at its foundation. The medical examination of the experience of self-cultivation will further clarify the mind-body relationship, that is, the correlative connection between the psychological and physiological functions within the living human body. This connection exists latently in a deep dimension with more intimate correlativity than has previously been known. The scientific study of *ki,* which recently has been vigorously pursued in China and Japan, holds a key to open the door. Moreover, this study suggests, through its biological and physical energy measurement of the living human body that there latently exists an invisible exchange of life between the living human body and the environment, that is, between a human being and the world, which transcends the surface relation established through consciousness and sensory perception.

We find here a field of study with universal significance for original human nature, one that transcends the cultural differences between East and West and which will probably demand of philosophy the task of a new critique of epistemology. Previously I have examined the fundamental characteristics of Eastern mind-body theory from such standpoints as contemporary philosophy and psychology.[1]

The present work is fruit gathered from study conducted over the last ten years or so. Through the rapid promotion of scholarly exchange between China and Japan in recent years, the research achievements on *ki*-energy as related to Eastern medicine and *qìgōng* training have been widely disseminated and have become known. New research in these fields is introduced in part III, but its study will probably have to await the future for proper academic evaluation. The study of *ki*-energy may, however, inaugurate the opening of a new perspective on both philosophy and science.

Since this book was written primarily with a Japanese audience in mind, there are few explanations on Asian religions and cultures in part I and II. I am afraid that many points may be unfamiliar to the Western reader, but I hope that he or she will not become bogged down by historical details. What I have sought in the present endeavor is a universal human truth that goes beyond differences of historical and cultural background.

When viewed historically the Western tradition of philosophy and science has since the medieval period developed paradigms of metaphysics based on observing and investigating the physical universe or outer nature. This situation has not changed since the nineteenth century when science became independent of philosophy and started to surpass it. In contrast, the Eastern tradition of philosophy and science has emphasized, not the observation of outer nature, but the investigation of inner nature based on practical, lived human experiences of self-observation. Thus the tradition of philosophy in the East possesses the character not of meta-physics but rather of what may be termed meta-medico-psychology. The study of *ki*-energy developed in East Asia has this historical background. Thanks to modern developments in psychology, medical science, and biophysics we have gained the means to reinterpret and reevaluate the ancient legacy of Eastern philosophy and science from a contemporary perspective.

Human beings are situated between two heterogenous orders, that of outer nature and inner nature. If we are biased toward either of them, a correct investigation of human nature would probably be impaired. The study of outer nature investigates the existing facts whereas the study of inner nature will, in the final analysis, lead us to question the meaning, value, and spirituality of human beings living in this world. It is unlikely that future science can avoid encountering these philosophical questions.

I would like to express my heartfelt appreciation for the endeavor and friendship of Professors Shigenori Nagatomo and Monte Hull, who translated this work into English. In addition to the task of translation they have given me many valuable suggestions concerning the issues that needed to be addressed in this work. If the present work proves to be of any use for mutual understanding between East and West, it will be a joy commonly shared by both the author and the translators.

Yuasa Yasuo
Summer, 1992

PART I

Eastern Mind-Body Theory and the Contemporary Period

CHAPTER 1

Eastern Mind-Body Theory

I. INTRODUCTION

While primarily studying Eastern intellectual and cultural history with my research centered on Japan, I have been interested in the mind-body relationship as conceived in philosophy, psychology, and medicine. Owing to this orientation I have developed an interest in the idea of a unique mind-body relationship running through the Eastern intellectual tradition. In the present work I would like to discuss the significance of the Eastern mind-body theory from a contemporary perspective.

To be more specific, I have developed a special interest in the problem of self-cultivation [*shugyō*][1] as found in various Eastern religious traditions. In Japan self-cultivation methods have been established and transmitted to later generations ever since Buddhism's acceptance in ancient times. Zen self-cultivation is one example that has become well known worldwide. In addition, there are many other self-cultivation methods which vary from school to school. For example, some people must have heard of the *shugendō* of mountain ascetics which developed in synthesis with the old mountain worship,[2] or *kaihōgyō,*[3] which was handed down at Mt. Hiei.[4] These Buddhist self-cultivation methods greatly influenced the development of artistry and the martial arts. Systems of self-cultivation, slightly different from those of Japan, have been transmitted in Buddhist and Daoist traditions in China, and in the Yogic tradition in India.

II. THE EASTERN TRADITION OF SELF-CULTIVATION AND WESTERN MIND-BODY DUALISM

To begin with a general remark, a connotation of the Japanese term "*shugyō*" or simply "*gyō*" (self-cultivation) is that of training the body, but it also implies training, as a human being, the spirit[5] or mind by training the body. In other words, "*shugyō*" carries the meaning of perfecting the human spirit or enhancing one's personality. Therefore, it seems to imply that mind and body are inseparable.

Corresponding to "*shugyō*" is "*tapas*" in the Indian tradition.[6] It is usually translated into Japanese as "*kugyō*" (austerity), but its etymological meaning is "fire" or "heat," that is, the function of heating things. However, it is used metaphorically or symbolically as internal heat or mental fire, rather than designating literal fire or heat. For example, a poet receiving an inspiration writes a beautiful poem, and this is attributed to the power of *tapas*. *Tapas* is said to refer to the *internal warmth* which creates something new from within oneself, just as a bird hatches its chick by warming an egg. Noting this sense, researchers in the West have translated *tapas* as "creative heat." In short, it may be understood as an energy that gives birth, through training various capacities of the body, to awakening a new self from within one's soul, or to a new function of the spirit. The Japanese terms "*shugyō*" and "*gyō*," I think, carry approximately the same sense as *tapas*.

Since this sort of idea has been germane to us Easterners for generations, it is relatively easy to understand that training the body means simultaneously training the mind (spirit). However, this idea is not necessarily easy for Westerners to understand. Take, for example, the idea of modern sports or modern medicine. Generally speaking, the training methods in sports aim at enhancing bodily capacities, or to be more specific, they aim at enhancing the motor capacity of the muscles in the limbs. They lack the goal of training the spirit or enhancing the personality. Naturally, it is conceivable that perseverance of hard training can bring forth the effect of strengthening spiritual power and nurturing strong will power. Teachers engaged in the practical guidance of students in physical education and martial arts probably know this fact through their own experience. Nonetheless, modern sports, at least insofar as they are viewed theoretically, have a bearing only on health and leisure, and do not embrace the goal and meaning of training the spirit or of enhancing the personality.

According to the idea of modern medicine, which was developed rapidly after Louis Pasteur (1822–1895) and Rudolf L. K. Virchow (1821–1902) in the nineteenth century, sickness means an abnormality of the body in its organs or functions, and is unrelated to the problem of mind. In other words, the fundamental attitude which modern medicine has assumed is that of treating the mind and body separately by dividing them up, and it has only studied the organization of the body and its functions while disregarding the problem of mind. Some call this type of model "biological medicine."

A dualism is presupposed here, or more precisely a dichotomy, which separates mind from body. René Descartes (1596–1650) established the mind-body (or mind-matter) dualism, and it has played a role in directing the way modern philosophy and empirical science have been developed. Historically speaking, the idea of dualism seems indigenous to the tradition of Western thought. According to the traditional view of Christianity, after its authority was established in the ancient Roman Empire, a human being was conceived as a being in which two principles, "spirit" and "flesh," are conjoined. The orthodox position in Christianity was that the "flesh" was the principle of sin, and the "spirit" the principle leading to God.[7]

The period in which Descartes lived was a time when science, arising after the Renaissance, had achieved rapid development, and when the storms of the Inquisition were raging. Descartes sought to make religion more rational and at the same time to provide a foundation for modern science. When Descartes' project is judged from the vantage point of intellectual history, his dualism separating spirit from matter (and consequently mind from body), was a project to arbitrate the conflict between religion and science, which represents an opposition between spirit and matter, by eliminating the religious connotation from the Christian, spirit-flesh dualistic view of the human being. Descartes attempted thereby to bestow separate roles to religion and science. Subsequently, however, religion gradually lost its power, and modern science entered a golden age. Today the value of material substance and the flesh, which were debased during the medieval period, has been raised high to the point where technology is welcome and freedom of sex is proclaimed.

In the contemporary period this tendency has been carried to the extreme. It is a reversal of the medieval view of man which valued the "spirit" while disdaining the "flesh." However, the reversal of value demonstrates that the *dualistic* way of thinking is still maintained, for *reversing* value means to emphasize one side while neglecting the other. It is probably our task in the contemporary period to develop a way to harmonize the dualism by overcoming the dichotomy of either-or alternatives, such as either mind or body, either spirit or flesh. In this respect, the tradition of the Eastern mind-body theory is an historical legacy of important value today.

I have previously published *Shintai: tōyōteki shinshinron no kokoromi* [The Body: Toward an Eastern Mind-Body Theory], which my friends in the United States and in France have translated.[8] When I examined its translation, the Japanese term "*shugyō*" seemed to have troubled the translators, and is rendered as "cultivation." Looking this word up in the dictionary, I learned that it means "to prepare land for raising crops, or to till," and derivatively it encompasses such meanings as "to refine, to culture, and to educate." It appears difficult for European languages to express the connotations embraced by the Japanese word "*gyō*," which carries the sense of strengthening the mind (spirit) and enhancing the personality, as a human being, by training the body.

In Christianity, there are terms such as "austerity" and "asceticism" which are rendered into Japanese respectively as "*kinyoku*" and "*kugyō*." These terms originally designated performing systematically organized "prayer, meditation, and work" at a monastery, and are close in form to the meaning of the Japanese word "*shugyō*." Behind these terms, however, is the spirit-flesh dualism in which the spirit is to be saved by torturing the flesh, the principle of sin. For this reason, these European terms introduce traditional Western values, which, by separating mind from body, place importance on the mind (spirit) while neglecting the value of the body. In contrast, mind and body are taken to be inseparable in the Eastern tradition, and training the body has been given positive meaning and value as a technical means of enhancing the spirit and personality. Here we can find a difference in the view of human being between the Eastern and Western traditions which is not a mere linguistic problem.

III. MEDITATION IN STILLNESS AND IN MOTION

Historically speaking, it was during the Heian period (794–1185) that Buddhist cultivation methods were appropriated on a large scale in Japan. There is a book called *Makashikan* [Chin. Móhē zhǐguān] which is valued in Tendai Buddhism.[9] It was written by the Chinese Tendai Master, Chigi (538–597), and deals with self-cultivation methods and medicine. Generally, it is considered a basic text in Buddhist medicine. The various cultivation methods described in this book greatly influenced Buddhism in the Heian period. Chigi broadly distinguishes two cultivation methods, "*samādhi*[10] through continual sitting" [*jōza zanmai*] and "*samādhi* through continual walking" [*jōgyō zanmai*].[11] Simply put, "*samādhi* through continual sitting" is "meditation through constant sitting," and "*samādhi* through continual walking" is "meditation through constant walking."

Meditation through constant sitting refers to the method of stilling the movements of mind, as in Zen meditation, by concentrating consciousness (thought-image) on a definite object while assuming a specific seated posture and dispelling wandering thoughts.[12] Sometimes sutras may be read or the name of Buddha recited in order to dispel wandering thoughts. "Continual" in "*samādhi* through continual sitting" means "repetition," and therefore carries the sense of "training."

Heian Buddhism developed with Esoteric Buddhism [*Mikkyō*][13] assuming a central role, and in this sect of Buddhism the body-mind function is called "the three mysteries" [*sanmitsu*] of "the body" [*shin*], "the mouth" [*ku*], and "the intention" [*i*], and it is explained in terms of "body mystery" [*shin mitsu*], "mouth mystery" [*ku mitsu*], and "intention mystery" [*i mitsu*]. "*Shin*" refers to the lived human body or one's own body [*karada*], "*ku*" refers to speech, and "*i*" to mind. *Mitsu* designates a *secret function*. The cultivation method of this Buddhism is explained in terms of these three functions.

The first, "body mystery," is an effect or function of bodily posture. It is called "*mudrā*" in Sanskrit. The hand gesture of a Buddha image is determined by iconographic rules depending on the kind of Buddha depicted. The hand gesture, then, is a *mudrā* [*in*]. In referring to the whole body of a Buddha, the term "*Maha mudrā*" is used. In Yoga, various postures for meditation are referred to as "*āsana*" (posture), and the "body mystery" of Esoteric Buddhism is approximately the same as "*āsana*." The next, "mouth mystery," designates an effect of respiration training vis-à-vis reading sutras and reciting sacred sounds, called "*mantra*" or "*dhāraṇī*." And the last, "intention mystery," since it is a function of the mind, may be understood as the *psychological effect* of meditation which enables a meditator to concentrate his or her consciousness (thought-image) and to dispell wandering thoughts. The cultivation method of "*samādhi* through continual sitting" consists of the combination of these three elements.

The next one, "*samādhi* through continual walking," designates the cultivation method which mainly utilizes bodily movements. The cultivation method called "*hanshu samādhi*,"[14] which appears in the *Makashikan*, became well known since it was practiced at Mt. Hiei. With this method the cultivator walks in a circle around an image of Amitābha Buddha,[15] enshrined in the "Jōgyō Samādhi Hall," while reciting words of praise for the Buddha. This sounds simple when explained, but in actuality the practice is rather difficult. The cultivator repeats the same movements while praising the words of the Buddha for many hours, except when taking food and short rests, continually for one hundred days. Shinran[16] (1173–1262) was a monk at Jōgyō Samādhi Hall when he was young, and I assume that he probably practiced this method. When this method of cultivation was spread among the populace, and was stylized while being transformed into an artistic form, it came to be known as "dancing *nenbutsu*" [*odori nenbutsu*], which consists of recitation of the name of Amitābha Buddha while dancing.[17] This is one of the original sources for popular folk arts in Japan. Dancing around a donjon while clapping hands in unison during the Bon festival in August is probably a vestige of "dancing *nenbutsu*".

There is a cultivation method called "*rōzan gyō*" (mountain retreat practice), practiced even today at Mt. Hiei, which consists of "throwing the five parts of the body on the ground" [*gotaitōchi-rei*].[18] The practitioner worships the Buddha while lying flat on the floor with both arms extended, then gradually standing up from this position, worships the Buddha with both hands joined together, and then returns to the initial position. Everyday the practitioner repeats this several thousand times for a period of several months. This method may also be considered as an example of "*samādhi* through continual motion," a method of self-cultivation emphasizing bodily movement.

At Mt. Hiei there is also a famous cultivation method called *kaihōgyō*. It is reportedly initiated by Sōō (836–918), a disciple of Great Master Jikaku Ennin (794–864),[19] but when assessed in light of intellectual history, it was invented by combining the mountain worship of ancient Shintōism with Buddhist meditation.[20] In this method a cultivator, while regarding the mountain peaks as sacred regions where Buddhas and gods are seated in stillness, walks continuously through the mountains every day for many miles. The formally prescribed period of this cultivation method is one thousand days, with the cultivator attempting one hundred days each year and taking ten years to complete. The practice is truly demanding with such regimens as reciting *mantra* for seven days without food and sleep at Myōōin by the Katsura River in the mountains of Hira. This is practiced when the cultivator has passed the seven-hundredth day out of one thousand days.[21] It may also be considered a developed form of the cultivation method of "*samādhi* through continual walking."

"*Samādhi* through continual walking," which I have translated as "meditation through walking," may also be translated in more general terms as "meditation in motion" [*undōteki meisō*]. The same psychological effect as in seated meditation is accomplished by means of bodily movement. For example, while constantly repeating the monotonous movement of walking in the mountains, the cultivator holds an image of the Buddha in his or her mind the whole time. The recitation of a *mantra* is the same. As the cultivator continues this bodily movement, the mind will gradually cease to respond to outside sensory stimuli, and will concentrate only on the mental image. In short, the repetition of bodily movement is here a means of meditation.

The term "*samādhi*" appears in both "*samādhi* through continual sitting" and "*samādhi* through continual walking." The Japanese term "*sanmai*" or "*zanmai*" is a transliteration of the Sanskrit word "*samādhi*," and its original meaning designates the state of a completely transparent mind in which, as a consequence of deepening meditation, no wandering thoughts occur. It is comparable to "no-mind" [*mushin*] or to "no-self" [*muga*] in which the consciousness of an "I" has completely disappeared. Colloquial Japanese, by adding the word "*zanmai*," uses such expressions as "chess *samādhi*" [*igo zanmai*], "reading *samādhi*" [*dokusho zanmai*], and "luxury *samādhi*" [*zeitaku zanmai*] to refer to the state of being immersed in activity. These expressions are borrowed from the original meaning of "forgetting the self."[22] Meditation training aims at experiencing the state of "*samādhi*"

FIGURE 1.1
THE MIND AND BODY RELATIONSHIP BETWEEN CONTINUAL SITTING AND CONTINUAL WALKING

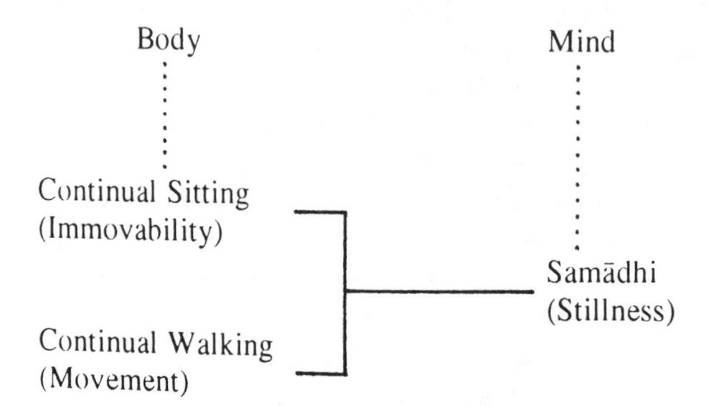

in which the mind is entirely transparent without any wandering thoughts. When examined psychologically, this means becoming aware of the movements of mind characteristic of and unique to oneself (that is, the habits or patterns of the mind/heart), and gradually transforming them by gaining control over them (see Fig. 1.1). I would like to point out here that on the one hand "*samādhi* through continual walking," which emphasizes mainly bodily movement, is referred to as "*sanmai.*" On the other hand, "*samādhi* through continual sitting" demands, as it were, an immovable "stillness" of both mind and body, because this meditation assumes an immovable seated posture. Therefore, this form of meditation may be called "meditation in stillness" [*seishiteki meisō*]. In contrast, the method of "*samādhi* through continual walking" gradually leads the mind to the state of transparent no-mind by means of *continuous* bodily movement. Thus, this method may be called "meditation in motion." Meditation in motion, and the philosophy behind it, soon greatly influenced the artistry and martial arts of Japan.

IV. MEDITATION AND PSYCHOTHERAPY

Now, I would like to examine briefly the meaning of meditative training from a psychological viewpoint. As is well known, the motto of Zen meditation is often called "no-thought, no-image" [*munen musō*]. By sitting for a long time without thinking anything at all while gazing at the tip of the nose with the eyes half closed, one endeavors to let the welling up of wandering thoughts and delusions gradually disappear. Zen meditation sometimes utilizes the breathing method called "observation of breath count" [*sūsokukan*] in which the meditator counts an inhalation as one and an exhalation as two, but it does not, generally speaking, employ a complicated breathing method. However, the cultivation method of Heian Buddhism[23] is more complicated and utilizes various techniques. Among the prominent ones are those in which the meditator concentrates on a specific image in the mind. For example, the meditation method called "*aji kan*" (letter A meditation) requires the meditator to imagine the Sanskrit letter "A." Another one is "*gachirin kan*" (moon meditation) in which the meditator imagines the moon, and then develops it from crescent to full.

These methods are collectively referred to as "*sādhana*" (method of accomplishment) in India, and designate techniques for achieving satori. For example, in the case of Acalanātha[24] *sādhana,* the cultivator, thinking to oneself that one has become an Acalanātha [*fudō myōo*], imagines various parts of his body: the skin of Acalanātha is like the color of a red flower, one of his eyes is slanted, from his mouth fearful looking fangs stick out, his face is ornamented with jade, a wreath hangs around his neck, and he holds a sword in his right hand. Around the sword coils a white serpent. His waist is covered by a tiger hide, ornamented with jade, and his whole body shines like the sun. In this manner the cultivator uses one's imagination in minute detail to concentrate the mind on these images.

In the temples of Esoteric Buddhism, brightly colored mandalas of many Buddhas, bodhisattvas, and heavenly beings are put up, and Buddha images are painted in shining gold as well. All these give off a colorful impression, quite appropriate for this religion born in tropical India. These mandalas and Buddha images were originally tools [*yantra*] for the self-cultivating monks to meditate on. People in ancient India believed that real Buddhas and divine beings dwelt in the invisible heavenly world.[25] Mandalas and Buddha images are the invisible heavenly gods made visible on earth to the naked eye. By worshipping these mandalas and Buddha images and reciting words of praise for them, while concentrating the mind on a Buddha image, and by entering into a

FIGURE 1.2
RED ACALANĀTHA

deep ecstatic state, the cultivator trains oneself to actually experience, while awake, scenes of the heavenly world where these beings dwell. Psychologically speaking, one attains a vision of the Buddhas as a kind of hallucination. The *Makashikan,* quoted earlier, states that, "the meditator sees Buddhas, now dwelling in the ten directions of the world, appear before one's eyes. It is just like a person with good eyesight seeing shining stars in a clear night sky."[26] This experience is called "seeing Buddhas in meditation" [*jōchū ken butsu*].

When examined from the standpoint of depth psychology, this meditation method is training to weaken the suppressive power operative on the surface of consciousness in order to activate the unconsciousness energy latent beneath it. In our ordinary waking state, the function of consciousness perceives an object in the external world and responds to it. However, when stimuli from the outside are shut off, the energy of the mind directed towards the outside decreases, and consequently the energy of the mind, latent beneath consciousness, becomes active in the course of training.

This is the same psychological mechanism as having a dream. When one is asleep, the function of consciousness is arrested, and consequently the unconscious energy suppressed and concealed beneath consciousness starts to surface, and appears as images in dreams. Meditation is training to experience freely the mechanism of this state while still awake.

Naturally, a little training in meditation will not usually bring the expected experience of an image. Some people experience various hallucinatory states while in meditation, but most states resist interpretation as to their meaning, and moreover the hallucinatory states, unlike dreams, do not usually contain a coherent story. Hallucinations often occur with schizophrenic patients, but the pathological hallucinations usually occur involuntarily, accompanying pain. In meditative cultivation, however, the hallucinations are usually experienced only during meditation, and once meditation is stopped, the hallucinations also cease. However, as training in meditation deepens, the hallucinatory experiences start carrying a sense of reality, inducing in the meditator strong emotions and feelings of ecstasy.[27] Among contemporary psychotherapies, there are some which have incorporated the old meditation techniques. One such example is Schultz's autogenic training, which is widely used today in Japan. In autogenic training, one relaxes with the eyes closed and imagines such things as the hands getting warm or seeing a red color. Ordinarily, one or two out of ten people can see a red color through training. Like this psychotherapy, meditation is a method of letting surface the emotions and complexes hidden in the unconscious, and by dissolving them, one acquires free control over the unconscious energy.

As previously mentioned, a little training in meditation does not easily bring the appearance of the Buddhas and gods of the heavenly world, nor scenes like a dream. Although there has been a tendency in modern Japan to deny the value of traditional meditative methods, a boom has recently arisen in the United States and the other countries. There is an interesting story that goes with it. Jung called the method of meditation which he invented himself "active imagination." It resembles the Eastern meditation method which utilizes images as the *sādhana* mentioned previously. This seems to have been suggested to him by a Daoist meditation method.

Because Jung's psychology spread rapidly in the United States in the seventies, when *gurus* from India and Tibet were disseminating Eastern meditation methods, it played a strong role for Americans in bridging an understanding with the East. Since this movement was initiated by the hippies, it is said that one of their motivating interests was the popularity of drugs. For example, when one takes a drug such as LSD or mescaline, things start shining like precious stones, and one experiences an ecstatic state or hallucinates strange dreamy images. Out of this experience people developed an interest in the function of the latent energy possessed by the unconscious. An ordinary person cannot have this kind of hallucination without recourse to drugs, but through long training, persons with a certain disposition can freely experience hallucinations.

As so far seen, there are common points between psychotherapy and meditation, but the fundamental ideas are slightly different. Although they share the same psychological mechanism, the beginning points and goals differ. Psychotherapy was originally devised as a therapy to cure neuroses, and it attempts to restore to a normal state the struggle and split arising between the conscious and the unconscious. The term "complex" means "compound or composite," but more accurately it is an abbreviation for "emotionally colored complex" [*gefühlsbetonter Komplex*]. An example would be a state where a person is always being haunted by an anxiety or fear of something. A neurosis is a symptom with which consciousness is helpless because some power causing these feelings (complexes) is always active in the unconscious. Psychotherapy is a way of freeing and dissolving an "emotional complex."

Nevertheless, there is no one, not even a normal person, who does not have any complexes. Generally speaking, a complex is related to the character or disposition, or to the pattern of movements of the mind/heart,[28] unique to each individual. With an ordinary person, it simply means that the complex is not brought to an abnormal, pathological state requiring the attention of a counselor or therapist. At any rate, the beginning point in psychotherapy is a patient's abnormal, pathological state of mind, and the goal is to restore a normal, healthy mind by curing the abnormality.

In contrast, the meditative method of self-cultivation is not aimed at curing a sick patient. Starting from the normal state of mind in our everyday life, it aims at achieving a higher, transformed state. Psychosomatic medicine and psychiatry sometimes use the term "altered state of consciousness" (ASC) to designate collectively psychological states, such as hypnosis, hallucinations, and the ecstatic states accompanying meditation, which differ from ordinary, everyday states. "*Samādhi*" may then be considered in this terminology as an altered state of consciousness.

As the cultivator continues meditative training, however, there are times when he or she is suddenly overcome by a pathological state. Some time ago, a young Zen monk came to visit me. As he had continued his meditative training he developed symptoms analogous to depersonalization (that is, a state of anxiety where one is unable to feel one's own existence, or where one loses a sense of the reality of external things). Or, he would fall into a quasi-neurotic state in which he was overtaken by anxiety while walking down the street, and could only walk at the edge of the street. This kind of state is called "Zen sickness" [*zenbyō*] in Zen Buddhism and "a demonic state" [*majikyō*] in Tendai Buddhism. In other words, the energy which can trigger these kinds of states exists latently in the unconscious region even with a "normal" person. (In some of the drug-induced cases, a huge spider or a monstrous crab may appear, depending on the person.) To overcome these pathological states, it is necessary to receive guidance from an experienced master (*guru*).

As we have seen, there are differences between psychotherapy and meditation in regard to their beginning points and goals, although both deal with the same psychological mechanisms. Psychotherapy is a method of restoring to a normal level a neurotic patient, that is, a person who has fallen into an abnormal, pathological state. By contrast, self-cultivation through meditation is a method of training that strengthens and enhances the function of the mind to a higher level than the ordinary state, just as the practice of hygienic method and motor training heightens bodily capacities. In other words, psychotherapy is a method for adjusting a discrepancy created between consciousness and the unconscious, whereas the purpose of self-cultivation is to strengthen the power which synthesizes the functions of consciousness and the unconscious, while learning to control the emotional patterns (the habits of the mind/heart) and complexes characteristic of oneself with the view to further transform the mind.

We may say that appropriating the power to synthesize the unconscious within consciousness by controlling the former means, more concretely, to become a person who can relate oneself to another with love in calmness. This occurs by correcting distortions of one's mind, such as timidity and temperamental dispositions. Yet in the course of meditative training, the cultivator can run into artificial neurotic states, and if the training goes wrong, one can actually become neurotic. A master, like a psychoanalyst treating a patient, must clearly observe the disciple's psychological state and guide the disciple so that he or she can overcome it. Analogically speaking, it is like producing an immune system in the body by artificially creating a slight sickness through vaccination. Once the cultivator breaks through this artificial neurotic state, the power of one's spirit will become increasingly strong. When training is practiced over a long period, the cultivator approaches a matured state of personality.

V. MEDITATION AND MIND-BODY ONENESS

As previously mentioned, Buddhist cultivation methods can be broadly distinguished into two types: "*samādhi* through continual sitting" (meditation in stillness), and "*samādhi* through continual walking" (meditation in motion). The former concentrates one's thought on the interior movements of the mind by placing the body in an immovable (still) position, while the latter trains one to look into the interior of the mind by placing the body in continual motion (movement).

Buddhas and gods are not originally found in the sensible thing-events [*jibutsu*] of the external world, but are rather the experiences of images within one's mind. Therefore, when they are examined psychologically, they may be regarded as *an autonomous power* existing latently in the unknown region of the unconscious, which are projectively understood as entities existing independently of consciousness. The power or energy of the unconscious is activated independent of the function of consciousness, and when it does appear in consciousness, one experiences it as various images as in the case of hallucinations and dreams. When those images are idealized, they take on the forms of Buddhas and gods. The numerous Buddhas and gods in Eastern religions are classified into various levels with their corresponding characteristics, and generally speaking, they represent perfected stages of the ideal human spirit. Meditative training concentrates the power of consciousness on these ideal, perfected stages, and integrates unconscious energy, functioning independently of consciousness, into these ideal states. When this takes place, the power of the unconscious region will be activated and become alive for consciousness, leading the cultivator into a world of experiences hidden from everyday consciousness.

The meditation method of Heian Buddhism often uses a technique of artificially creating visual images (states of so-called visual and other hallucinations) through the active imagination. For example, in the case of "*samādhi* through continual walking" (meditation in motion), the mind is constantly concentrated on a Buddha, while one orally recites a *mantra* and places the body in constant motion. In other words, it integrates unconscious energy by activating it through repetition of a specific bodily movement.

How then does this training change the mind-body relationship? Zen Buddhism often uses the phrase "body-mind oneness" [*shinshin ichinyo*]. This phrase appears among historical Japanese texts as early as Eisai's[29] (1141–1215) *Kōzen gokokuron* [Discourse on Promoting Zen and Protecting the Country].[30] He refers to a deepened state of meditation after entering into *samādhi* as "all engagements are discarded, everything is put to rest; in body-mind oneness there is neither movement nor stillness." We find in Dōgen's (1200–1253) fascicle "*Zazengi*" [Rules for Meditation] in *Shōbōgenzō* a description of the preparatory attitude for doing seated meditation.[31] Echoing Eisai's characterization, Dōgen states, "Discard all engagements, and put everything to rest. Think neither evil nor good. Seated meditation is not an operation of consciousness."[32] "Discard all engagements, and put everything to rest" means to abandon the attitude of mind directed toward the thing-events of the external world. In other words, when one meditates, all connections (or engagements) with the external world are cut off and forgotten, and one focuses exclusively on the movements of the mind arising from within its interior. In situations of everyday life, our attention is drawn to the thing-events of the external world toward which the energy of our minds flows. For this reason, we make judgements as to whether other people's speech and action are good or bad, and create the distinction between good and bad (which is contrary to Dōgen's words, "think neither good nor evil"). By stopping all such conscious judgments, meditation delves exclusively into the inner world of the psyche. Viewed psychologically, it is a technique for controlling unconscious functions by weakening the functions of consciousness which respond to stimuli from outside, and for redirecting the energy of the mind into its interior in order to activate the unconscious. When a meditator continues training for a long period of time, wandering thoughts disappear, and the mind, becoming empty, experiences the state of *samādhi* in which there is no consciousness of an "I."

In Zen Buddhism there is the term "*kenshō*" (seeing into one's own nature). It designates the initial experience of satori, which is the first experience of a transformed state of consciousness. Although the terms "satori" and "*samādhi*" encompass various phases and stages, generally speaking they correspond to the states of "no-mind" [*mushin*] and "no-self" [*muga*]. They include such ecstatic experiences as not being able to determine where one's body is, and the state in which one's consciousness leaves the body. (The latter is sometimes referred to as "out of body experience.") It is difficult to generalize, but some experiences accompany hallucinations and others do not. Eisai refers to these kinds of experience as "body-mind oneness" [*shinshin ichinyo*]. Myōe (1173–1232) uses the phrase "body-mind crystallization" [*shinshin gyōnen*] in *Yume no ki* [The Record of Dreams], which contains the record of his own cultivation experiences.[33] Interpreted philologically, "body-mind oneness' [*shinshin ichinyo*] designates a state in which mind and body become as one without separation, and "body-mind crystallization" [*shinshin gyōnen*][34] designates a state in which both the mind and body congeal into one. In an ordinary conscious state one is aware of the condition of one's own body (bodily sensation or coenesthesis), and along with it one also knows that the mind is in an active state different from the body. When the body is sitting quietly, the mind experiences various movements. Expressions such as "body-mind oneness" and "body-mind crystallization" probably designate states in which the mind and the body become one when the multifarious movements of the mind disappear. Moreover, Dōgen calls the *kenshō* experience he had while doing seated meditation in China "casting off body and mind" [*shinjin datsuraku*]. It probably refers to a felt lack of distinction between mind and body.

In our ordinary state of consciousness, bodily sensation is experienced as different in kind from the narrow sense of mental states such as thinking and imagining. Bodily sensation refers to the sensations we have of the conditions of our hands, legs, or internal organs, including internal sensations of change in bodily states such as itching or feeling cold in the hand. Broadly speaking, bodily sensation belongs to consciousness and in this respect is a state of the mind, but functions indigenous to the mind, such as thinking and emotion, are experienced as activities different from bodily sensation. Even though no change occurs in bodily sensation in the initial phase of meditation, wandering thoughts arise one after another. In such a state, body and mind are felt to be distinct. An ecstatic state is an experience in which this distinction has disappeared.

Of interest in this regard is the case of meditation in motion. Meditation in motion is a method of achieving an ecstatic experience, as is the case of meditation in stillness, through constant repetition of bodily movement. We may cite the "dancing *nenbutsu*" [*odori nenbutsu*] initiated by Ippen (1239–89) as a relatively easy example for understanding this point. "Dancing *nenbutsu*" takes the form of continuously dancing, swinging hands and legs, while reciting the phrase "*namu amidabutsu*" (I entrust myself to Abmitābha Buddha). In our contemporary period, when young people dance continuously at a disco, the constant bodily movement generates a kind of pleasant sensation and ecstatic feeling. Analogously, meditation in motion attempts to achieve a highly transformed state of consciousness through training the motor movement of the bodily organs (especially the hands and legs). The method of meditation in motion has extremely important significance for assessing characteristics of Japanese culture.

VI. SELF-CULTIVATION AND ARTISTRY

The theory of Buddhist self-cultivation has greatly influenced Japanese cultural history. It was incorporated into the arts toward the end of the Heian period (794–1185), and from the beginning of the Kamakura period (1185–1333) and extending into the Muromachi period (1338–1573), it shaped theories of artistry in such areas as *waka* poetry,[35] Nō or *Nōgaku* theater,[36] and *Sadō*[37] (the way of tea). Furthermore, the theory of self-cultivation influenced the martial arts from the period of Warring States (1467 to c. 1568) to the beginning of the Edo period (1603–1876), giving rise to the theory of *Budō* (the way of the samurai warrior).[38]

Generally speaking, artistic expression may be characterized as the pursuit of beauty. *Waka* poetry and literature express an aesthetic sensibility through the use of language or words, while sculpture, painting, and music express it through various sensible materials. In contrast, *Nōgaku* or Nō theater and *Sadō* attempt to express beauty through bodily movement. The artistic expressions of any ethnic culture are known to have an intimate connection with its religiosity when their origins are traced back, and in Japan a tradition was established to understand the essence of the arts based on the Buddhist self-cultivation theory.[39]

Generally speaking, the goal of self-cultivation is to pursue "satori," and the goal of the arts is to pursue "beauty." Accordingly, the ultimate, ideal condition of aesthetic experience has been sought in analogy or comparison with the experience of satori. The term "*yūgen*" (profound, suggestive mystery) is a case in point. FUJIWARA Shunzei (1114–1204), a poet toward the end of the Heian period, was the first to use this term, which was suggested by the Tendai text *Makashikan.* (As previously mentioned, this text is a basic text on self-cultivation in Tendai Buddhism.) In short, Fujiwara Shunzei reasoned that a poet can achieve the ideal aesthetic state of beauty, or *yūgen,* just as a monk achieves satori through self-cultivation.

In the Kamakura period (1185–1333), however, *waka* poetry was widely theorized in analogy with *dhāraṇī* in a theory called *waka-dhāraṇī. Dhāraṇī* refers to sacred spells used in Buddhism, and in this case, means a sacred word symbolically expressing the world of Buddhas. According to this theory, an excellent *waka* poem expresses the state of *yūgen* in words, just as *dhāraṇī* expresses the state of satori which ordinary people cannot easily achieve. In this case, a poet pursues beauty, expressed by the word *yūgen,* through the practice [*keiko*] of poetic composition, that is, through *training the mind* in attempting to compose better poems, just as the monk attempts to achieve satori through self-cultivation. Accordingly, the theory was formulated such that a poet can reach beauty by training and polishing his or her mind.

This is the theory of "*kadō*," the way of *waka* poetry composition, which regards the method of poetic composition as a kind of culturing and nurturing of the personality.

During the medieval period, this theory had an enormous influence on Nō, which was representative of the theatrical performances of the time. Since beauty is expressed through bodily movement in theatrical performance, unlike the case of *waka* poetry, the mind-body relationship became an important theme in this theater.

Zeami (1363–1443), a great systematizer and formulator of the Nō theatre, symbolically expresses beauty in Nō theatre by the word "flower" [*hana*]. The term "flower" corresponds to "*yūgen*" in the way of *waka* poetry composition. In other words, Nō is an art which attempts to express the "flower" through the use of the body. Fundamental to this theatrical art are its performing techniques, which Zeami calls "*waza*," and its training "*keiko*" (practice). Moreover, he understands "*keiko*" as corresponding to Buddhist "self-cultivation" [*shugyō*]. In other words, just as a monk endeavors to achieve satori through self-cultivation, so a Nō performer endeavors to make the "flower" blossom on stage by repeated practice of performing techniques. How, then, does the practice of performing techniques change the mind-body relationship?

When we are healthy, we do not think about our body, believing that we can move our body as our mind wishes. However, during infancy, a toddler has difficulty walking and is incapable of using even a pair of chopsticks. We have embodied or appropriated how to move our hands and legs through training [*keiko*] since childhood. A craftsman's skill and an actor's performance are acquired by professionally training their bodies in their respective fields, and their freedom of movement is expressed accordingly. With an amateur, the body does not easily move in accordance with the mind's wish. When I was a student, I learned a little dancing for Nō theater, and I recall that it was very difficult for me to synchronize my hands and legs with a song. However, accomplished and masterful performers execute their performing techniques decisively. In short, they can execute their bodily movements as their minds intend without the least miscalculation.

At the beginner's stage, whether in a theatrical performance, dance, or sport, the student tries to move his or her body first by thinking, as it were, through the head. In other words, the student intellectually understands and calculates the teacher's instruction, according to which he or she then tries to control the body. Nevertheless, the body does not move as one's mind wishes. Here, mind and body are lived *dualistically.* The mind *qua* thinking consciousness and the body, which is moved following the command of the mind, are understood separately. However, if one continues to train oneself repeatedly, the body gradually comes to move in accordance with the mind's wishes. When this occurs, the student understands the meaning of the teacher's instructions. This is because the "body" has learned. When this process is repeatedly and diligently practiced, the student comes to move his or her body freely and unconsciously. The ideal state can be referred to as "body-mind oneness." There is no gap between the movement of the mind and that of the body in the performance of a master, for the master's mind and body are one.

This process of training is, needless to say, the same in Western theatrical performance and sports. However, since the tradition of a mind-body dualistic pattern of thinking is strong in the West, as previously mentioned, there is a strong tendency to train the body through conscious calculation. That is, the assumption is that training proceeds from mind to body, or from mind to form. Contrary to this order, the tradition of Eastern self-cultivation places importance on entering the mind from the body or form. That is, it attempts to train the mind by training the body. Consequently, the mind is not simply consciousness nor is it constant and unchangeable, but rather it is that which is *transformed* through training the body.

A point to be noted in this regard is that beauty in the arts is appreciated by an observer. In a theatrical performance, the audience is aesthetically moved by the drama performed on stage, and this is different from the pursuit of satori in self-cultivation. The pursuit of satori is related to the cultivator himself and not to other people. In contrast, the arts, whether Eastern or Western, presuppose the human relationship between producer and appreciator. Traditional theories of art in the West have understood beauty by emphasizing the standpoint of the observer. For example, according to Aristotle's theory of art, which is the classic theory of theater, the essence of tragedy is catharsis of the soul. The audience watching a tragedy empathizes with the mind of an actor playing a role in the drama, and is led to feel sorrow or lamentation, thus being emotionally moved. Catharsis of the soul refers to this function of being emotionally moved.

Eastern theater, of course, cannot disregard the audience's standpoint. The "flower," which is beauty in Nō theater, is that which the audience feels. However, a characteristic of Japanese artistry is that its fundamental emphasis is placed more on the *standpoint of the performer* than on that of the audience. The theory of *waka* composition maintains that a poet achieves the state of *yūgen* through training in *waka* poetry, and Zeami's theory of Nō theater teaches the embodiment of "flower" by a performer. The theory of artistry explains the *catharsis in the soul of the performer* achieved through artistic production; the standpoint of the art appreciator is only secondary. The artist requires the catharsis and enhancement of his or her mind in pursuit of beauty, just as does the cultivator in pursuit of satori.

Zeami characterizes the relationship between the mind and body as "flower is mind, and its seed is performing technique."[40] Performing techniques [*waza*] are bodily expressions. Special attention is needed here to understand the expression "flower is mind." In order to make flowers blossom, one must sow seeds. The bodily training of performing techniques is comparable to sowing "seeds." When seeds are nurtured and cared for over a long period, flowers will blossom in due time. Zeami contends that the flower which blossoms through bodily training is the Nō mind, the mind of Nō performance. In Zeami's understanding, the mind-body relationship is taken in an order proceeding from the performing techniques [*waza*] *qua* the seeds to the "flower," that is, from the body or the form to the mind. Therefore, the mind is understood as that which is transformed and reborn constantly through the form, as the flower grows and blossoms.

Zeami calls the ideal state of "flower," "no-mind" [*mushin*] or "emptiness" [*kū*]. It is freedom in dancing without consciousness of its performance. In other words, it is a state of "body-mind oneness" where the movement of mind and body become indistinguishable. It is a state of self-forgetfulness, in which consciousness of oneself as the subject of bodily movement disappears and becomes the movement itself that is dancing.

In philosophical terminology, mind and body in ordinary circumstances are in the relation of subject and object. The most representative objects are material substances found in the external world, that is, things. Our body, too, exists as a kind of a material substance or object in this world (space). In contrast, the subject is that which cannot become object; that is, it is the bearer of conscious functions which can move or cognize the object. The mind in this sense is a subject (or more precisely the function of a subject). In short, the mind that is subject dominates and moves the body that is object, and this is conscious bodily movement.

In the state of body-mind oneness, as mentioned above, the mind moves while unconsciously becoming one with the body. That is, there is no longer a felt distinction between the mind *qua* subject and the body *qua* object; the subject is simultaneously the object, and the object is simultaneously the subject. The movement of the object that is the body is such that it is wholly the movement of the mind that is subject. The philosopher NISHIDA Kitarō (1870–1945) refers to this state as "pure experience" [*junsui keiken*] or "acting intuition" [*kōiteki chokkan*]. Nishida maintains that "acting" is at the same time intuiting emptiness (absolute nothing [*zettaimu*]).[41] He characterizes it as "becoming a thing, and penetrating into things."[42] The mind becomes entirely a "thing," that is the body, demonstrating to the fullest the capacities and possibilities endowed in the body (a thing), and it moves penetrating things around it. The center of this bodily movement is a "stillness" in the midst of dynamism, just as the center pin of a top spinning at full speed remains stationary. Zeami calls this state "no-mind" [*mushin*] or "emptiness" [*kū*].

VII. CHARACTERISTICS OF THE JAPANESE MARTIAL ARTS

I will now examine the Japanese way of the *bushi,* or samurai warriors. There are many Japanese martial arts, including *jūdō,* swordsmanship [*kendō*], archery, and horseback riding, all of which originated in the distant past, and *karate* and *aikidō* which have developed in modern times. Both *jūdō* and *aikidō* are disseminated worldwide today, but they spread from Japan even though they originated in China. Why did these martial arts not spread directly from China rather than by way of Japan? There seems to be a reason indicated in the intellectual history of the respective countries.

Confucianism has flourished in China (also in Korea) since ancient times, and Buddhism and Daoism have been accorded lower status. Confucianism was linked to cultural education such as knowledge of the classics, rites, poetry, calligraphy, and painting, or to use contemporary divisions, to education in the humanities such as philosophy, literature, and arts, which the aristocrats [Jap. *bunkan;* Chin. *wénguān*], called "*shitaifu*" [Chin. *shìdàfū*], were required to study. The *shitaifu* were aristocrats who controlled political power, holding it both in China and Korea all the way until the modern period. For this reason, the military class was treated as an object of disdain by Confucian aristocrats. It is symbolically epitomized by the phrase, "Respect for Letters, Disdain for the Military" [*sūbun keibu*] as it is exemplified in Korean Neo-Confucianism. The military class was one of professional martial artists, which corresponds in modern terms to military personnel. The martial arts, being mere techniques, have traditionally been regarded in the history of both China and Korea as having a lower value than the classics and the arts. However, in Japan the *bushi,* or samurai warriors, came to dominate political power toward the end of the Heian period (794–1185). This situation of the military class seizing political power for a long period of time did not occur in China or Korea until the modern period. However, in Japan, since the medieval period, the *bushi* continued to hold power for seven-hundred years.

As we have just seen, dominance by the *bushi* continued since the time of the Kamakura government for a long period, and so they needed to educate themselves spiritually as a controlling class. The upper class *bushi* during the Kamakura period (1185–1333) devoted themselves to the self-cultivation of Esoteric and Zen Buddhism. During the Muromachi period (1338–1573) knowledge of the arts such as *waka* poetry, linked verse [*renga*], and the way of tea were required even of the *bushi,* whose attitude was epitomized as "Both Ways in Letters and Military" [*bunbu ryōdō*].[43] Because there was a long period when the tradition of "letters" and that of the "military" interacted in Japan, the martial arts were not simply techniques, but gradually acquired a high artistic sensitivity and spirituality. "Letters" here designates religion, scholarship, and the arts, and is the product of the activities of the mind such as knowledge and aesthetic sensibility. In contrast, "military" designates training in bodily techniques. Alternatively, "letters" and "military," or "mind" and "body," have traditionally been considered inseparable in Japanese history. For this reason, the Japanese *bushi* way is intimately related to Buddhism and the arts, and has the characteristics, as it were, of a high, inner spirituality. The idea that training to perfect performing techniques nurtures a faithful mind and promotes spiritual exchange with others can be observed, for example, in building a god-shelf for worship in a practice hall, in the custom of exchanging greetings after worshipping the god, and in votive matches performed on the grounds of shrines and temples. The depth of spirituality observed in the Japanese *bushi* way is a unique cultural product born of the history of Japan. I know several foreigners who are learning the martial arts, and one of the reasons that the Japanese martial arts have attracted the interest of many foreigners lies, I think, in the deep spirituality which the martial arts embody.

The *bushi* way, like the way of the arts, was profoundly influenced by Buddhist self-cultivation methods, predominantly those of Esoteric and Zen Buddhism. The theory of the *bushi* way was formulated at the beginning of the Warring State period (1467–c. 1568), and continued into the beginning of the Edo period (1603–1867).

How, then, does the theory of the *bushi* way understand the mind-body relationship? According to my research, its fundamentals were inherited from Buddhist self-cultivation methods, particularly "meditation in motion" (or "*samādhi* through continual walking"). The goal of the *bushi* way, in general, is to reach the state of "no-mind" or "*samādhi*" which opens up through training bodily movement as meditation deepens. For this reason, a center of calm "immovability" (*fudō*), called "no-mind" or "*samādhi,*" is always found in the midst of bodily dynamism.

Takuan (1573–1645), a Zen monk in the beginning of the Edo period and Zen master to Shōgun Iëmitsu[44] (1604–1651) and YAGYŪ Munenori[45] (1571–1646), explains the mental attitude required in the *bushi* way.[46] Takuan calls the psychological state of an amateur, unskilled person, "desires residing in ignorance" [*mumyōjūchi bonnō*], which is a dark state of living in delusion.

He defines it as a condition in which the movement of mind is captivated by the things before one's eyes.

> If one places his mind on the [opponent's] sword, the sword will take hold of his mind. If one places his mind on timing, the timing will, again, take hold of his mind. And if one places his mind on his striking sword, that will take hold of his mind. All this is stagnation of the mind and will result in opening up a weak spot before oneself.[47]

Takuan explains that a swordsman cannot execute his techniques as long as he is captivated by the movements of his opponent's sword, or by the opponent's bodily movements, or to put it generally, as long as he is distracted by the changing situation. In contrast, Takuan calls the condition of the skilled master "the immovable wisdom of Buddhas" [*shobutsu fudōchi*]. It designates a state in which the mind moves freely in all directions, forward, backward, right, and left as it wishes without becoming stagnant. Here, the movements of the mind do not remain at any one spot and flow freely. At the center of these movements is "immovable wisdom." Because the center is immovable, captivated by nothing, the mind can in turn move freely without stagnation.

Takuan uses such terms as "right mind" [*shōshin*], "original mind" [*honshin*], and "no-mind" [*mushin*] to characterize this state. In contrast, the amateur's state of "desires residing in ignorance" is characterized as "imbalanced mind" [*hen shin*], "delusory mind" [*mōshin*], and "having a mind" [*u shin*]. Takuan says this is a state of extreme fixation where the mind stiffens by pondering on something. Therefore, practice in the *bushi* way releases one from the mind's tendency to get fixated and captivated by something, and it trains one to achieve a state of freedom of movement without captivation by anything. If one continues training, Takuan claims, it is possible to reach the "rank of no-mind and no-thought" [*mushin munen no kurai*]. "In the ultimate rank, *the hands, legs, and body learn,* and the mind does not interfere with anything at all."[48] That is to say, when there is repeated training in the practice of performing techniques, and the body-mind is disciplined, then the state of conscious movement changes into one in which the hands, legs, and body unconsciously move of themselves. This is the state of "no-mind." What Takuan calls "immovable wisdom" designates this state of no-mind. There is an immovable point at the center of the free bodily movements, just as the center shaft of a top maintains a quiet immovable position while it is spinning at full speed. This is what Takuan calls "immovable wisdom." The theory of the Japanese *bushi* way, as expressed by Takuan, inherits the cultivation method of "*samādhi* through continual walking" (or "meditation in motion") in the tradition of ancient Buddhism [*kodai bukkyō*], and concretizes it in the martial arts.

Consequently, "body-mind oneness," as discussed above, applies directly to the mind-body relationship as it is understood in the *bushi* way. When I hear the phase "body-mind oneness," my association is of the beautiful performing technique of a master in the martial arts. To take contemporary examples, we may associate "body-mind oneness" with the performance of an excellent gymnast or figure skater. A neophyte or a person with awkward motor nerves cannot move his or her body as the mind wishes; the movement of the mind and that of the body are totally discordant. However, with repeated training, the movements of mind and body gradually coincide with each other in a way that is unique to each person, depending upon one's efforts and innate disposition. If one reaches what is called a perfect performance, one achieves a state in which one can move the body freely without intending it. Here the movements of mind and body are one; there is no distinction between one's mind and body. To move one's body without conscious effort suggests that a person is approaching the state of no-mind while letting ego-consciousness disappear.

There is an important difference between modern Western sports and the Japanese *bushi* way, however. Training in sports aims at developing the body's capacity, or more specifically, the motor capacity of the muscles in the four limbs (hands and legs), and does not include the spiritual meaning of training the mind's capacity. On the other hand, the original goal in the *bushi* way is to develop mental (or spiritual) capacity. Psychologically, this suggests an important difference. Modern sports, with its goal of developing the motor capacity of the muscles, ignores the problem of the unconscious. The function of the unconscious is most clearly manifest in the activity of emotion, and the latter has nothing directly to do with the motor capacity of the muscles. Yet the Buddhist cultivation method of "meditation in motion" (or "*samādhi* through continual walking"), which gave rise to the *bushi* way, is originally designed with the goal of strengthening the synthesis between consciousness and the unconscious by controlling unconscious emotional functions. Therefore, an ultimate goal in the tradition of the ancient *bushi* way [*kobudō*] is to achieve a mature personality which can control emotion.

According to the *Heihō kadensho* [The Family Transmission of the Military Method], which belongs to the Yagyū school of martial arts, the human mind is distinguished into "original mind" [*honshin*] and "deluded mind" [*mōshin*], and their relationship is explained as follows. "Original mind" refers to the true self endowed in all human beings, corresponding to the Buddhists' "buddha-nature" [*busshō*], or to what Zen calls the "original face before one's father and mother were born" [*honrai no memboku*].[49] In contrast, "deluded mind" is referred to as "I," or as "*kekki*" [literally, "blood and psychophysical *ki*-energy"]. "*Kekki*" refers to an easily agitated mind, and "I" refers to egocentric feeling and emotion.

> Blood, rising up, changes the facial expression, and issues out in anger. Moreover, if the other hates what "I" love, "I" get angry and become spiteful. Or, if the other person hates what "I" hate, "I" become pleased, forcing the unreasonable [*hi*] into the reasonable [*ri*].[50]

The "deluded mind" then is that state in which a person is bound to the egocentric movement of the emotions, and is captivated by love and hatred. When it is at work, nothing goes right for a *bushi* or samurai whether he tries swordsmanship, archery, or horseback riding. The *Heihō kadensho* maintains that practice in the *bushi* way aims to overcome the activity of the deluded mind and endeavors to actualize the functioning of the original mind.

> The deluded mind [*mōshin*] is a sickness of the mind. To depart from the deluded mind is to depart from the sickness. Once this sickness is left behind, the mind is free from sickness. The mind free from sickness is called the original mind [*honshin*]. When the original mind is attained, such a person is a master in the military method.[51]

To put it differently, a master of the *bushi* way, like an accomplished Zen meditator, is a human being who is not swayed by his or her emotions and can control them. The ultimate goal that the *bushi* way seeks is, as in Zen self-cultivation, the development of a mature personality.

As we have seen in the foregoing, the Japanese *bushi* way came to possess techniques for disciplining and enhancing one's spirit. The sword was originally a weapon. It was a tool for self-protection or for killing people. It was produced with the purposes of opposing, competing with, and conquering others. However, the ultimate purpose of training in swordsmanship was changed to conquering oneself rather than others. In the *Heihō kadensho* this transformation is characterized as a change from "the sword to kill others" [*satsujinken*] to "the sword to save others" [*katsujinken*]. *Aikidō*, which developed in modern times, was devised by pursuing the implication of this idea to its logical conclusion.

Aikidō does not aim at competing with and beating an opponent in a match. The term "*aiki*" designates making one's *ki* (psychophysical energy) agree with that of an opponent, that is, bringing about an agreement of the opponent's body-mind movement with one's own. To put it more generally, the goal of *aikidō* is to reach a state in which oneself and the other are one through harmonizing and accommodating each other. The martial arts with their initial purpose of opposing and conquering others underwent a change, as we have just seen, to the technique of conquering oneself, and further to the technique of harmonizing with others so as to become one with them. Here we can discern the important significance of the Japanese *bushi* way in Japanese intellectual history.

It would not be an exaggeration to say that, fundamentally, modern Western sports aim at competition in a game, or at winning over others in a match. This is true in all competitive games, and for this reason, the record becomes important. Also, competition arouses thrill and excitement in the viewers, from which is generated the idea of sports as a show, and we are now in the golden age of professional sports. Today, sports such as Olympic skiing and marathons have come to share a large market as a means for making money.

In this trend, the traditional Western pattern of thinking is still alive. A philosopher in ancient Greece distinguished three kinds of people who gathered at the Olympia. First is the observer, second the competitor, and third the seller. Among the three, the observer was regarded as the most valuable human being, because the observer occupied a position, like the gods dwelling in the Olympian pantheon, from which to observe the competition. The position of the observer was called "*theōria*" (to see, or to observe). "*Theōria*" is the etymological origin for the term "theory." In contrast, those who competed were in the position of "*prāxis*" ("practice"). Accordingly, in the West those who practiced were given a lower status than those who observed. And those vendors catering to the audience were given a still lower status than those who practiced. (As mentioned earlier, the standpoint of the observer assumed a fundamental position in the theater of the West.)

However, the relationship among the above three gradually underwent a curious reversal in Western history. During the Roman period, fighting between man and ferocious animals attracted the enthusiasm of the populace, and the emperors supported the fighters in order to win popularity. Competitive fighters were created and became famous in this manner. In contrast, the observers were now the nameless mass, while the competitors rose to a higher, glorified status. Today, financial power has become important for organizing competition and theatrical performances, and the power of capital has assumed the highest position. Accordingly, the relative relationship among the observer, the performer, and the financier has been completely reversed from that of ancient times.

By way of contrast, the standpoint of the performer or competitor has been valued as most important in Japanese artistry and the *bushi* way. In other words, the standpoint of *prāxis* has been regarded as more important than that of *theōria*. To put it in still simpler terms, the standpoint of the observer is disregarded. The goal of Japanese artistry and the *bushi* way is for the competitor or performer to discipline one's spirit by using one's body. And by transforming one's mind, a flower blossoms, whereby one achieves the state of "no-mind." The self ascends to the height at which it is no longer one's self, but is the self which harmonizes and accommodates others; it becomes one with the world and with the universe. This idea embedded in the Japanese *bushi* way seems especially valuable for the contemporary world. Looking at the condition of contemporary civilization in the advanced countries, it seems that the more affluent the world has become materially, the poorer it has become spiritually: contemporary civilization is on the verge of losing its spiritual wealth. But, isn't the most truly important thing for human beings the act of enhancing one's own mind and heart, while nurturing the soul which harmonizes with others?

CHAPTER 2

Beyond the Contemporary Period

I. FROM DISJUNCTIVE MIND-BODY DUALISM TO CORRELATIVE MIND-BODY DUALISM

In chapter 1 I articulated characteristics of the Eastern mind-body theory in light of an historical perspective. I would like now to examine the problem from the standpoints of contemporary medicine and physiological psychology.

As previously stated, modern medicine (biological medicine) since its establishment in approximately the nineteenth century has presupposed in its orthodox form the Cartesian mind-body dualism (derived from the spirit-matter dichotomy), which views mind and body disjunctively. Consequently, ignoring the issue of mind, modern medicine has studied exclusively the anatomical organization and physiological functions of the body. This model of thinking defines sickness as an abnormality in the organs which make up the organization of the body, or as an abnormality in their physiological function. The cure is to dissolve the abnormal condition either by surgical operation or by medication.

Starting in this century, the methodological presuppositions of modern science have been questioned by scholars in various ways. One may mention three major trends. The first started with depth psychology and has developed into psychosomatic medicine. The second is Hans Selyé's stress theory. The third is a movement in neurophysiology which has taken a new perspective in dealing with the mind and brain relationship. All of these recognize an intimate correlation between the mind and body in place of the Cartesian disjunctive mind-body theory.

Sigmund Freud's psychoanalysis made clear that there is a sickness which is caused by a complex in the mind (unconscious). He initially studied hysteria, and learned that when hysteria occurred a sharp pain was felt in the pupils, together with a convulsion and stiffening in the limbs, although there was no abnormality in the physiological organs. In short, since neurosis is a sickness with no recognizable physiological abnormality, it cannot be explained unless the problem of mind is taken into consideration. Moreover, many psychoses are attributable to inner dispositions in which there are no clearly recognizable organic disorders in the organ (the brain). Therefore, in order to understand the mechanism of mental diseases it is necessary to hold a view of the human being which presupposes a correlativity between mind and body, and which incorporates the function of mind in its methodological procedure.

Psychosomatic medicine, which has incorporated both depth psychology and physiology, is now being accepted. It deals primarily with sickness associated with internal medicine, closely related to the internal organs, rather than with sicknesses of the mind such as neurosis and psychosis. It includes such illnesses as psychosomatic disorders and dysfunctions of the autonomic nervous system. When the balance of the autonomic nervous system is disturbed, the function of internal organs is rendered dysfunctional. Abnormality in the autonomic nervous system is often caused by psychological stress. Today, mind-body correlativity is found even among sicknesses which can become objects of surgical operation. For example, there is the discovery of cancer caused by psychological factors. Various psychotherapies are now being applied, in combination with medication, to sicknesses of the internal organs which previously were treated only through medication.

Second, Hans Selyé's stress theory started with the study of endocrine secretions (around the pituitary-adrenocortical axis). The term "stress" is originally taken from terminology used in mechanics to designate "distortion." Stress is an extreme, tensed condition in the physiological function generated by a force as, for instance, when a spring is compressed with full force. The stimulus which triggers this condition is called a stressor and there are physical as well as chemical stressors. For example, it is possible to trigger a stressful condition in a physiological function by applying an outside physical stimulus.

Selyé discovered in his study on ovarian hormones that a psychological stressor can trigger a stressful condition. A new idea arising from stress theory is that various kinds of stressors (for example, physical, chemical, or psychological) can trigger an identical stress. In other words, there is not necessarily a one-to-one correspondence between cause and effect, and there can be various causes for an identical effect (that is, the general adaptation syndrome). Yet it is common to understand stress theory as referring to psychological stress, since it had not been previously anticipated that a psychological stressor could trigger a stress. (The term "stress" used today usually refers to psychological stress.) Psychological stress brings about abnormality in the hormonal secretions of the endocrine glands, and influences the activity of the nervous system, particularly the autonomic nervous system. Therefore, stress theory has given strong support for the abovementioned psychosomatic theory.

The third noteworthy trend is a development in brain physiology in which many scholars have begun to question the validity of the hitherto accepted organ-oriented medicine. Brain physiology in the first half of this century was dominated by the localization theory of brain functions. The theory of cerebral localization is that the centers of various physiological and psychological functions are localized somewhere in the brain, and by collecting them together, one can explain all of the mind-body functions. It is true that many important research results have been accomplished by accepting this theory. Physiological organs (such as the eye and ear) regulating sensory functions (for example, visual and auditory functions) are localized, and it is relatively easy to find out where their centers are in the brain. The theory of cerebral localization applies to a considerable extent even to the motor organs (for example, the hand and legs). However, it has gradually become evident that it cannot sufficiently explain psychological functions such as thinking and remembering.

One of the presuppositions concerning the mind-body theory which organ-oriented medicine has held since the nineteenth century can be characterized as reductionistic. This has the following two meanings. One is that the whole function of the brain is supported by the sum of all parts of the brain functions, which reduces the whole to its parts. The other is that the essence of the function of the mind is reducible to the physiological activities of the brain. For example, the conditioned-reflex theory which was initiated in the USSR in the beginning of this century, insists that what is understood as the function of consciousness designates the activities of the nerves. As research in transmission substances of the nerve impulse (for example, dopamine and endorphins) has developed in recent years in biochemistry, it has become clear how a secretion of chemical substance correlates with a psychological state. These discoveries seemed to strongly support the presupposition that various psychological functions are reducible to biochemical nerve activities. Descartes' mind-body dualism, which separates matter (the body) from spirit, had rendered them totally unrelated, and the reductionism which flourished from the nineteenth century to the first half of this century went one step further: it advanced to the monism of matter by claiming that the function of spirit (mind) is reducible to the function of matter.

Most brain physiologists today still carry on their research with the disjunctive dualism of Descartes or with reductionistic presuppositions, but in recent years there have arisen some brain physiologists who question reductionism. Those researchers include, for example, Wilder Penfield, John C. Eccles, Roger Sperry, and Karl Pribram.[1] They have moved to a new perspective for understanding the mind and brain after realizing that some of the psychological functions could not be sufficiently explained in terms of the theory of cerebral localization. The theory of localization is appropriate within a limited scope, but it cannot explain everything.

Penfield and Pribram have focused on the function of *memory*. The center for the function of memory is difficult to localize (that is, an engram). Recollection of a memory presupposes a relationship between consciousness and the unconscious. In other words, the center of the unconscious which functions as memory storage is difficult to localize in the brain. They ran into this fact and concluded that the essence of the mind cannot be reduced to the mechanisms of the brain, rather the mind is a substance (a being) which functions independently of the brain while maintaining a close correlation with it. (When we assume this standpoint, it is possible to take a view different from the hitherto accepted theory concerning the relationship between the transmission substances of nerve impulses and their psychological function.) The reductionistic view holds that the secretion of a certain biochemical substance as a cause produces a psychological function as its effect. But what we find here is merely a *correlation* between the two, and it is not clear whether or not a causal relationship exists between the states of matter and mind.

I must add that those who hold to this new perspective are a minority in the field of brain physiology. Penfield and others started out as rationalists upholding the reductionistic position, but they have gradually recognized its limitations, which I feel is a new movement in contemporary mind-body theory.

The new contemporary dualism, which considers the mind and brain as different, differs from Descartes' dualism. The former has gone through the period of reductionistic monism of matter, and it recognizes a close correlation between the mind and brain, that is, between the spirit and body (or matter). Yet this new dualism does not reject *in toto* the previously accepted reductionism. For example, the theory of cerebral localization certainly is valid *within a specifically limited area.* If we analogically compare the hitherto accepted organ-oriented medicine to the worldview espoused by Newtonian physics, the new dualism may be compared to the worldview proposed by quantum physics. The former approach is not mistaken so long as we realize that it deals with the mind-body issue in approximation, but if a more exact method is called for, we cannot conceive the functioning of the body while disregarding the mind.

As I have indicated above, thinking out the mind-body relationship today has become a new problem. The problem has changed from the disjunctive mind-body dualism (the Cartesian dichotomy) to a dualism of mind-body correlativity. Following this model of mind-body correlativity, it is possible to study the body in its physiological functions and its various organs by dividing the whole into numerous parts in light of anatomical classification. This is the reason that clinical medicine is divided into many specialized areas such as internal medicine, surgery, and otorhinolaryngology. This kind of classification, however, cannot apply to the mind. Although the mind is usually believed to be in the brain, the function of the mind is not only related to the brain but also influences the functions of all the organs in the whole body. Consequently, when we take mind-body correlativity as our standpoint, the reductionistic attitude, which first divides the whole into its parts and then understands it as the sum of its parts, is clearly insufficient. For this reason, a holistic standpoint is advocated today which takes note of the holistic function of the mind-body. This is designated by the terms "holistic medicine" and "holistic health."

It is noteworthy at this juncture that a number of the Western psychologists and psychiatrists who pioneered the perspective of mind-body correlativity have shown an interest in Eastern self-cultivation methods. For example, one can mention C. G. Jung, Erich Fromm, and Medard Boss. Jung studied, with wide interest, the cultivation methods of Daoism, Esoteric Buddhism, Zen Buddhism, and Yoga.[2] Fromm was particularly interested in Zen Buddhism and studied the relationship between Zen and psychoanalysis. Boss thought that the meditative methods of Zen and Yoga have important significance for Western psychotherapy. The therapeutic method of Schultz's autogenic training, which was briefly mentioned in chapter 1, is said to have been suggested by yogic techniques.

As seen above, many Western psychiatrists and psychotherapists have started paying attention to Eastern self-cultivation methods. Why have they become interested in Eastern self-cultivation? The answer from a practical, realistic viewpoint is that they have recognized the same therapeutic effect in the techniques of Eastern self-cultivation as in psychotherapy. In short, it is because the application of various techniques employed in self-cultivation methods is useful to psychotherapy.

Going a step beyond these therapists and psychiatrists, we can discover in the traditional mind-body theory, which is based on Eastern self-cultivation methods, an interesting theoretical problem which needs to be examined afresh for contemporary people. Meditation, as I have characterized it in the previous chapter, has the effect of dissolving complexes in the unconscious while transforming the habits of the mind/heart (psychological structures or patterns). How are these issues related to the mechanism of the body when examined from the standpoint of contemporary physiological psychology?

II. THREE INFORMATION SYSTEMS IN THE BODY

It is convenient to understand holistically the function of the body in light of the nervous system, for the nerves are a kind of information system controlling and regulating the physiological functions of the various organs of the body.

When we categorize the nerves in the manner of a medical textbook, we can broadly distinguish two groups: the central nerves (CN) which consist of the brain and the spinal cord, and the peripheral nerves (PN) that branch out from the central nerves and are distributed throughout the organs. There are three representatives of the peripheral nerves: *the sensory nerves* and *the motor nerves* together with *the autonomic nerves,* which branch out from the brain-stem (the connecting area between the brain and the spinal cord) and have a center in the area below the cerebral cortex. Of these three, the sensory nerves and the motor nerves are the systems that govern the sensory organs and the motor organs respectively, that is, the animal functions of the body. The autonomic nerves are a system primarily governing the function of the visceral organs, that is, the vegetative functions (respiration, circulation, nutrition, excretion, and procreation) which maintain the life of an individual body.

When we take the body as a system of information, it can be grouped into the following three systems. The first is an information system relating the body to the external world. A kind of information circuit is established between the body and the external world by means of the sensory organs which receive stimuli from the environment, and by means of the motor organs which act on the outside. When sensory organs such as the eyes or ears receive a stimulus entering from outside, they send it to the brain by converting it to an impulse (an information input) traveling through the sensory nerves (for example, an optical nerve). If we take this circuit as centripetal (afferent), the hands and legs, which are motor organs, can be regarded as a centrifugal (efferent) circuit. When the brain receives a sensory stimulus from the distal organs, various sensory centers in the cerebral cortex respond to it, and synthesizing the information in the frontal lobe, the brain forms a judgment. When a situation in the external world is recognized by means of this process, the frontal lobe sends out a centrifugal impulse (an information output) by way of the motor nerves which control the muscles in the limbs. In short, the body can take the action appropriate for a situation in the external world in virtue of the fact that the sensory nerves function *passively* for the stimulus coming from outside, and the motor nerves function *actively* on it (see Fig. 2.1).

The philosopher Henri Bergson (1859–1941) calls the above information system "the sensory-motor apparatus" (*les appareils sensori-moteurs*).[3] According to him, this apparatus is organized

FIGURE 2.1
EXTERNAL SENSORY-MOTOR CIRCUIT

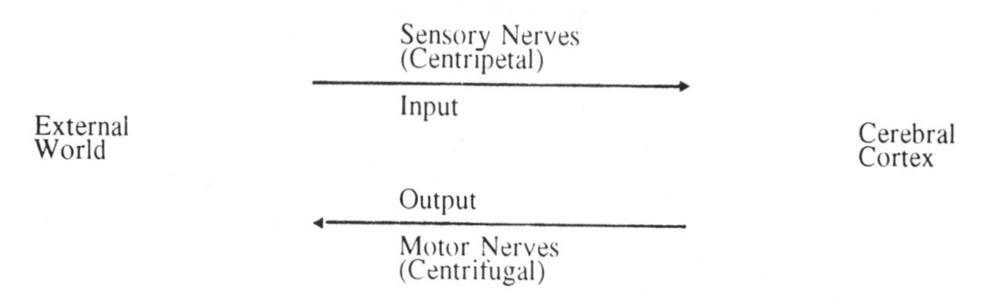

for the "utility of life," which refers to daily activities such as moving about and eating foods, for which this "sensory-motor apparatus" is necessary. Moreover, Maurice Merleau-Ponty (1908–61), another philosopher, following the idea suggested by Bergson, calls the relationship between the sensory nerves and the motor nerves that deal with the external world the "sensory-motor circuit" (*un circuit sensori-moteur*). This is a habituated information system for action relating to the external world. Penfield, a brain physiologist, characterizes the same idea as the "automatic sensory-motor mechanism."

These days it is fashionable to regard the brain as a kind of information management system, comparing it to a computer. Furthermore, by combining the computer's information management and the motor apparatus, various kinds of robots have been produced. In contrast with the system of the body, a robot is a mechanization of the function of this external sensory-motor circuit [*gaikai kankaku undō kairo*] centered in the cerebral cortex. The stimuli received through the sensory organs from outside (for example, light, sound, tactile sensation, and olfactory sensation) are information inputs to the computer, which is the brain, of data concerning situations in the external world. The computer, that is, the cerebral cortex, reads off the data to give a response, and sends a command to the motor organs through the circuit of motor nerves thereby initiating an action. This mechanism uses the same principle as that in a robot. When seen in this way, the training of bodily capabilities is to enhance the potential capacity of the sensory-motor circuit, that is, to develop the capacity to respond more swiftly to stimuli from outside, or to embody a capacity to manage more data.

The second information system of the body is *an internal information apparatus* about the condition of the body itself, and chiefly consists of two circuits. First is the information apparatus concerning motion. The motor nerves are the circuit through which the cerebral cortex sends commands to the four limbs (the hands and legs), which are the distal motor organs. The muscles and tendons in the motor organs, such as the hands and legs, are equipped with sensory motor nerves which inform the brain of their condition. In this case, the motor nerves are a centrifugal (efferent) circuit while the motor sensory nerves are a centripetal (afferent) circuit. Those who excel in sports or in the performing arts have the capacity of this circuit well developed: the information carrying the conditions of the hands and legs is rapidly conveyed to the center of the brain through the sensory-motor nerves, and the center, in turn, immediately sends commands responding to the conditions to the distal organs of hands and legs. In virtue of this circuit, they are capable of performing well. This is the body's "circuit of kinesthesis" [*undōkankaku kairo*] and is the information system which supports the first external sensory-motor circuit.

Among philosophers, there were some who took note early on of the fact that this second circuit plays a role in supporting the first external sensory-motor circuit. Edmund Husserl (1859–1938), the founder of phenomenology, paid attention to the kinesthesis of the body existing latently at the base of the intentional function of consciousness.[4] Philosophers referring to "ego-consciousness," as represented by Descartes' "I think, therefore I am" (*cogito, ergo sum*), tend to associate it with a narrow sense of the functions of mind such as thinking, willing, feeling, emotion, and imagination. However, behind these functions is found the kinesthesis of the body directed toward the external world. When we take Descartes' *cogito* as the central function of ego-consciousness, motor sensation lies at its periphery. Inheriting this idea from Husserl, Merleau-Ponty proposed the concept of "body scheme" (*le schéma corporel*), which brought a new perspective to mind-body theory. His body scheme is a kind of biofeedback apparatus which supports the whole of the first information system, the external sensory-motor circuit. (I will explain his concept in chapter 4.)

Another circuit concerning the condition of the body is the *splanchnic nerves.* These nerves send information to the brain about the conditions of the visceral organs, but since their corresponding area in the neocortex or neoencephalon of the brain is rather small, a splanchnic sensation cannot be clearly felt in ordinary circumstances, unlike motor sensations which can be localized. When we are healthy we cannot have a distinct sensation of the abdominal cavity which would distinguish its various parts such as the lungs, heart, or stomach. (In contrast, motor sensations in the hands and legs can be brought to such clear awareness that we can distinguish the state of each fingertip. This is because there is a larger area in the cerebral cortex corresponding to the distal organs.) When we take motor sensation to be at the periphery of ego-consciousness, the splanchnic sensation is further behind it, formed at the base of a vague, dark consciousness.

However, when an abnormality is detected somewhere within the interior of the body, that is, when a sickness occurs, this splanchnic sensation informs the central nervous system of its abnormality in the form of pain. In such a situation, an extremely strong internal sensation is generated—a symptom that makes one aware of the sickness. Based on this information, a doctor tries to locate the problem. The splanchnic nerves are a centripetal circuit conveying the condition of the distal organs (in this case, the visceral organs) to the central nervous system. In addition to splanchnic sensation, we can enumerate the sensation of balance and dermal sensation as constituting the internal information apparatus concerning the condition of the body. The cerebral cortex synthesizes all the information and constantly checks the interior condition of the information apparatus (computer) that is the body.

I shall collectively call this internal information apparatus concerning the condition of the body centered around the splanchnic sensation, the "circuit of somesthesis" [*taiseinaibu kankaku*]. (Somesthesis is translated into Japanese as "*taiseinaibu kankaku,*" which includes dermal sensation, bathyesthesia, the sensation of balance, and splanchnic sensation. Furthermore, the whole, combining kinesthesis and somethesis, is referred to as "coenesthesis" [*zenshinnaibu kankaku* or *shintai kankaku*] (see Fig. 2.2).

This second circuit of coenesthesis can be compared to a feedback apparatus. It is like a thermostat in which a red light goes off

FIGURE 2.2
THE CIRCUIT OF COENESTHESIS

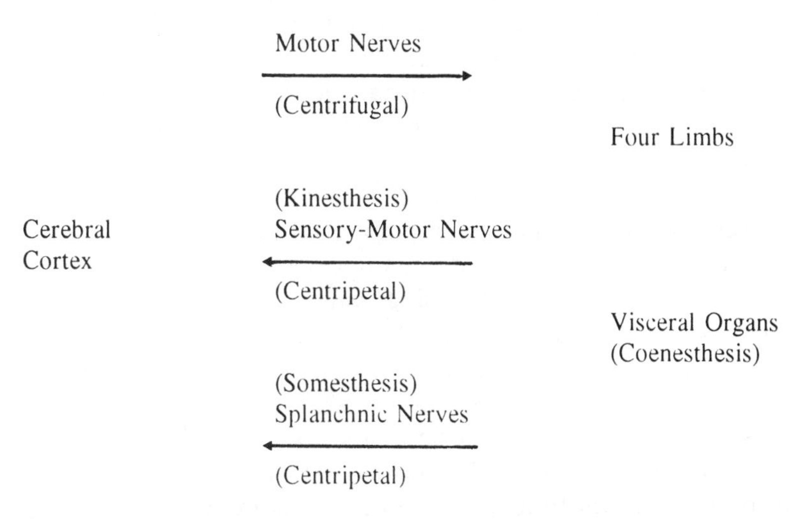

when the interior is heated, cutting off the supply of electric current, and thereby bringing the temperature down; when the interior becomes cold, the red lamp goes on again, allowing the electric current to flow in the interior. In other words, a change occurring in the interior is conveyed to the central nerves and in order to respond to the change, the central nerves send out a command to the distal organs. In short, coenesthesis is conscious awareness of one's bodily condition. I will call it *consciousness of self-apprehending sensation,* that is, awareness of one's own body.

Incidentally, all bodily movements are closely related to the mechanism of memory. Take the example of playing a sport or the piano. One improves one's skill through repeated exercise, and once the knack is learned, the player becomes proficient in its performance. If one reaches the state, to use an expression unique to the Japanese language, in which "the body learns," such a person is a full-fledged player. When one achieves skillful performance, one can instantly judge how to move one's hands, legs, or waist. Or even without the consciousness of judgment, the body moves unconsciously. Interpreting this mechanism psychologically suggests that at the base of the consciousness of judgment there exists a kind of automatic memory apparatus where past data is stored in such a way that it is sent to consciousness, checking the failures, so as to have a successful execution next time. The exercises repeat this process. In other words, exercises are to *habituate* the body in a specific direction. For this purpose, it is necessary to enhance *the capacity of this memory apparatus.* What is needed for this activity is the second circuit of coenesthesis.

The fundamental structure of the second circuit is its feedback system as mentioned above, but its precise mechanism is not sufficiently understood (for example, the mechanism of pain and bathyesthesia, or deep sensibility). This is because the relationship between memory, which is a psychological function, and the physiological function of the body has not been sufficiently clarified. Memory is a function connecting consciousness and the *unconscious,* which stores the data of past experiences. Therefore, a study of the unconscious is imperative for examining the mechanism within this second circuit.

Next, the third information system of the body is the circuit related to the autonomic nervous system. The autonomic nerves control the visceral functions in order to maintain life, such as the respiratory organs (lungs), the circulatory organ (heart), and the digestive organs (for example, the stomach). The autonomic nervous system is divided into sympathetic nerves and parasympathetic nerves, and the visceral organs can maintain their normality when these two nerves maintain a balance between being tensed and relaxed. When an extremely tense situation is prolonged, an abnormal condition occurs because of stress.

There are both centripetal and centrifugal circuits in the autonomic nervous system, but unlike the first two circuits they do not have separate circuits. The centripetal and centrifugal fibers are intermingled within the fibers making up the autonomic nerves. The centripetal circuit sends information concerning the state of a visceral organ to the center of the brain. What we need to pay special attention to here is that this circuit *does not reach* the cerebral cortex. This suggests that the activities of the visceral organs are performed below a conscious level. In contrast to this centripetal circuit, in the centrifugal circuit the brain converts a stimulus received through the sensory organs into *an emotional response* (pleasure or pain), that is, into information of stress, and sends it to the distal visceral organs.

The third circuit is the circuit for maintaining life. When the first external sensory-motor circuit is destroyed, one is often called a "vegetable." This occurs, for example, when a blood vessel in

FIGURE 2.3
EMOTION-INSTINCT CIRCUIT

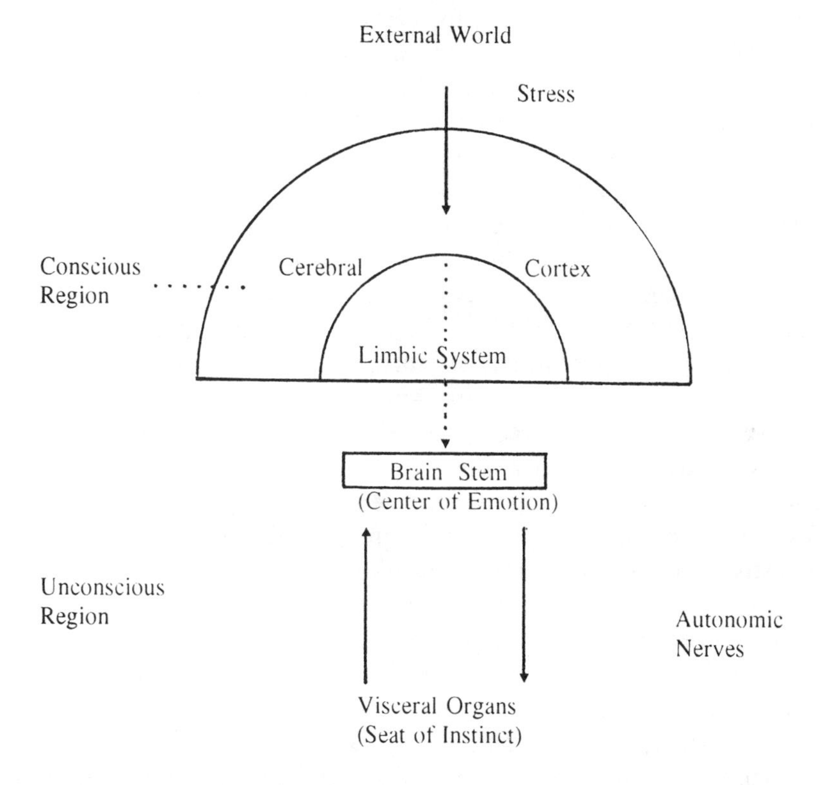

the brain ruptures, or when the motor nerves, which activate the motor movements of the body, are paralyzed. Yet the life of the patient can still be sustained if assistance from others is available. When the third circuit is destroyed, however, the individual's body is bound for death. In this sense, the circuit is the most fundamental for maintaining life rather than the body. This circuit is closely related to human instincts such as appetite and sexual desire. Thus, I will call it the "emotion-instinct circuit" [*jōdō honnō kairo*]. See Figure 2.3.

I will now examine the relationship between the mind and the above three information systems. The center for both the first external sensory-motor circuit and the second circuit of coenesthesis is located in the cerebral cortex. They are located in specific areas of the cortex. For example, the optical nerves, beginning in the retina of the eyes, are connected to the optical area in the occipital region of the cerebral cortex. The center for the motor nerves of the hands and legs is concentrated in the somatotropic area of the cerebral cortex. In contrast, the center for the autonomic nervous system is not in the cerebral cortex, but rather is in the brain stem (the region extending from the interbrain or diencephalon to the medulla oblongata) below or inside of the limbic system, or what is called the paleoencephalon. Psychologically interpreted, it is closely related to emotion. The frontal lobe is where consciousness becomes aware of the function of emotion, but the location where emotion originates is in the section called the hypothalamus in the interbrain. Unlike the first external sensory-motor circuit and the second circuit of coenesthesis, the autonomic nerves, in both their centripetal and centrifugal circuits, terminate below the cortex without reaching it. Thus, the function of emotion is not experienced under normal circumstances as a localized sensation in a specific part of the body.

This is an extremely important point psychophysiologically. The representative functions of consciousness (mind) are three, namely, sensory perception, thinking, and feeling (emotion). Among them, both sensory perception and thinking can be mapped onto specific areas of the body. For example, visual and auditory perceptions are perceived in specific organs such as the eyes and ears, and the internal sensation of the hands and legs (motor organs) can be distinctively experienced as in the case of the clear and distinct sensation of each finger. In short, the perceptual function is the function of consciousness connected to a localized, specific section of the body. Moreover, the thinking function occurs primarily in connection with the frontal lobe of the cerebral cortex although, unlike sensory perception, it is difficult to specify its location exactly. However, emotions such as anger and sorrow are holistic, and cannot be localized in a particular section of the body. In this sense, emotion is a holistic function of the mind. Therefore, the standpoints of psychosomatic medicine and holistic health take the function of emotion to be extremely important.

The relationship among the foregoing three circuits may be schematized as in Figure 2.4. A sensory stimulus from outside enters through the first external sensory-motor circuit, which is in the uppermost surface in the scheme, passes through the second circuit of coenesthesis, and reaches the third emotion-instinct cir-

FIGURE 2.4
THE RELATIONSHIP AMONG THE THREE CIRCUITS

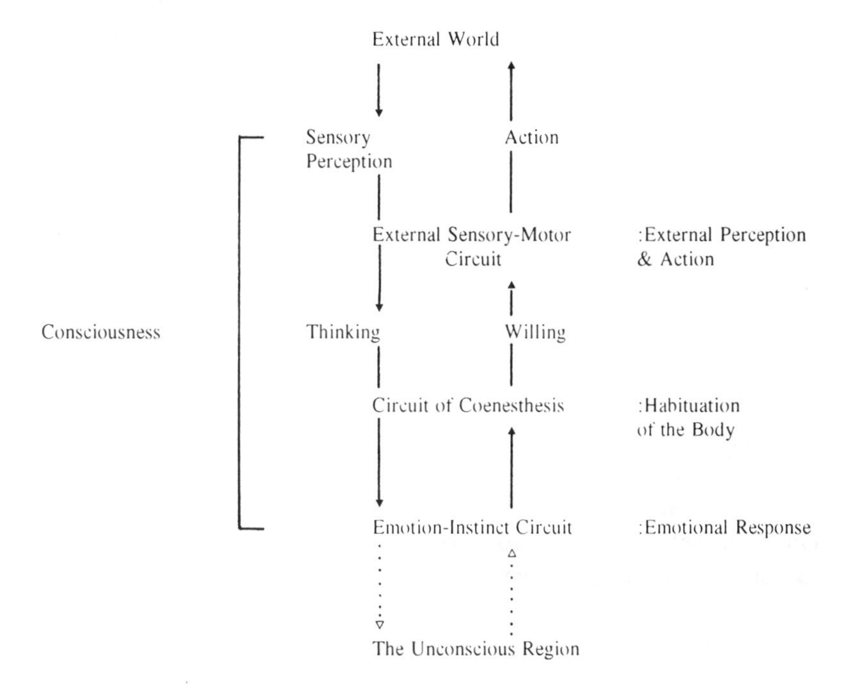

cuit, which is the lowest in the scheme, where a response of pleasure or pain is generated. This response returns to activate the second circuit, and further activating the first circuit it is expressed as bodily action in the external world.

In light of the history of philosophy, it is noteworthy that Western philosophers have paid attention since early on to the first circuit and to the kinesthesis of the second circuit, but they have not sufficiently focused on somesthesis and the third circuit. Depth psychologists and psychiatrists with an interest in Eastern self-cultivation methods first noticed the important significance of the third circuit for the body. This is a point to keep in mind when examining the contemporary significance of the Eastern mind-body theory. As clarified by discoveries in depth psychology, the unconscious emotional complex is active in a way which consciousness cannot control, and which can induce neurosis. This is because emotion originates below the cerebral cortex, and consciousness connected to the cortex suppresses emotion into the unconscious region. The unconscious function, when seen from the viewpoint of psychophysiology, cannot be specifically located in a section of the brain or body. For now, the unconscious can be conceived of as storage for memory, though as I have already indicated, it has become evident that the theory of memory localization is difficult to maintain as brain physiology has progressed in its development.

Because of this difficulty, Penfield and the others have abandoned reductionism and moved to correlative dualism taking the mind to exist independent of the brain (the body). Penfield in his later years, arrived at the idea that the mind might continue to exist even after departing from the body, and went so far as to maintain the old, traditional faith which recognizes the immortality of the soul after death. Starting with the idea that the function of memory is holographic, Pribram gradually came to hold the idea of a potential order, which consciousness cannot know, behind the empirically known order. Early in the beginning of this century, the philosopher Henri Bergson proposed the idea of "sheer duration" (*durée pure*), using the problem of memory as its clue. This is a forerunner to the correlative dualism which contends that the mind is a substance independent of the brain (the body), and it is also commensurate with Freud's concept of the unconscious.

From a philosophical standpoint, the function of memory has a bearing on the foundation of the concept of ego-consciousness. It is the mental activity which enables a human being to confirm self-identity, that is, that *I am my self.* For example, we can continue to live because we can recall, as the need arises, information such as techniques and knowledge acquired in our past and our life-history. A person suffering from amnesia or mental blindness cannot identify him or herself nor recall a place where he or she used to live. In this sense, the problem of memory (and consequently the problem of the unconscious) has central importance for human nature and personality. There are still many unresolved issues concerning the problem of memory which remain for future investigation, but since the Eastern mind-body theory deals with knowledge of the world beneath consciousness as its important task, I expect that the Eastern mind-body theory will offer suggestions or direction to the contemporary situation.

Now I would like to summarize the relationship between the foregoing three circuits of the body and the Eastern mind-body theory which I outlined in chapter 1.

The capacity of the external sensory-motor circuit with its center in the cerebral cortex does not have a direct connection with the function of emotion. For example, anger or sorrow does not immediately impair eyesight nor muscle power. The capacity of the first external sensory-motor circuit (the level of activities in the sensory organs and motor organs) is dependent primarily on the second circuit of coenesthesis. This circuit is connected to the mechanism of the habituated body. Those who can move their body freely and unconsciously as a consequence of repeated training have heightened the level of activity in the second circuit through development of memory capacity. This habituates the function of various bodily organs, which in turn heightens the active capacity of the first circuit. Therefore, the third emotion-instinct circuit does not have a direct bearing on the first sensory-motor circuit, although they are not totally unrelated.

Take an everyday example. The practice of an art, or training in a martial art or sport, is preparation for performance before an audience. But in such an important situation one often cannot exert one's usual strength because of becoming too nervous. When one loses one's calm, movement of the body becomes stiff and wastes power in unwanted places. This is because the movement of the mind and body become discordant. In a martial arts match, if one were to get angry with an opponent's move, one would lose emotional equilibrium and expose a weak spot. To avoid falling into this state, one must train oneself to retain a calm mind in any situation. Therefore, training to maintain emotional stability is important even when examined from the standpoint of muscular movement.

Meditation training is related to this point. As I mentioned previously, meditative training aims at dissolving emotional complexes rising from the unconscious and at learning to control oneself as one's mind wishes. For example, an emotionally unstable or nervous person becomes too nervous or excited on an important occasion, and is unable in a formal match to exert the usual power that one can demonstrate during training. This means that the potential capacity of the external sensory-motor circuit is not operating to full capacity because it is hindered by the loss of emotional equilibrium. Or, there may be the opposite situation where one can exert more than usual power when developing heightened tension and eagerness. In the latter case the function of emotion serves as a lubricant for energy to run smoothly in the external sensory-motor circuit. Seen in this light, the self-cultivation through seated meditation that the *bushi* of the past devoted themselves to is a rather rational method.

Meditation corrects distortion, as it were, in the function of emotion, and trains one to freely control it. When overcome by fear on the battlefield, or when losing emotional stability in a match with an opponent, the body stops moving smoothly. However, repeated meditative training in everyday life prevents a person from becoming excited in these serious situations, and enables one to make balanced judgments.

As I stated in the beginning of the previous chapter, the fundamental characteristic of Eastern self-cultivation methods lies in training the mind by training the body. Control is gained in the capacities of the various organs of the body, with the most freedom in the motor organs. Specific performing techniques (bodily movements) can be embodied to a high degree through constant, repeated training. This means that the first external sensory-motor circuit is heightened through habitualization of the second circuit of coenesthesis. However, the goal of Western sports stops at this stage.

In contrast, self-cultivation by means of bodily movement aims at making the function of the third emotion-instinct circuit, the deepest circuit in my scheme,[5] work smoothly through habitualization of the second circuit of coenesthesis. Movement of the mind can be enhanced and developed, just like the performing techniques of the body, through constant, repeated training. For example, there is a practice in the esoteric self-cultivation method of reciting a specific *mantra* (sacred sound) tens of thousands of times while concentrating the mind on a Buddha image. The practices of "*nenbutsu*" and "*daimoku*,"[6] which were developed in Japanese Buddhism, derive from this esoteric method. In this instance, a vocal code is employed, but the principle is the same in using other bodily organs. The essential point is to work on the activity of the emotion-instinct circuit by training that habituates the circuit of coenesthesis. The goal of self-cultivation, then, is to transform the habitual dispositions of the mind, by controlling emotion, in order to integrate the power of the unconscious with consciousness.

As mentioned above, when one gets too nervous it is difficult to exert one's usual power and consequently one cannot move the body as one wishes. This happens because a disturbance in the emotional function prevents a smooth connection between the movements of the mind and body. It is comparable to a situation where parts of a machine stop working properly because the lubricant has run out. To put this conversely, if a person can maintain calmness without being swayed by emotion, the movements of the mind and body will coincide with each other smoothly and freely. In short, controlling emotion in self-cultivation enhances the *degree of correlativity* between the movement of the mind and body, and develops a more intimate relation of union between mind and body. And ultimately, the aim of controlling emotion in self-cultivation is to pursue the spiritual goal of developing a mature, all-around personality.

Having said this, my characterization may still sound abstract, so I will examine in more concrete detail control of the function of the autonomic nervous system, which is the emotion-instinct circuit.

III. CONDITIONED REFLEX AND CONTROL OF THE AUTONOMIC NERVES

As noted in the previous sections, the development of depth psychology brought the issue of mind into the field of medical science, which in turn produced psychosomatic medicine. The theory of conditioned reflex gave powerful support to the development of psychosomatic medicine. Since I have not elaborated on this point, I would like to examine in detail the idea of controlling the autonomic function in light of the theory of conditioned reflexes.

A major difference between the function of the external sensory-motor circuit and that of the autonomic nervous system is that the former is voluntary, while the latter usually is not. Anyone can freely exercise the will to move the hand and leg (i.e., motor organs) unless one suffers from a special functional disorder. In addition, we can shut off, to an extent, stimuli received through the sensory organs by closing our eyes or covering our ears. In contrast, the activities of the visceral organs, such as pulsation of the heart or the digestive function of the stomach, are performed by themselves independent of the will, and we cannot usually exercise our will over them. The term "autonomic" in "autonomic nervous system" means that an activity is self-regulated, independent of the will. That is, the activity of the various visceral organs which are regulated by the autonomic nerves operates independent of the function of so-called consciousness. Nevertheless, this does not mean that the function of the external sensory-motor circuit and that of the autonomic nerves have nothing to do with each other. The mind influences the activity of the autonomic nerves through the function of emotion as well as through the activity of the visceral organs.

It was Ivan Pavlov's (1849–1936) experiments on conditioned reflexes which first discovered the above mechanism from a physiological viewpoint. If a bell is always rung when a dog is given food, and if this is repeated, the dog starts salivating upon just hearing the bell (a sensory stimulus). A secretion of saliva occurs in virtue of the activity of the parasympathetic nerves in the center of the medulla oblongata. This is usually an autonomic function occurring reflexively with food in the mouth as a stimulus; that is, it is an unconditioned reflex occurring independent of consciousness. There is no direct relationship in terms of the physiological function between hearing the bell (a sensory stimulus to the cortex) and the secretion of saliva (an activity of the autonomic nerves). Contrary to this situation, a conditioned reflex, which occurs only upon repeated reception of a stimulus (food), will be formed only with the sound of the bell. This is a reflex conditioned through habituation. In this case, the stimulus to the sensory organ and the activity of the autonomic nerves are connected by the function of *emotion* rooted in instinct. In the above example, the dog's *appetite* (its desire to eat) is stimulated.

To explain this mechanism in light of the preceding three circuits, the information entering the first external sensory-motor circuit reaches the third emotion-instinct circuit. An emotional response to this information rebounds back to the second circuit of coenesthesis which habituates the body, the process of which establishes a connecting passage among these three circuits.

As previously mentioned, the sensory nerves which control the sensory organs have centers in the cerebral cortex, and the autonomic nerves have a center beneath the cerebral cortex (in the brain stem). Although their respective centers are located in separate sections of the brain, the mechanism of conditioned reflexes demonstrates that a temporary connection is established between the cerebral cortex and the cortex beneath it, or between the neoencephalon and the paleoencephalon. The important point in this case is that the function of *emotion* creates a new temporary circuit which connects the cerebral cortex (the sensory nerves) with the cortex beneath it (the autonomic nerves). Here, the theory of conditioned reflexes makes it clear that it has discovered the same fact as depth psychology, although they have approached the problem from quite different perspectives.

When the mechanism of conditioned reflexes is examined from the position of depth psychology, the emotional complex suppressed beneath consciousness upsets the balance in the autonomic nerves, and produces a dysfunction in the visceral organ. The theory of conditioned reflexes explains the same fact as a stimulus entering through the sensory organs from outside forming a temporary connection with the autonomic nerves in the form of a conditioned reflex. It has now been discovered that conditioned reflexes are formed not only in the mechanism of the secretion of saliva but in the activities of various visceral organs. Although depth psychology and the theory of conditioned reflexes have taken completely different philosophical positions—idealism for depth psychology, and materialism for the theory of conditioned reflex—the problem on which they have focused is the same clinical fact.

In short, when a distorted emotional complex becomes *psychologically* fixed, triggering a disorder in the activity of the autonomic nerves, it means *physiologically* that a temporary connection is formed by means of a conditioned reflex between the function of the cerebral cortex (the sensory and motor nerves) and the function of the autonomic nervous system.

Here we need to examine the relationship between the body and its environment. In our daily life, we receive various physical and psychological stimuli (stresses) from our surrounding environment, and the manner of our response differs individually depending on personality. Personality may be defined psychologically as the unique way a particular person responds to stimuli. In other words, it is the pattern of emotional response (or habit of the heart/mind) unique to a particular person. When this emotional response is excessively distorted, a complex is formed resulting, for example, in a neurosis. In this case, the stimuli from outside enter the body through the external sensory-motor circuit, and proceed to influence the functioning of the autonomic nerves. At any rate, what is of importance is the following: the activity falling under the cerebral cortex (sensory-motor system) and the activity of the autonomic nervous system which operates independent of will are not totally unrelated, but rather they are *connected through the function of emotion.* Consequently, it is possible to form various temporary connections through learning or conditioning which bear on the function of emotion. This point is related to Eastern self-cultivation methods, particularly to meditation training. Meditation training controls unconscious emotion. Roughly speaking, it means developing the functions of both the autonomic nervous system and emotion to *a higher degree,* or in a way conducive to living. This is based on a conditioned connection between the activity of the conscious-cortex order and the activity of the unconscious-autonomic order.

Of note here is that meditative training in Eastern self-cultivation in many cases starts with a breathing exercise. Although a distinctive feature of Zen meditation is that it does not employ a complicated breathing method, it nevertheless uses the method of "observing breath count" [*sūsokukan*]. In Yoga meditation, there are many special breathing methods (*prānāyāma*), although Yoga itself is divided into two groups, one emphasizing meditation and the other emphasizing bodily exercise. In Chinese Daoist self-cultivation there is also a special breathing method called "*shōshūten*" (small circulation of light breathing).[7] That control of breathing is useful for controlling emotion is probably wisdom born naturally out of experience.

Everyone has had the experience of breathing deeply to appease an excited mood. Of special note here is that the respiratory organ, when viewed physiologically, is governed by both *motor nerves* and *autonomic nerves.* Both voluntary and involuntary muscles are attached to the lungs. Thus, breathing can be controlled to a certain extent by will, as in the case of deep or rapid breathing. Therefore, continuous training in breathing method would seem to be useful for forming a temporary conditioned-reflex connection between the cerebral cortex and the autonomic functions.

In recent years, experimental research in biofeedback has been extensively carried out. Soon after World War II, Dr. HIRAI Tomio and Dr. KASAMATSU Akio, both psychiatrists at Tokyo University, measured the brain waves (EEG) of Zen monks in meditation and discovered that they frequently emitted α waves during meditation.[8] Dr. Kamiya, a second-generation Japanese-American, took note of this report and performed follow-up experiments to confirm this fact. Consequently, Kamiya designed an apparatus which can convert the α wave into a sound. Using this apparatus, a subject trains oneself to concentrate one's thought in such a way that the α wave will appear (that is, so the sound will be heard). As previously mentioned, feedback is an automatic control system. That is, it is a way of self-control by converting a process occurring within the subject's body (in this case, an occurrence of the α wave) into sensible information (the sound) so that the subject becomes aware of it. Using this as a guide, the subject can in turn control the process occurring inside his or her mind-body. This kind of research has enabled us to pursue empirical, scientific study of the relationship between the unconscious functions of the mind and physiological processes occurring inside the body.

Biofeedback research has now made it clear that consciousness can control various physiological functions, not only brain waves, but also the electric response of the skin and the heartbeat, including blood volume. This research clarifies the meaning of Eastern meditation and self-cultivation methods together with their value for the human mind and body in developing health.

Biofeedback research is based on the same principle as the theory of conditioned reflexes in that it deals with controlling the activity of the autonomic nervous system. Some years ago, our research team measured a *yogin* (a Hindu cultivator) who was visiting Japan from India. He had a reputation for an ability to control his heartbeat. We prepared equipment to amplify his heartbeat into a speaker system, and his electrocardiogram was projected onto a television screen. We asked him to concentrate his thought so that he could control his heartbeat. Measurements taken at the time indicated no change in his electrocardiogram, but we could not hear his heartbeat at all. When we asked him to stop his concentration, his heartbeat was then heard. We repeated this experiment several times, and the same results were obtained.

According to a report by an Indian scholar who X-rayed this *yogin,* his heart was reportedly transformed into a tubular shape during meditation. Probably no heartbeat was heard because the blood volume in his heart was dramatically decreased by the contraction of the heart. (More advanced *yogins* apparently can slow the rate of their heartbeat.)

Although we need to gather many more cases like this, it does represent an instance of self-control. At any rate, it is clear that either meditation with a breathing exercise or training the mind, can influence the physiological function of the autonomic nervous system which the so-called free will is otherwise incapable of controlling. The function of the autonomic nerves is intimately connected to pleasure and pain, or to both positive and negative emotions such as anger, sorrow, hatred, pleasure, love, and peace. When negative emotions are always reinforced, a pathological state will ensue, but on the other hand if positive emotions are reinforced, they help develop a healthy mind-body and nurture a more mature psychological character (emotional patterns as habits of the mind/heart). Meditation means integrating the function of consciousness with the activity of energy in the deeper layer of the unconscious, while eliminating distortions in the emotions. Accordingly, self-cultivation delves into the deeper, unknown layer of the mind or unconscious, and by controlling its power heightens potential mind-body capacity.

One point must be added in this connection. The various exercises handed down in Eastern self-cultivation methods such as Yoga are designed to enhance the functioning of organs governed by the autonomic nervous system, unlike Western-style exercises which aim at enhancing the capacity of the motor organs (muscles). For example, a particular posture (*āsana*) is good for the liver or for strengthening the capacity of the stomach.[9] For this reason, although I have used the term "exercise," yogic *āsanas* do not call for vigorous movement of the arms and legs, but rather require a posture to be held still for a certain amount of time.

Western-style exercises and sports aim at strengthening the muscles of the arms and legs, but no care is taken to relate them to the organs regulated by the autonomic nervous system. When interpreted psychologically, this shows that Western training of the body lacks the idea of controlling the function of emotion and instinct.

IV. A METHODOLOGICAL REFLECTION

In examining the Eastern mind-body theory we must also include in our investigation the theory of Eastern medicine. I will discuss this in chapter 4, but here I would like to provide a methodological reflection from a philosophical standpoint.

What are the fundamental differences between the modern Western pattern of thinking and the traditional Eastern pattern of thinking? To approach this question in light of the mind-body function, modern Western medicine uses for its standard the normal condition of the great majority of people, that is, *an unspecified, large number of cases*. For example, by observing cases of normal people that "this" organ functions in a certain way or "that" drug has a particular effect, an empirical law is formulated. Generally speaking, modern empirical science adopts this method. For this reason, a modern scientific law has general validity. This approach, however, tends to ignore or treat lightly the exceptional cases.

In contrast, Eastern medicine follows the principle of prescribing medication differently from patient to patient; even though the illnesses dealt with may seem identical, it is not uncommon for prescriptions to differ between patients. This is because Eastern medicine does not formulate an empirical law by generalizing as its standard the cases of an unspecified, large number of people.

Applying this attitude to the mind-body relationship, the traditional Eastern pattern of thinking takes as its standard people who after a long period of training have acquired a higher capacity than the average person, rather than the average condition of most people. It proceeds to investigate the mind-body relationship in light of exceptional cases such as, for example, a genius or the masters of various disciplines. Traditional scholarship in the East has generally taken this approach. A law derived therefrom indeed lacks the general validity of the laws of modern science, but it has instead the advantage of grasping a deeper, potential mechanism which otherwise would remain incomprehensible.

One of the shortcomings of the modern pattern of thinking is the tendency to regard the unspecified, large number of cases as "normal" and all that which does not conform to it as "abnormal." This gives rise to a problem in psychiatry. Psychiatry takes as its object of research pathological, abnormal conditions such as psychosis and neurosis, and "abnormal" in this case carries a negative sense of "pathological." With the distinction between "normal" and "abnormal" based on the pathological, a genius or a master is a human being who does not fit the standard based on an indeterminate number of ordinary people, and is in this respect "abnormal." Both a genius and a madman will end up equally being treated as "abnormal." Since medical science obtains information mainly from sick people, it has a tendency to identify "the abnormal" with the pathological.

In the history of psychiatry there was a theory, held for example by Cesare Lombroso (1836–1909), that a genius is identical with a madman. According to this theory, a genius is essentially a kind of madman. It is true that, relatively speaking, many geniuses possess abnormal innate dispositions, but it is not legitimate to make the value judgment that "normal" is good and "abnormal" is bad based on a distinction that takes the average of an indeterminate number of people for its standard. For example, if we measure IQ or physical strength among the majority of people and draw a statistical graph, we will obtain a normal distribution shaped like a mountain peaking in the center. In this case, if we take the indeterminate number of cases as a standard mean, the normal is the average majority in the middle, whereas the minority on each side is abnormal. However, what we fail to realize is that there are two kinds of "abnormality" in terms of its value: a positive abnormality and a negative abnormality. Those few on the right side of the distribution scoring higher should be regarded as "abnormal" or "supernormal" in a positive sense.

It is said that "the exception clarifies the essence." The exceptional, abnormal condition is useful for clarifying the essence of things which otherwise remains incomprehensible in an average condition. One instance of this saying is that medical science has clarified the mechanism of the body through the study of sickness. In the East, the mind-body problem has been approached focusing always on the exceptional, elite experience.

At any rate, Eastern mind-body theory attempts to understand the ideal state based on the experiences of the elite who through long periods of training have acquired a high degree of mind-body ability, which cannot be observed in the average person. It is both the ideal state and the potential state which promises a *possibility* to all people. Here we discover a fundamentally different approach compared to modern, Western, mind-body theories. This difference has a bearing, for example, on how to understand "health."

When we adopt the dichotomous viewpoint of regarding the cases of an indefinite number of people as "normal" and those falling outside of it as "abnormal," only a negative definition can be given to "healthy": it is the state in which no sickness or no pathological abnormality is present. However, according to the Eastern viewpoint, "health" and "sickness" are not states which can be clearly demarcated in terms of their quality, but are taken to be a *difference of degree*. In other words, any human being is potentially a sick or a healthy person to a certain degree, and health has various levels. Eastern theory takes as preventive medicine the approach of enhancing, through constant and repeated training, the degree of health so as not to contract sickness.

To use a simple metaphor, the modern Western pattern of thinking is a kind of "democratic" theory taking the majority as its standard. By contrast, the traditional Eastern pattern of thinking is an "elitist" theory with a goal which only a few can reach through their efforts.

Democracy and the majority principle may be important in the world of politics, but human dispositions and capacities vary from person to person when seen from the medical and psychological standpoints. It is impossible to make them equal by means of political power. What is important is rather to find a way of enhancement appropriate to each person's capacity and disposition. The fundamental principle is the same in regard to issues such as bodily capacity, health, and growth of personality (or mind). In each one cannot enhance one's endowed potential capacity unless one makes an effort. It cannot be left up to medical doctors. In this respect, the Eastern elitist view of human being does not take the essence of human nature simply as a given, but takes it as an unknown which needs to be practically investigated. Self-cultivation is an endeavor to discover the true self through this practical investigation and to actualize it.

In connection with this observation, I would like to draw attention to another difference between traditional patterns of Eastern and Western thinking which concerns the relationship between theory and practice. According to the modern Western pattern of thought, theory and its application are in principle distinguished. The usual procedure in this model is to construe a theory by observing an indefinite number of cases and then to apply the theory to actuality. On the other hand, theory and practice are not distinguished in the Eastern model. There is a strong tendency to formulate theoretical constructs following practical experience. To put this in the context of the mind-body relationship, a theoretical viewpoint is formulated by investigating the cases of persons who have acquired the experience and supernormal capacity which an average person cannot imitate. For example, the experience of "body-mind oneness" or "casting off mind and body" is available only to those who have spent a long time training and cultivating their mind-body, and using this experience as a standard, the mind-body relationship is theorized.

Therefore, Western mind-body theories have a strongly held attitude of asking theoretically what *is* the relationship between the mind and body, but Eastern mind-body theory takes the attitude of asking how the mind-body relationship *becomes* or *changes* through training and practice. And based on how the relationship has developed through practice, the theory asks in turn what is the *original* relationship between mind and body. Since the modern Western pattern of thinking first seeks to formulate a theoretical paradigm of the mind-body relationship, it tends to ignore those cases which do not fit the paradigm, disregarding them as exceptional or abnormal. On the other hand, the Eastern model takes the attitude of investigating the mind-body relationship through practical experience, starting with the idea that a true mind-body relationship is unknown in the everyday, normal state.

It is necessary to keep in mind this implicit philosophical presupposition in investigating the meaning of the Eastern mind-body theory. Western philosophers have so far advanced many theories concerning the mind-body relationship. After the dualism of Descartes, parallelism, epiphenomenalism, and the theory of the human as a machine were advocated. Parallelism maintains that there is a one-to-one relationship between the functions of mind and body. Epiphenomenalism takes the activity of mind to be an epiphenomenon accompanying the function of the body where the latter is central. Ivan Pavlov, who discovered the conditioned reflex, adopted materialism and insisted that what is considered the function of the mind is reducible to a higher nerve activity by means of the stimulus of the secondary sign system (such as languages).

The identity theory, which was initiated in the 1960s in the United States, maintains that consciousness is reducible to brain activity; that is, the state of mind is identical with the state of the brain. To be more specific, an explanation of the state of the mind is the same as that of the state of the brain, and their only difference is that the former uses inaccurate ordinary language while the latter employs precise scientific language. The identity theory is an extension of the theory of humans as machines.

There are many interesting points made in these theories, but I always feel that in these philosophers' arguments there is a question about whether these theories stop at the argument of how to appropriately formulate a theoretical paradigm.

In the future this attitude will change, I hope, since as indicated in the previous chapter there has been an increase in the number of Western researchers who have started to pay attention to Eastern meditation and self-cultivation methods. In the case of biofeedback, for example, theoretical investigation is impossible unless there is training (*practice*) by a subject with no bifurcation between practice and theory. The traditional mind-body theory in Eastern philosophy seeks to know a deeper, unknown mind-body relationship which resists understanding as long as we remain in our everyday field of experience. At the same time it examines the experience of how the mind-body relationship changes through the process of self-cultivation and the psychological experience accompanying this process. Therefore, it is not simply a matter of a way of thinking. Since practice and theory are inseparable from the outset, training the body is training the mind. Thus, Eastern mind-body theory is connected to the problem of human ways of living as they pertain to the enhancement of the mind, that is, to growth of personality and the transformation of human nature.

PART II

Ki *and the Body: Martial Arts, Meditation Methods, and Eastern Medicine*

CHAPTER 3

Ki *and the Body in the Martial Arts and Meditation Methods*

I. INTRODUCTION

The concept of *ki* [Chin. *qì*], as exemplified in part in the Sung-Ming *riki* [Chin. *lǐqì*][1] philosophy, is an important concept running through the history of Chinese philosophy.[2] In the historical background of *riki* philosophy are interactions among Confucianism, Buddhism, and Daoism. Although on several occasions there were subtle conflicts regarding their philosophical worldviews, at their base was a common fundamental experience. This is the self-cultivation method [*shugyōhō*], or the mind-body disciplinary training method, which Confucians call "quiet sitting" [*seiza*], Buddhists "seated meditation" [*zazen*], and Daoists "kneading medicine"[3] [*rentan*] or "guiding *ki*" [*dōin*]. Their contents may be referred to collectively as meditation methods [*meisōhō*].

We have seen gradual clarification of the meaning of these meditation experiences through the knowledge of modern psychology as depth psychology developed. I wonder if the problem of *ki* may be approached afresh from this new perspective?

Moreover, the concept of *ki* has fundamental importance for the view of the body which is held by traditional Chinese medicine and which has been handed down from ancient times to the contemporary period. When meditation methods are seen from the standpoint of today's individually specialized sciences, however, they belong to the field of psychology, while Chinese medicine seems to have a close connection to the field of physiology. The former is concerned with the problem of mind and the latter with the problem of body. These two fields cannot be properly connected with the thinking model of modern science, which has followed the mind-matter dichotomy since Descartes. For some time

I have been pondering how to see this relationship. As I became acquainted with the practitioners and researchers of Eastern martial arts (the old way of the martial arts [*kobudō*]), I came to realize that the concept of *ki* has played an important role even in the martial arts. Since ancient times, martial arts training has been regarded as a method for disciplining and enhancing the mind, or spirit, as well as bodily capacities. As I started examining the martial arts, I came to understand that the cultivation method of the martial arts bears an intimate connection not only with meditation methods but also with Eastern medicine. Therefore, in the following I would like to investigate the relationship among the martial arts, meditation methods, and Eastern medicine, using *ki* as a pivotal concept. Through this I would like to elucidate the Eastern view of human being and the world.

II. UNIFYING MIND AND *KI*-ENERGY

The ultimate secret of Japanese martial arts is said to lie in letting the mind unite with *ki* [*shinki icchi*], which I learned from Mr. KAWASE Ken'ichi, a researcher in the martial arts. According to Kawase, Japanese martial arts have since ancient times regarded their ultimate secret to be the "unification of mind, *ki,* and power."[4] In the terminology of books on the martial arts, "power" refers to performing technique or body skill [*waza*]. Kawase interprets a performing technique as successfully executed when mind and *ki* become unified. But what does it mean to say that mind and *ki* become unified?

Since mind/heart [*shin*] means *kokoro*[5] in Japanese, it may be taken for the present purpose as consciousness. In contrast, *ki* is a nebulous concept rather difficult to grasp, and yet in the martial arts it designates the "mind" in the lower abdomen (the so-called "*seika tanden*").[6] Cultivating this *tanden* is fundamental to all the martial arts. This traditionally originated in the self-cultivation methods of Daoism (breathing and meditation methods) as well as in the theoretical system of Eastern medicine, which has a close connection with Daoism. It also designates a practical training method. To use the name of the acu-point[7] utilized in Eastern medicine, the area of the *tanden* in the lower abdomen is called the "ocean of *ki*" [*kikai*], which approximately corresponds to the solar plexus. The fact that the term "mind" [*shin*] means at the same time the "ocean of *ki*" in the lower abdomen gives us a clue for examining the meaning of the unification of mind and *ki*.

The *postures* of the body are foundational in the martial arts as well as in self-cultivation methods. In the so-called natural posture of the body [*shizentai*], the practitioner tries to settle the gravity of his or her body into the lower abdomen, while relaxing the upper half of the body and straightening the spinal cord. One tries to maintain this posture in seated form when doing breathing exercises and meditation. This is a beginning step in training the mind-body to relax. It is fundamentally the same in the martial arts; the only difference is that in the martial arts the natural posture of the body is standing and facing an opponent. Meditation trains one to direct one's mind within while maintaining this posture as long as possible in a state of silent stillness (immovability) so that wandering thoughts, welling up from the bottom of the mind, disappear. To put it differently, meditation is training to gaze into the *inner world*. Assuming the same posture in martial arts, the practitioner goes out to the *outer world*. This point suggests that the meaning of the unification of mind and *ki* may be sought in the relationship between "inner" and "outer" worlds. Historically speaking, the martial arts and meditative methods are closely related.

Here we enter a somewhat intricate philosophical issue. The contrast between the "inner" and "outer" worlds has so far been used as metaphors. In the martial arts, however, the "outer" world refers to *outside one's body,* and this is not a metaphor. There, various things, including the other's body, are found. This environment is "outside." By contrast, when we say that meditation is training to gaze into the inner world, the "inner" is not, strictly speaking, the interior of the body, but rather means the mind [*kokoro*] or the world of the psyche [*tamashii*]. Since mind does not have a visible form, when its state is explained to others it must be expressed in terms of its relationship to sensible thing-events [*jibutsu*]. This being the case, the world of mind is metaphorically referred to as the "inner world." Nevertheless, the term "inner" is not entirely metaphorical, because consciousness comes naturally to gaze within the interior of the body when in meditation sensible stimuli from outside are shut off as much as possible.

At any rate, what is here referred to as "inner" means, to use a broad division, the world of mind, and "outer" means the world of matter [*mono*]. In other words, the contrast between "inner" and "outer" will mean the relationship between mind and matter, or between spirit and material substance (matter found in the external world). What then is the status of the body? Does it belong to the "outer world?" Or, is it something else? In Western languages, the term "body" covers both "one's own body" [*karada*][8] and "material substance" or "matter" [*buttai*]. In Japanese, "one's own body" and "material substance" are altogether different. We do not think that "one's own body" is a material substance. If another person treats it as a material substance no different from the things around us, we will be upset. We feel that it has characteristic qualities different from material substances found in the outer or external world. In other words, we have the feeling that "one's own body" is an *intermediary being* between "mind" and "matter," and that it is a mediating system of organs connecting the world of spirit to the world of material substance. What distinguishes "one's own body" in this case from matter (material substance) is the feeling of "being alive." In "one's own body" there is "life" [*inochi*] or vital force [*seimei*], whereas there is no feeling of "being alive" in an inanimate object.

In short, "one's own body" exists as an intermediary being between and connecting mind and matter, and within it is found the feeling of "life." The Eastern theory of the body is in essence an attempt to investigate the structure of "life" in "one's own body" from the perspectives of both mind and matter.

To put it a little more accurately, modern Western medicine's theory of the body first anatomically classifies the body into various organs, and then by examining their physiological functions, it conceives of the mechanism of the body. The mechanism in this case is understood objectively in the same manner as the mechanisms of matter. (I shall for now call the body-image which is thus obtained the "object-body" [*kyakutaiteki shintai*][9]). However, the body can be apprehended not only from this objective viewpoint but from its interior, that is, from an incarnate subjective viewpoint. (In the preceding I have already indicated the sense of "interior" when dealing with the "inner" world.) An issue emerging in this connection is *the sensation of the body* [*shintai kankaku*] or *coenesthesis* [*zenshinnaibu kankaku*]. It refers to sensations we have of the condition of our own body.[10] It is made conscious primarily through the motor-sensory nerves which inform the brain of the muscular condition of the limbs (arms and legs), which are the motor organs, and through the splanchnic sensory nerves which inform us of the state of the internal organs. (In addition, there are special sensations of the body such as the sensation of balance and dermal sensation. Stomach pain and itching indicate abnormal conditions in the sensation of the body.) I shall collectively designate these sensations as "coenesthesis" [*zenshin naibu kankaku*] or "somatic sensation" [*shintai kankaku*].

Broadly speaking, these sensations belong to the state of consciousness (that is, the mind). However, we ordinarily distinguish them from the narrow functions of the mind such as thinking and feeling. They concern the feelings in (or of) "one's own body." When a doctor diagnoses a patient, he or she asks about the condition of this body, using it for clues to understand the state of the object-body. In other words, the body can be distinguished into two aspects: the objective aspect when observing the other's body from outside, and the subjective (incarnate) aspect when feeling one's own body from within. A characteristic of the Eastern theory of the body lies, in view of this dual aspect, in emphasizing the subjective self-apprehending sensation that is felt from within one's own body.

Now let us return to the subject of *ki*. It is known that cultivators in the martial arts have in the past trained themselves well in breathing exercises. Breathing methods are variously called, "adjusting *ki*" [*chōki*], "using *ki*" [*fukuki*], "embryonic breathing" [*taisoku*], and "going *ki*" [*kōki*], although they are all basically the same. "Embryonic breathing" is a method of breathing which slowly prolongs each exhalation and inhalation, like the gentle and soft breathing of a baby. "Going *ki*" is a method of breathing to distribute *ki* to the hands and legs in accordance with inhalation and exhalation. Kawase mentions breathing methods handed down in various schools of Jūjitsu, but they have only minor differences. As the above terminology indicates, breathing and *ki* since ancient times have been conceived as holding a close relationship. Although the term "*ki*" is sometimes used in the sense of "air," it has been generally thought to differ from it. In "going *ki*," one actually just imagines in one's mind that he or she is "circulating" it. This point is difficult to understand for modern ways of thinking.

In Eugen Herrigel's *Zen in the Art of Archery* there is an interesting story concerning the relationship between breathing methods and training in the martial arts.[11] When Herrigel was teaching philosophy at Tōhoku Imperial University, he studied Japanese archery under AWA Kenzō, a reputed master, and obtained as high as the sixth degree certificate. He was initially instructed in the knack for releasing the arrow. When he pulled the bowstring he was to let the work be done by the hands themselves without using the power of his whole body. He was to loosen up the power in the muscles of the arms and shoulders, while closely observing the activities of both hands as if they were completely unrelated to him. The master told Herrigel that once he learned this technique, he would fulfil a condition for "spiritually" releasing the arrow when pulling the string. However, unlike the Western bow, the Japanese bow requires of the beginner the full strength of the body to pull it. This is because in Japanese archery an arrow is cocked with both arms extended high above the head, and then the arms gradually separate as they are brought down, whereas in Western archery the bow is brought to a halt at the level of the shoulders. Both hands are gradually set apart, and the left hand holding the bow is brought down to the level of the eyes while separating the arms. The hand of the right arm, bent in pulling the string, is stopped at the joint of the shoulder. The arrow head sticks out a little over the front of the bow. Maintaining this posture, an archer must sustain an immovable position for a while, calculating the appropriate time to release the arrow.

Herrigel trained himself in this manner, but his hands started shaking within several seconds while he was separating the bow and string, and he experienced difficulty breathing. The tip of his arrow did not remain stable, and he could not enter the state of stillness; he was far from becoming "spiritual" about the whole thing. No matter how many times he tried, it was in vain. The master told him to "loosen up." At last, Herrigel told the master that he could not perform in accordance with what he was instructed. The master instructed him that his failure lay in the wrong pattern of breathing. According to the master, after inhalation Herrigel should gradually push his breath down so as to distend his abdomen appropriately. At this point, he should hold his breath for a while, and then, slowly breathe out rhythmically. After a brief rest, he should inhale the air in one stroke. The master instructed him that, as he continued to practice the rhythm and pattern of inhalation and exhalation, he would find a source of spiritual power through this breathing method. He would discover that the source of this spiritual power would well up abundantly, and in proportion to the degree to which he loosened up, *the spiritual power would readily be infused into, and flow through, his hands and legs.* What the master referred to here as "spiritual power" is *ki.*

Herrigel then started training himself in this breathing method without using the bow. At first, he felt as though for no reason his head was going blank, although this was soon cured. The master emphasized the manner of exhalation, which is to breathe out in such a way that the breath disappears as gradually and slowly as possible. When Herrigel tried the bow after training himself in this breathing method, he discovered that it was useful for holding the upper part of his body in a still posture, but as he loosened up his arms and shoulders in pulling the bowstring, he found that now his legs would stiffen up. The master warned him that his leg muscles were stiffening. Herrigel retorted that he was trying to hold himself while loosening up. The master said "that's the problem," adding that he should forget everything and concentrate exclusively on his breathing while doing nothing else. After training himself in this manner, Herrigel reached the experience of a certain mood where he felt that it was not he who was breathing, but instead he was passively made to breathe. (This passive mood of being breathed also accompanies a deepened state of meditation. For example, Sū Dōngpō (1036–1101), a well-known poet during the Sung period, recorded in a note describing *ki*-training that one reaches a state called "*súi*" (to follow) after long training in breathing. It refers to a state where one is passively made to breathe, rather than voluntarily breathing.) As Herrigel experienced this passive breathing, he could gradually pull the bow string as he loosened his whole body, while at the same time maintaining the posture of stretching the bowstring. Herrigel related that he had learned the meaning of "spiritually" pulling the bowstring.

This story exemplifies well the fundamentals of the cultivation methods handed down in various Eastern religions. Training in meditation also starts with a breathing exercise. It is training to relax mind and body, and to enter a still, immovable state. The

Daoist meditation method refers to this as "cultivating *ki*" or "cultivating *tan*". This is no different in the martial arts. Therefore, the unification of mind and *ki* would probably mean, at least for now, that the mind *comes to feel* the flow of *ki*. In other words, *ki* is not a function which can be perceived by ordinary consciousness in everyday life, but is a new function which consciousness (or mind) is gradually able to perceive through mind-body training in meditation and breathing methods. Herrigel felt *ki* to be a kind of spiritual power. In recent years, depth psychology has probed into Eastern self-cultivation methods, and from such a perspective, the problem of *ki* is probably related to *the domain of the unconscious*. For now, *ki* may be conceived of as a function intuitively apprehended as a sensation of power rising from the base of coenesthesis.

Incidentally, Eastern medicine regards *ki* as a kind of energy, unique to the living body, that flows in the so-called meridians.[12] According to Kawase, both meridians and acu-points are to be cultivated in martial arts; they are at the same time both killing and saving points. For example, one offensive strategy for controlling an opponent is to attack on the meridians or acu-points where an opponent's *ki* is emitted. *Kikō* or *qìgōng* (*ki*-training),[13] now flourishing in China, is a hygiene, a therapy, and a training method, based on the theory of the body uniquely transmitted in the East. In Japan, new martial arts such as Aikidō have been developed in modern times, and they are spreading worldwide. In short, the martial arts of the East have thought that for successful excecution of correct technique the mind must apprehend the feeling that the flow of one's *ki* has become unified with that of an opponent; that is, a unification of the mind and *ki* is achieved. Moreover, from a medical perspective it has been thought that the flow of *ki* is closely related to a healthy state of both mind and body. I shall now proceed to investigate this issue of *ki*, first, from an historical perspective in way of preparation, and later, in chapter 4, I will examine it from a contemporary perspective.

III. MEDITATION TRAINING TRANSFORMS *KI*

In the Daoist cultivation method, the term "*ki*" is often found juxtaposed with "*shin, ki,* and *sei*" [Chin. *shén, qì,* and *jīng*]. For example, in Wáng Yángmíng's *Denshūroku* [Chin. *Tánxílù*] the following dialogue is found:

> QUESTION: I would like to ask what the Daoist's primal *ki*, primal *shin*, and primal *sei* are.
> MASTER REPLIES: They all mean one thing. When it is flowing, it is *ki*, when it is concentrated, it is called *sei*, and when its function is spiritually subtle, it is called *shin*.[14]

In his youth Wáng Yángmíng studied Zen Buddhism and the Daoist technique of guiding *ki* [*dōin*], and he is said to have obtained considerable paranormal ability. It is a well-known story that at the age of thirty-seven he experienced satori at Lung-ch'ang in Kuei-chou province. During the Sung and Ming periods Buddhists were engaged in seated meditation [*zazen*], Confucians in "quiet sitting" [*seiza*], and Daoists in "*ki* guiding meditation" [*dōin*]. They were competing among themselves in their respective meditation-cultivation methods. Various philosophic theories of *riki* were formed, as represented by Zhūzǐ and Wáng Yángmíng, taking as their foundation the experience of the whole personality by methods utilizing body and mind. Their written works remain for us today as a legacy of their intellectual activities, but their experiences are gone. By attempting these kinds of cultivation methods ourselves, however, we can to a degree relive their experiences.[15]

Although it appeared that the tradition of these cultivation methods had died out in mainland China, once China opened itself up to foreign countries after the Cultural Revolution, it became evident that they had survived after all. Moreover, the values in these old mind-body training techniques are in recent years recognized under the name of *qìgōng* [Jap. *kikō*], that is, *ki*-training. "*Qìgōng*" is a recent neologism collectively designating the various hygienic methods closely related to meditation, the martial arts, and Eastern medicine. (The "*gōng*" in "*qìgōng*" is taken from "*gōngfū*," meaning "to train.") It includes, in one body of knowledge, medicine, the martial arts (physical education), psychotherapy, and religious philosophy. (I shall explicate this *qìgōng* later.)

The "*ki, shin,* and *sei,*" mentioned above in Wáng Yángmíng's dialogue are called "*sānhé*" ("three rivers") in the Daoist cultivation method. "*Hé*" means flow. Erwin Rousselle, a sinologist, wrote an essay concerning the relationship of *ki, shin,* and *sei* basing his interpretation on his own personal experience of self-cultivation.[16] He went to China after receiving guidance from the depth psychologist C. G. Jung and the sinologist Richard Wilhelm. He learned actual Daoist self-cultivation methods in Beijing, associating himself with a Daoist organization called *Dàodéxuéshè*. Although it is not clear how much technical knowledge he had of psychology and physiology, I would like to sketch his explanation.

According to Rousselle, *shin, ki,* and *sei* may roughly be regarded respectively as "spiritual power," "life power," and "power for procreation" (or "power for immortality"). Meditation is training to control these three powers. The meditator first controls the flow of *ki* together with training in breathing. By means of this he or she sublimates the flow of *sei,* which becomes a seed for satori, and further transforms it into a spiritually subtle flow of *shin.* This explanation, like that of Wáng Yángmíng, states that *shin, ki,* and *sei* are fundamentally the same. It will be easy to understand the basic division among them, following Wáng Yángmíng, if we interpret *ki* collectively as a flowing energy divided into *sei ki* and *shin ki.*

Rousselle further explains the meaning of meditation training as follows. Although the flow of *shin, ki,* and *sei* does not exactly correspond to the body's physiological dimensions, it does influence them and is its psychological expression. (Needless to say, there is no hint of the modern mind-body dichotomy implied in this explanation.) *Sei* is an energy of impulses directed toward the external world, and has the function of producing things. It is often used to mean sexual energy. It attempts to attract to itself *ki*-energy, which is a psychic power. According to the traditional Chinese view, the human soul consists of two parts, an earthly "somatic soul" [*haku;* Chin. *pō*] and a heavenly "spiritual soul" [*kon*; Chin. *hún*]. The function of the "somatic soul" affects the flow of *ki,* and it attracts the heavenly "spiritual soul" into the orbit of its own function. To paraphrase it in modern terms, *sei* is desire and instinctive energy which tend to move toward the thing-events of the external world. Because of the strength of its power, our ordinary state is one in which the creative function latent in the psyche ("*shin*") is not activated. Daoist meditation recognizes this state as a *predominance* of *yīn over yáng*. Meditative training prevents *sei* energy from falling into such a state, and by concentrating one's thought-image in order not to waste the energy, it gradually purifies and purges the power of *ki.* In virtue of this process, *ki* will be transformed into *shin.* Along with this transformation, the heavenly "spiritual soul" will be released from the shackle of the power of the "somatic soul," thus enabling the meditator to reach an understanding of imperishability through the transformation of his or her personality, and to become connected with the sacred source of being (*Tàijí* or *Dào*). Rousselle says that when this occurs, the meditator will initiate a new and different association with society and the cosmos.

In view of the above summary explanation, the basic idea of meditation can be stated in roughly the following way. Meditation training changes the function of *ki,* latent in the mind-body, from its state of a more materially-based quality ("*sei*") moving toward the thing-events of the external world, to an inward direction. By training and controlling this process, meditation training transforms and sublimates *ki* to energy of a more spiritually purified state (*shin*). Through this training, the meditator actualizes a sublime, creative energy latent in the region of the unconscious and achieves a highly transformed state of personality.

When viewing this transformation in light of its somatic dimension, it is necessary to note the three so-called *tanden* [Chin. *dāntián*]. *Tanden* refers to a place to concentrate one's thought-image in meditation. The representative ones are the upper *tanden* in the center of the forehead, the middle *tanden* in the region of the heart, and the lower *tanden* in the lower abdomen. These are usually called the three *tanden.* (The term "*tanden*" means "a place to knead medicine" [*tan*]). It approximately corresponds to *cakra* in yogic meditation. Yoga, however, postulates six or seven *cakras* along the spinal cord.)[17] According to Rouselle's explanation, the upper *tanden* is the seat of light residing within ultimate, though latent, human nature [*seikō;* Chin. *xìngguāng*]. The middle *tanden* is the abode of the "spiritual soul," which is the heavenly awakened soul. And the lower *tanden* in the lower abdomen is the seat of the lower portion of the soul, the "somatic soul." Consequently, meditation is training to sublimate the energy of instinctive desire (sexual libido) indicated by the lower *tanden,* and by transforming the latter, it activates the function of the middle *tanden* and further awakens the latent, original human nature of light which is dormant in the upper *tanden*. In view of the transformation of *ki,* we may also characterize meditation as follows. Meditation is training to purify the power of *sei ki,* which is active primarily in the lower *tanden,* and to transform its nature to a creative quality, awakening and activating the power of subtle spiritual energy (*shin ki*) latent in the upper *tanden*.

This is a rough summary of meditation training viewed from its somatic dimension. This explanation, however, presupposes a premodern theory of physiological psychology. From today's physiological viewpoint, the lower abdomen is closely related to the reproductive function, and the forehead is associated with the frontal lobe of the brain, a seat of higher mental activity. According to the modern mind-body dichotomy, relating the lower abdomen to "*sei,*" and the forehead to "*shin*" may be taken as a kind of metaphor or symbolic expression for explaining a transformative process in psychological experience. But it seems unlikely that it can be interpreted simply as a metaphor or symbolic expression. The physiopsychological system of Eastern medicine is built upon the accumulation of clinical and curative experiences of over one thousand years, and Daoist meditation has been devised on the basis of the accumulated inner experiences of many people since ancient times. There we can find, I believe, a fount of valuable discoveries for medicine and psychology. Stored within it is an essence irreducible to the modern mind-body dichotomy. We must elucidate its meaning as best as we can from a contemporary perspective so that we can discover a new theory of the body which goes beyond the mind-body dichotomy.

When we adopt for present purposes the viewpoint of depth psychology, we see that "*sei*" approximates Freud's concept of libido. Freud interpreted the unconscious as the seat of suppressed, inferior instincts (especially, the sexual instinct). Jung took it to be the "shadow" in conformity with the inner experience of images. Often entering the region of the shadow is the power symbolized by sexual images, which Jung called anima or animus. According to Jung, however, the region of the unconscious is not simply dominated by the power of the "shadow." He says that a higher, creative, intuitive function is latent there. The idea of "*shin*" coincides with Jung's view.

Here I must explain my terminology. Jung calls the higher region, or the power emitted from it, the *Selbst*. "*Selbst*" is often translated as "Self" but this rendition is not clearly distinguishable from the self of self-consciousness (*Selbstbewusstsein*) when considered in relation to philosophy. In philosophy, self-consciousness and ego-consciousness are synonymous, but "self-consciousness" in Jungian terminology is a contradictory concept.[18] Existential philosophy makes a distinction with regard to the self (*Selbst*) between "inauthentic self" (*uneigentliches Selbst*) and "authentic self" (*eigentliches Selbst*). Heidegger took the former as the "I" in the field of everyday experience. The authentic self, which is different, is the true mode of being a self sought through one's own existential resolution. The sense of Jung's "Self" is close to this idea. Therefore, I would like to render "*Selbst*" as "authentic self" or "self-nature." Although this rendition is explicable in analogy with the concept of ego, it is not the center of conscious functions (the field of consciousness); rather, it is the latent center of personality apprehended through feeling in the region of transcendental experience which cannot be explained in terms of the standpoint of everyday consciousness. For example, the "original nature" [*honzen no sei;* Chin. *běnránxìng*] of which Zhūzǐ speaks in his philosophy is the authentic self as defined above. It is also commensurate with the "Buddha-nature" [*busshō*] of Buddhism, "Dao" in Daoism, and "Puruṣa" in Yoga. For simplicity's sake, I shall employ the rendition "self-nature."

The above depth-psychological interpretation is illustrated in figure 3.1. The ego is the center of the field of consciousness and controls various functions that surface in the mind. However, beneath consciousness exists the undisclosed region of unconsciousness. Separating them, and serving in the role of a filter, is Freud's concept of superego. (Jung calls it the *persona.* Simply put, the *persona* is the masked personality.) The superego is a psychological function that is appropriated and internalized as the power of social and moral constraints which are inculcated from infancy to suppress instinctive desires. Beneath this filter are suppressed the instinctive powers of the shadow, such as sexual desire and aggressive impulses (anger and hatred). It corresponds to the Buddhist concept of "*kleśa*" (desires and delusions). The "nature of *ki* quality" [*kishitsu no sei;* Chin. *qìzhìxìng*],[19] of which Neo-Confucian *riki* philosophy speaks, points to the psychological structure of this everyday state of experience. However, the religious tradition of the East maintains that there is a pure world of light at the

FIGURE 3.1
THE STRUCTURE OF THE PSYCHE

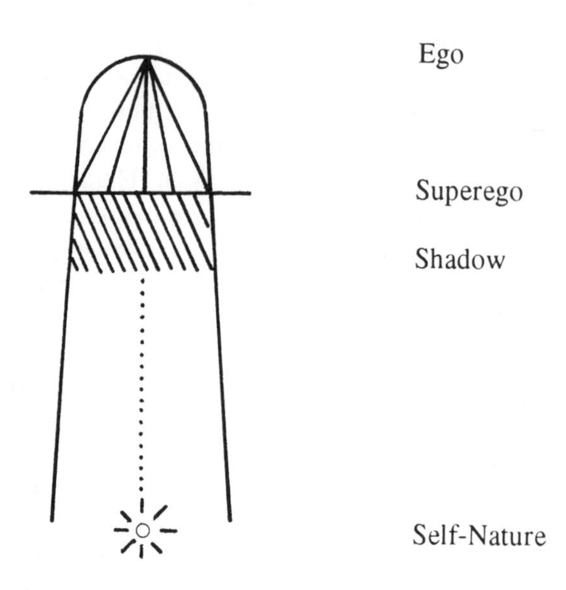

depth of this dark region. "Buddha-nature" and "the nature of the originally thus" [*honzen no sei;* Chin. *běnrándēxìng*] are terms designating such a latent dimension. Jung's "self-nature" is ambiguous and defies clear definition,[20] but it seems to be suggested by the above-mentioned Eastern concept. In figure 3.1 this is shown by the symbol of light, but it may be appropriate to characterize it as the region of higher experience. In short, ego and self-nature are separated by the instinctive region of shadow. Meditation training endeavors to integrate the function of ego and the dimension of self-nature, which are otherwise separated in the ordinary, everyday state, and to establish a correlative relationship between them. *Ki* is a key concept for clarifying the meaning of this training not only physiologically but also psychologically.

IV. THE TRANSFORMATION OF *KI*

We shall next examine various aspects of meditative experience in more concrete terms in view of the issue of *ki*. Roussselle explains in the latter half of his paper the fundamentals of breathing and the meditation method, which are more or less the same as the ones found in *The Secret of the Golden Flower* [Chin. *Tàiyījīnhuázhōngzhǐ*], a Daoist book of meditation. (This treatise became known in academic circles through the joint work of Richard Wilhelm and C. G. Jung. Hereafter, the title is abbreviated as *The Secret.*) So, I shall investigate the issue of *ki* following the explanations given in this treatise.[21]

The first chapter of this treatise is entitled "Heavenly Mind" [*ten shin;* Chin. *tiānxīn*]. "Heavenly mind" signifies "Dao" and is a symbolic designation of the ultimate, original nature of human being, although in this work it is explained as a "heavenly light" [*ten kō;* Chin. *tiānguāng*] latent between the eyes. This explanation defies comprehension by readers accustomed to conventional philosophical works. "Between the eyes" refers to the previously mentioned upper *tanden.* In Buddhist terminology, this is called the "curled white hair" [*byakugō;* Chin. *baíháo*] seen between the eyebrows in images of the Buddha. As legend has it, when Shakyamuni attained satori, the area between his eyebrows opened up and emitted a light. The Eastern meditation method has traditionally placed importance on the area of the upper *tanden.* The method of concentrating thought-images on this area, known as the "curled white hair meditation" [*byakugōkan:* Chin. *báiháoguān*], was widely used in Buddhism in China during the T'ang dynasty (618–907) and in Japan during the Heian period (794–1185). An example can be found in Genshin's *Ōjōyōshū* [*Essentials for Attaining the Pure Land*].[22]

The Secret refers to meditation training as "circulation of light" [*kaikō;* Chin. *huíguāng*] and states that fundamental to this meditation is the performance of a circulating movement of light in a reverse direction. In *The Secret* we read that "training in the circulation of light uses an entirely reversed method."[23] This reverse movement has the following two meanings. One is to reverse the function of consciousness which, in an ordinary state, is directed to the thing-events of the external world. That is, it redirects consciousness inward through concentrating on a thought-image between the eyes (the upper *tanden*). Simply put, meditation reverses the flow of mind-body energy which tends toward the outside, by concentrating its flow in the direction of one's own interior.

The other meaning of reversing the movement requires a somewhat complicated explanation. It signifies a method of concentrating on a thought-image, while synchronizing the act of concentration with the rhythm of breathing. This method is usually called the "small circulation of light" [*shōshūten*]. According to the traditional theory of the body that Chinese medicine espouses, the front of the body is regarded as *yīn,* and the back as *yáng*. It is maintained that in an ordinary state *yáng ki* flows from top to bottom in the back of the body, and *yīn ki* from bottom to top in the front of the body. In other words, *ki* alternates between *yīn* and *yáng* polar phases, with this polarity admitting ambiguity. When it descends along the back it fundamentally displays a *yáng* quality, and when it ascends along the front, it shows a *yīn* quality. The *Huìmìngjīng* [The Wisdom of Life Sutra], another treatise contained in *The Secret,* demonstrates diagrammatically these two pathways in terms of the two representative meridians, the *nin* ventral meridian [Chin. *rènmài*] and the *toku* dorsal meridian [Chin. *dúmài*] (see fig. 3.2). These two meridians are closely connected with Eastern medicine's theory of the body; the *nin* ventral meridian runs through the center of the front of the body, while the *toku* dorsal meridian is located in the back along the spinal cord. Accordingly, in an ordinary state *yáng ki* descends the back of the body, and in turn becoming *yīn ki,* it ascends the front of the body through the *nin* ventral meridian.[24] (The details are shown in Fig. 3.3.)

Here I must explain the alternation of *ki* in light of the relationship between "*sei ki*" and "*shin ki*." In an ordinary state, a person is caught up by instinctive desires for the thing-events of the external world, and for this reason, wastes his or her mind-body energy. In this state "*sei ki*" is strong and the power of "*shin ki*" is suppressed. As mentioned earlier, the Daoist meditation method considers this state to be a *predominance of yīn over yáng.* To put it simply, *yīn* indicates a bad or negative state. The alternation between *yīn* and *yáng* may be thought as analogous to the relationship between an artery and a vein. The *yīn ki,* like blood circulating through a vein after supplying nutrients to the various parts of a living body, is a flow of *ki* returning to the center. In contrast, *yáng ki* may be compared to fresh blood in the artery positively promoting the function of the living body. In short, *yáng ki* may be taken, for our present purpose, to be good, positive *ki.*

When the power of "*sei ki,*" the energy of instinctive desire, is strong in the ordinary state, *ki* as a whole has a strong tendency

FIGURE 3.2
THE *NIN* VENTRAL MERIDIAN AND *TOKU* DORSAL MERIDIAN

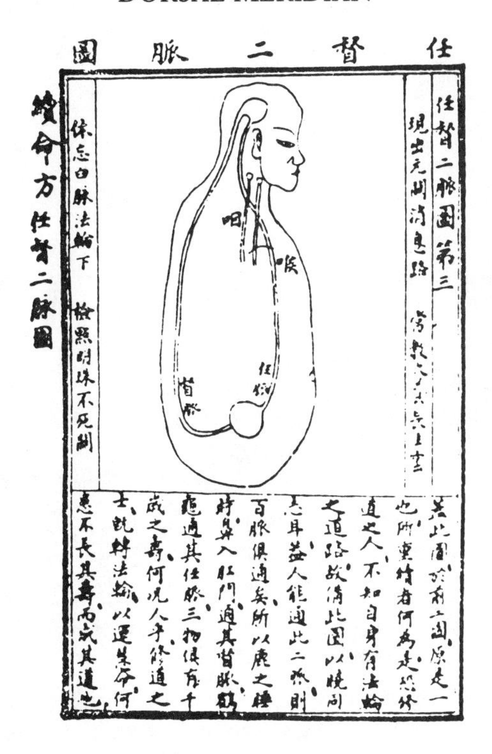

toward the *yīn* quality while the *yáng* quality is weak. This is the state in which *yīn predominates over yáng*. In order, then, to strengthen the *yáng* quality it is necessary to reverse the flow of *ki*. This then is the meaning when *The Secret* states that the "circulation of light is a reverse method." Figure 3.4, taken from the *Huìmìngjīng*, shows the "six seasons" [*rokukō*] of the intermediary points along the *nin* ventral and *toku* dorsal meridians. This seems to suggest important acu-points on these two meridians. They are apparently marked for a method which activates these points. When the meditator concentrates his or her consciousness to affect the flow of *ki*, *ki*-energy will be gathered into these points. (This method corresponds roughly to the Yogic meditation method for awakening the *cakras*.)

In the method of small circulation of light, the meditator imagines while inhaling that the invisible *ki* contained in the

FIGURE 3.3a
THE *NIN* VENTRAL
MERIDIAN

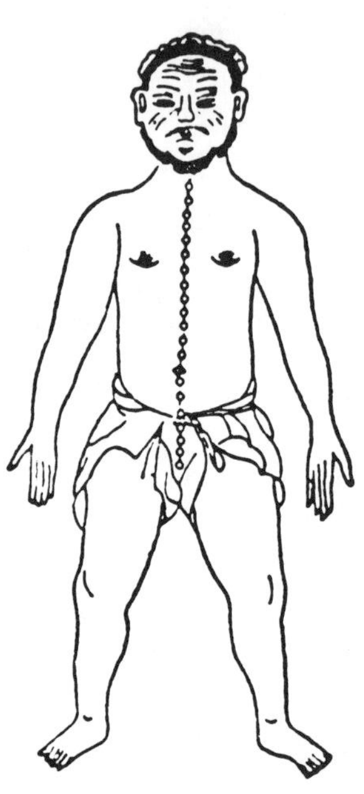

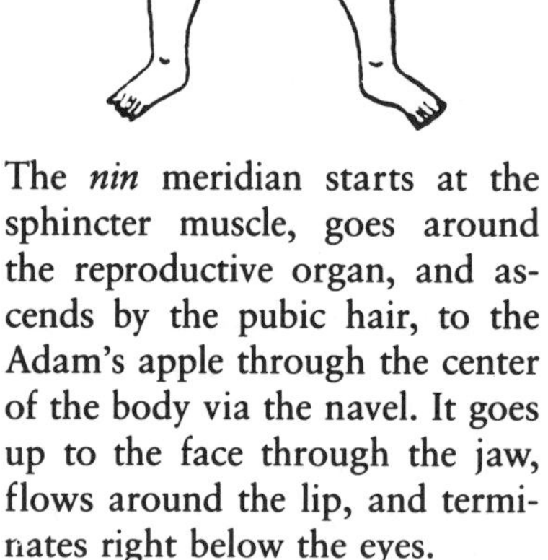

The *nin* meridian starts at the sphincter muscle, goes around the reproductive organ, and ascends by the pubic hair, to the Adam's apple through the center of the body via the navel. It goes up to the face through the jaw, flows around the lip, and terminates right below the eyes.

FIGURE 3.3b
THE *TOKU* DORSAL MERIDIAN

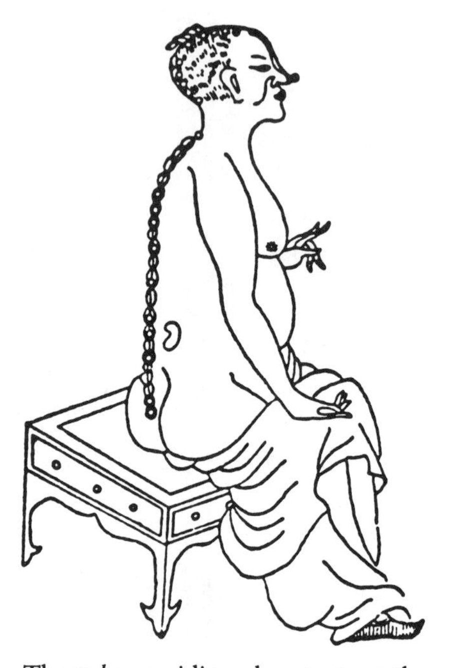

The *toku* meridian also starts at the sphincter muscle, ascends along the center of the back and branches right and left at the shoulder blades (merging with the bladder meridian). These branches merge again in the center, going upward to the head by way of the neck and come down the front, terminating in the upper teeth.

breath rises through the *toku* dorsal meridian, and that while exhaling it goes down the *nin* ventral meridian in the front of the body. The *Huìmìngjìng* shows this process in figure 3.4. This method seems to have the effect of dispelling the wandering thoughts which occur during meditation, and of heightening the degree of concentration of consciousness. The text says that repeated training in this method will gradually strengthen the power

FIGURE 3.4
SIX SEASONS OF THE DHARMA WHEEL

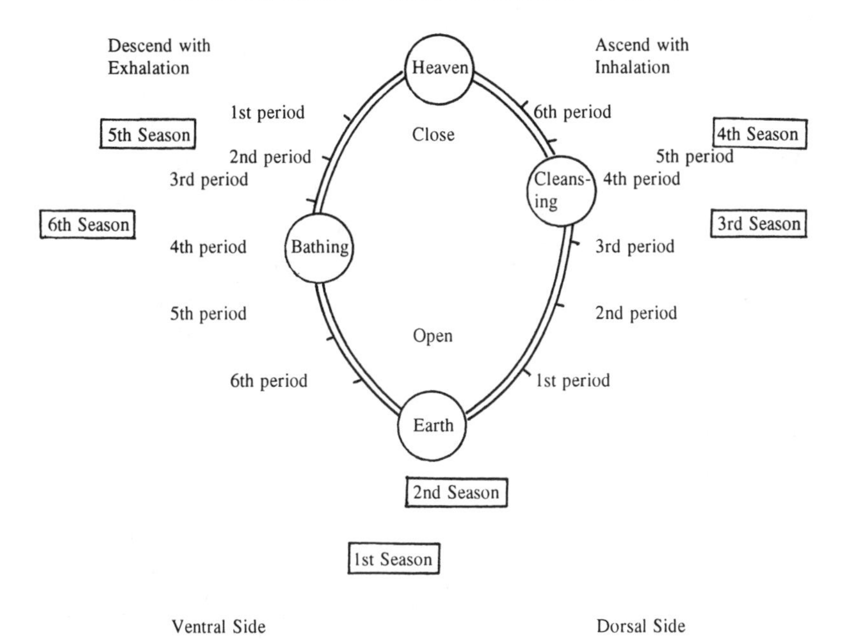

of *yáng*, and *ki* will approach the state of "true *yáng*" [*shin yō*] or "pure *yáng*" [*jun yō*]. In the "pure *yáng*" state the latent original light starts shining such that "*sei ki*" is purified and transformed into "*shin ki*."

The second chapter of *The Secret* explains the relationship between "primal *shin*" [*gen shin*] and "conscious *shin*" [*shiki shin*]. Richard Wilhelm translates the former as "primordial spirit" (*der ursprüngliche Geist*) and the latter as "conscious spirit" (*der bewusste Geist*). To use Jung's terminology, "primal *shin*" corresponds roughly to "self-nature" latently existing at the base of the collective unconscious, and "conscious *shin*" corresponds to the function of ego-consciousness. The text explains "primal *shin*" analogically as the Son of Heaven (the emperor) and "conscious *shin*" as a general who robs the Son of Heaven of his authority. The general exercises his authority in disregard of the Son of Heaven. In this state the power of "*sei ki*" is strong and the function of "*shin ki*" is suppressed. The cultivator must restore the original power endowed to the Son of Heaven by controlling the power of the general.

The third chapter of *The Secret* deals with "guarding the circulation of light in the middle" [*kaikō shuchū*]. "Guarding in the middle" means guarding "the middle Yellow" [*chūkō*] in Daoism, and guarding "the center where phenomena originate" [*enchū*] in Buddism.[25] Both expressions symbolically signify the latent, original nature of the mind. In other words, meditation means to guard and nurture ultimate human nature within the mind.

This chapter also describes a method of sitting posture. One sits comfortably in a correct posture with the eyes half-closed gazing at the tip of the nose. To sit for a prolonged period of time, the meditator must assume a comfortable posture with the back straight, and yet the mind must be alert. If the eyes are totally open, stimuli from outside will distract the mind. On the other hand, if the eyes are totally closed, the meditator is prone to fall into a drowsy, dreamy state. In order to avoid stimuli from outside while maintaining the concentration on the interior of the mind, the so-called half eyes are most appropriate.

The fourth chapter, "Circulation of Light in Adjusting the Breath" [*kaikō chōsoku*], deals mainly with the breathing method. It is essential to establish a mutually dependent relation between the movements of the mind and the rhythm of breathing. *The Secret* states that "mind and breath mutually depend on each other."[26] In other words, thought must be concentrated on the rhythm of breathing so as not to think of anything else. Breathing should be as slow and subtle as possible. Then, the meditator begins to feel that he or she is listening to the breath. It is not desirable to hear the sounds of inhalation or exhalation. When the sounds are heard, the breathing is rough and the mind slips into distraction. Through repeated training to maintain quiet, slow breathing, the mind can be sustained in an almost immovable state. When not receiving stimuli from outside, its movements become subtle and still. The text says that if the meditator continues this training for a long period of time, the mind suddenly becomes so still that its subtlest movements cease. Herrigel's testimony that, after extended training in breathing, he felt he was being breathed is probably an instance of this state. I have also had this experience.

In this connection, the text explains the relation between the mind and *ki* as follows. *Ki* is originally a transformation of the activities of the original nature of mind. *The Secret* states that "*ki* is a transformation of original mind."[27] Therefore, *ki* and the mind have an intimate relationship. The breathing method was devised and transmitted to us by sages who came to know the reciprocal influence between the movements of *ki* and the mind. The text describes this as "intercourse between mind and *ki*."[28] When mind moves, *ki* moves. When breathing is subtle, the movement of the mind is subtle. This is because *ki* moves with breathing, affecting the activities of the mind. Therefore, it is necessary to nurture *ki* in order to stabilize and still the mind. The text reads, "to stabilize the mind, nurturing of *ki* must precede."[29] This is the method of concentrating and maintaining the power of *ki*.

The fourth chapter also discusses unfavorable states into which the cultivator is liable to fall during the course of meditation. It enumerates two such conditions: "the depressed twilight state" [*konchin*] and "the dispersed and distracted state" [*sanran*]. These terms originated in Buddhism and are used in such works as *Abhidharmakosa*[30] and *Chéngwéishìlùn*.[31] "*Konchin*" refers to falling into such states as sleep and dark depression. It designates a depressed state in which the movement of the mind is captivated by the power rising from within its interior. Although the mind must be still, it must be a clear waking state of stillness, maintaining full alertness. "*Sanran,*" on the other hand, is a state of wandering thoughts, distracted by stimuli from the outside. If the meditator should fall into the state of "*konchin,*" he or she should rise from the sitting position and walk around a little. When the mood is cleared, one should return to a seated meditation posture.

When the cultivator continues the above training on a daily basis, the following states can be experienced. The cultivator starts experiencing something that is not a being in the midst of all that exists. *The Secret* writes "it is like a nothing in the midst of all beings."[32] Further endeavor brings an experience to the cultivator in which one feels that in addition to one's physical body there is another, different body. It is just like the feeling of something which should not be existing when there is nothing. The text reads, "it is like a being in the midst of nothing."[33] If the cultivator continues for one hundred more days, he or she will experience, though only to a degree, a subtle, spiritual fire (*shinka*). Still further endeavor brings the experience of seeing "one point of true *yáng*" [*itten no shinyō*] within the light of this fire, and one is suddenly aware that the seed of a yellow pearl is born in the lower abdomen. This is compared to the occurrence of conception when husband and wife have intercourse.

Although aspects of meditative experience vary from person to person, the states mentioned above are relatively easy to experience. For example, mild hallucinations occur such as a warm, bright sensation around the lower abdomen, or a pervading light around oneself. Many descriptions of these hallucinatory experiences of light are detailed in Myōe's *Yume no ki* [Record of Dreams]. The above mentioned experiences demonstrate instances of apprehending the feeling of *ki* in meditation. The experience of *kenshō* ("seeing into one's nature") in Zen meditation seems to be accompanied by an ecstatic feeling in addition to the abovementioned states.

V. ASPECTS OF INNER IMAGE EXPERIENCES ACCOMPANYING THE TRANSFORMATION OF *KI*

So far, I have introduced and commented on *The Secret* up through the fourth chapter. The remaining chapters deal mainly with inner images experienced in deepening states of meditation. Psychologically speaking, they describe hallucinatory images and their accompanying moods.

The fifth chapter, "Mistakes in the Circulation of Light" [*kaikō sabyū*], deals with pathological, hallucinatory states that are encountered in the course of meditation. The realm of trouble and perplexity in the cultivator's mind is where the five dark demons (the five demons of the *skandhas*[34]) are rampant and at play. If the cultivator falls into such a realm, his or her *ki* becomes cold and heavy, and a stagnant mood prevails. Although people tend to associate stilling the mind with a state analogous to a dead tree or cold ashes, it should actually be a heightened stillness as if one were welcoming a bright, spring day. When the cultivator is swayed by a depressive state, many chilling and enervating images will appear. The text says that these experiences indicate a transmigration into the lower beastly world. The commentary explains it as follows. When the cultivator sits in meditation with closed eyes for a prolonged period of time, he or she will experience the illumination of various lights and vivid colors, or see bodhisattvas, gods, and sages approaching, as well as various other hallucinatory visions. The cultivator should not peacefully remain in any of these experiences for they are nothing but demonic states which will trouble and perplex the cultivator.

These delusory hallucinations are fairly well studied from the standpoints of contemporary psychology and psychiatry. A person placed in isolation will often fall into an abnormal state and be set upon by hallucinations. The biography of Xuánzhuàng (596–664) records an hallucination he had while traveling alone in the desert in which he saw armed soldiers riding on horseback.[35] Victims in mountaineering accidents often hallucinate about houses and human figures.[36] Ritter, a female psychologist, recorded an experiment in which she lived alone for one hundred and sixty days in the Arctic. She describes her hallucinations, such as seeing a monster walking on the snow, clearly hearing a person skiing when nobody was there, and dissolving herself in the moonlight. Sensory deprivation experiments are designed to shut out all sensory stimuli, for example, by placing a subject in a dark room for a long time. It has been confirmed that when a subject is left in such a situation, hallucinatory symptoms are likely to occur. Since meditation trains one to concentrate the movement of the mind on its interior, it is not uncommon for a meditator to fall into these kinds of hallucinations.

When the hallucinations are examined psychologically, they show symptoms resembling neuroses. In our ordinary state, as explained by Minkowski, our minds consume our psychological energy by emotionally interacting with people or affairs around us.[37] The emotional interactions include, for example, the state of being soothed upon seeing a flower blossom, or a joyful mood while talking with a friend. However, once the emotional interaction is closed off, the flow of emotion loses its object and becomes stagnant, and a compensatory image (*Ergänzungsbild*) is created proportionate to the level of stagnation in emotional energy. Neurosis means falling into a lonely, autistic, psychological state, in which one is unable to establish emotional interaction with the environment, and projects outward a compensatory image of one's own creation. To be possessed by hatred, jealousy, melancholy, complaints and the like, means to be in this autistic state. In contrast, meditation purposefully creates a state resembling sensory deprivation, letting the power of the unconscious be released to surface on a conscious level, and so likely creating an autistic state.

The Secret warns that the meditator can fall into a heavy, depressive mood. This warning probably comes from actual experiences in meditation. We often find warnings against pathological states in Eastern self-cultivation methods. What is called "Zen sickness" resembles this pathological state. *Tendaishōshikan* [Chin. *Tiāntáixiǎozhǐguān*], a self-cultivation book of Tendai Buddhism, calls the pathological state "the demonic phase of the *skandhas*" [*inmasō*] or "the demonic realm" [*majikyō*].

From a depth-psychological viewpoint, the region of the "shadow" mentioned earlier separates the ego, which is the center of conscious functions, from the region of self-nature latent at the base of the unconscious (see Fig. 3.1). Therefore, to activate the creative energy latent in the region of self-nature, the meditator must first face the power of the "shadow" and go beyond it. The power of the "shadow" may here be taken as the function of Freud's sexual libido or Adler's aggressive impulse (inferiority complex). In the Eastern meditative tradition it has been well known since ancient times that these interferences often occur, although their remedies may differ among schools or religions. In the text under discussion we find the explanation that, "the meditation method of our school differs from that of Zen Buddhism. Once meditation is deepened a step, there is a confirmatory experience parallel to the step." The original reads, "Our school differs from the Zen school. For one step gained, there is a subtle experience corresponding to that step."[38] *The Secret* contends that since Zen speaks only of the ultimate state of satori, it takes the stance of rejecting the intermediary experiences leading to it. However, Daoism describes various experiences appearing in the process and guides the meditator toward progress while rejecting the pathological states.

Generally speaking, Daoism and the meditation method of Buddhism in the T'ang dynasty tended to value the experience of images, while Zen Buddhism, which flourished after the Sung dynasty, had a strong tendency to reject the value of all experience of images with the well-known motto, "no-image and no-thought" [*munen musō*]. This Zen attitude was probably influenced by Confucian philosophy with its tendency toward moral will, as is seen in the *riki* theory of the time, as well as by the rationalism of aristocrats. Zen, in other words, took the attitude of spiritual elitism which esteemed the paramount state of satori, while Daoism assumed an attitude close to the general populace. From the standpoint of today's psychology, it is easier to obtain clues for our research when there are descriptions about the experiences of images.

In the sixth chapter, "Subtle Signs in the Circulation of Light" [*kaikōchōken*], we find an explanation of the correctly deepened state of meditation, which is compared to the blossoming of a golden flower. There are many confirmatory experiences. The meditator finds oneself in a blissful state, quietly feeling a continuous connection with things, while one's mind and mood are heightened as if intoxicated. This is a sign of *yáng ki* circulating all over the body in harmony. Soon, all sounds disappear and stillness prevails, and the meditator begins to feel that the earth is a world filled with bright light, and that the moon with its silvery rays is hanging high in mid-heaven. This occurrence is a sign that the original substance of the mind is clearly revealed.

The following three states are mentioned as the confirmatory experiences accompanying the deepening of meditation. The first is the experience of hearing the god-man speaking in the valley. When this occurs, the meditator can hear clearly each person's voice even though people seem to be talking to each other in the far distance. The voice is heard like a reverberating echo in the valley. This is the experience called "the god-man exists in the valley."[39] This explanation was advanced in view of the well-known phrase "The goddess of the valley never dies" found in the sixth chapter of the *Dàodéjīng*. But the above state, in terms of its experiential content, has nothing especially to do with this phrase. We may regard it as an auditory hallucination, but in the Eastern self-cultivation method pathological and authentic cases are distinguished based on the experience. Yogic texts also contain descriptions of voices, and in Myōe's *Yume no ki* there are reports of hearing voices during meditation.

The second confirmatory experience is the following. In the stillness of meditation, the meditator experiences a flashing light in front of the eyes, everything starts shining white, and one feels as if one is in the clouds. Opening the eyes to try to find where one's body is, it can no longer be found anywhere. When this occurs, there is no distinction between inner and outer. This is an auspicious sign.

The third confirmatory experience is the following. In the stillness of meditation, the meditator feels that the physical body is wrapped in fundamental *ki* that is rising, and strings of white cotton threads feel like precious jade. Sitting in a meditative posture, one feels that one cannot stay in this position, as if being pulled upward. This is the experience in which "the *shin* returns to the heaven and reaches its apex."[40] When this experience is repeatedly had, the experience of ascent can actually be confirmed.

In general terms, can these experiences be regarded as ecstatic states? What is the state in the experience of "ascent" and the state in which the meditator cannot find his or her body even when the eyes are open? (The original reads, "opening the eyes, he seeks his body, but nothing is found."[41]) These descriptions alone are not sufficient for understanding these states. I wonder if they are analogous to the out-of-body experiences (OBE) which are discussed today. Out-of-body experience is a state in which ego-consciousness feels as if it has left its body. (see Fig. 3.5). According to the commentary inserted in *The Secret,* these states demonstrate the ascent of "*yō shin*" (a spiritually subtle function of *yáng ki*).

Concrete explanations of meditative experience end in the sixth chapter. Chapter seven, "Utilization of the Circulation of Light" [*kaikō kappō*], deals with the relationship between daily life and meditative training. Dealing with the business of daily life according to right-thinking is compared to formless, yet concrete, meditation. The text reads "it is circulation of light with no trace."[42] To put it in another way, the meditator can spend his daily life with the same feeling as in the experience of meditation. According to the commentary of the text, an accomplished meditator manifests subtle and hidden activities, and without forcing people in society to follow his way, he instead follows their ways. Just looking at the surface of his activities, it is impossible to see through to his true conduct and the functions of his hidden power. This is the Eastern sage's way of living.

Although the text goes on for several more chapters, I shall for now close my presentation of it here. I might add one further point, however. A passage in the text explains the process of meditation as a union of the male principle and the female principle. The text reads "it is intercourse between water [*kan*] and fire [*ri*]."[43] This idea is derived from the *Yìjīng*. "Kan" designates "water" [*sui*] and signifies femininity whereas "*ri*" designates "fire" [*ka*] and signifies masculinity. "Masculine-fire" [*rika*] lies in the

FIGURE 3.5
GOING OUT OF THE EMBRYO

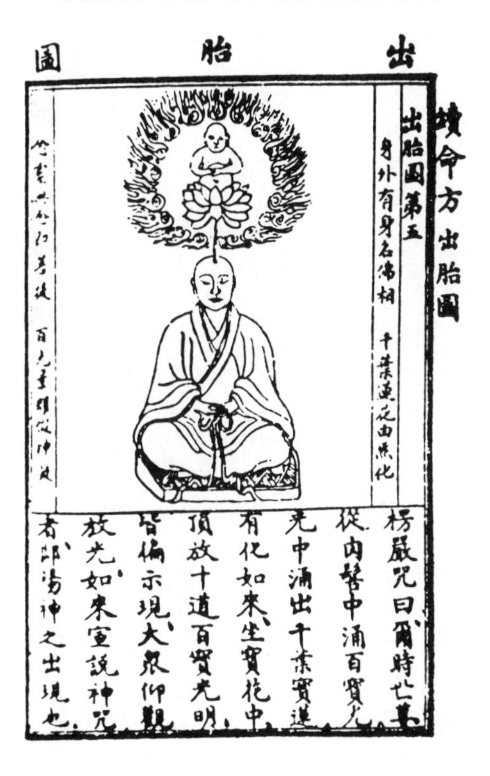

heart (the middle *tanden*) and "feminine-water" [*kan sui*] in the lower abdomen (the lower *tanden*). Their conjunction is referred to as "intercourse between water [*kan*] and fire [*ri*]." This explanation is suggestive when examining the Eastern meditation method from a depth-psychological standpoint. As I mentioned in the previous section, when one starts meditative training, there is in due time the sudden feeling of a fire flaring, for example, in the lower abdomen. *The Secret* calls this experience "one point of true *yáng*" and compares it to conception through intercourse between husband and wife. In the Daoist mediation method, it is called "the conception of a true person" [*shinjin jutai*] and is often shown in a diagram (see *Fig. 3.6*). This experience is probably similar to the initial *kenshō* of which Zen Buddhism speaks. Needless to say, the reference to this experience as conception through sexual intercourse is a kind of metaphor or symbolic expression, but

FIGURE 3.6
THE CONCEPTION OF DAO

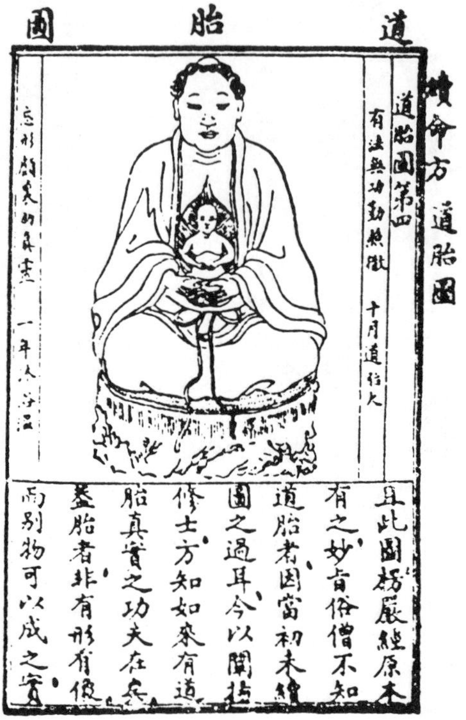

it is not just that. Sexual symbols are often employed in Yoga and Tantric Buddhism to explain the experiences of cultivation and satori. This suggests that the meditative cultivators of the East had knowledge of depth-psychological experiences and since ancient times have been well acquainted with the idea of the libido which Freud discovered from a modern perspective. Meditation is training that transforms and sublimates the libido.

Human beings without exception have sexual desire. Sexual desire is both psychological and physiological energy. Physiologically speaking, ejaculation is an emission of sperm and at the same time, it is accompanied by psychological pleasure. For this reason, a human being can easily indulge in sexual pleasure, but this indulgence, the text maintains, is the path leading humans to lose sight of the true and original human nature, because the power of "*sei ki*" weakens the power of "*shin ki*" in sexual indulgence. It is joyful and happy to have offspring, but one must refrain from the abuse of sex. In the view of Eastern meditation, sexual energy is the source of energy for a journey into knowing ultimate, original human nature. Gasoline is useful when it is appropriately used for travelling far, but it can become a source of disaster when it is made to explode.

The difference between Eastern self-cultivation and Western asceticism lies in this point. According to the tradition of the Christian view of humans in the West, "spirit" and "flesh" were separated, and the latter was regarded as the source of sin. An example is found in the story of the Garden of Eden in the Book of Genesis. Some maintain that the spirit-flesh dualism was an influence from Greek thought, and for this reason there has been a strong tendency to suppress sexual desire in the tradition of Western ethics. Carried to an extreme, it is prone to lead human beings into asceticism and rigorism, as is represented by Puritanism. In modern times, this tendency has been reversed; the satisfaction of desire and a denial of asceticism have come to be regarded as the appropriate way of life for human beings. Eventually, this idea has proclaimed sexual freedom. However, as suggested in the proverb "Extremes stop a person short," excessive asceticism is prone to produce neurotic symptoms, whereas excessive pursuit of desire wears out both mind and body. Since the Eastern tradition is well aware of this fact, it has taught people to make good use of sexual energy by accumulating it without indiscriminately releasing it. In short, transformation of "*sei*" into *shin*" by "kneading *ki*" means transformation of the libido.

VI. THE MEANING OF KNOWLEDGE IN EASTERN THOUGHT: AN INTERMEDIARY METHODOLOGICAL INVESTIGATION

I hope that the preceding elucidation of *ki* has provided the reader with at least some understanding of the meaning of the mind coming to feel and apprehend *ki*. But some readers may complain that the explanation is not fully convincing. While the preceding explanation describes experiences of consciousness transformed during the course of meditation, without the actual meditative experiences, it is naturally difficult to understand it. This points to a methodological characteristic of Eastern philosophy. Although it will be a short digression, I would like to add a methodological reflection here.

The books on self-cultivation methods in Buddhism and Daoism are not designed to give intellectual proofs or ratiocinations. Rather, they are guidebooks for attaining practical experience. The books dealing with theoretical doctrines are written by presupposing practical experience. Shakyamuni Buddha remained silent on the metaphysical disputes of the time. This is because intellectual disputes are useless for attaining satori (nirvana). What is of foremost importance is actually obtaining the *experience* of satori. Therefore, philosophical knowledge in the East is originally a kind of *practical knowledge* and is not mere intellectual knowledge or proof. Herein lies a point of difference from the Western philosophical tradition.

In the case of Eastern philosophy, it is important to acquire practical experience rather than an intellectual proof. In other words, it is important first to encounter the gods and bodhisattvas and actually to know their activities. Many sutras dealing with self-cultivation are designed to articulate the methods for achieving this goal. Books on theoretical doctrines are written presupposing practical knowledge or experience. When we look at, for example, Xuánzhuàng's *The Records of the Western Regions in the Great T'ang* [*Dàtáng xīyùjì*] and his biography, *Cíēntán,* we learn that there were both Abhidharmaists (philosophical theoreticians) and *yogācārins* (*yogins* or cultivating monks) in the temples of Theravada (Hinayana) Buddhism in India. Abhidharmaists construed theories in light of the experience of the cultivating monks. Abhidharma commentaries, which were an initial stage of Buddhist philosophy, were written in this manner.

Jung says the reason that no conflict or confrontation occurred between religion and science in the East is probably because Eastern religions are not based on faith, but have the character of a kind of cognitive religion (*die erkennende Religion*) or religious cognition (*die religiöse Erkenntnis*).[44] What is referred to here as "cognition" is not the cognition of the external world with which modern science deals, but is cognition of the inner world, of the depths of the world of the psyche. Therefore, Eastern religion has an experiential knowledge with *practical character,* and consequently, theory and practice cannot be separated.

CHAPTER 4

Ki *and the Body in Eastern Medicine*

I. INTRODUCTION

I shall now examine the problem of *ki* from the viewpoint of Eastern medicine. The traditional medicine of the East with its acupuncture therapy has more than a thousand years of history, but in Japan, since the acceptance of modern Western medicine it has been excluded from the system of medicine as being unscientific. Although it is recognized in virtue of its actual clinical effects, it has been regarded as unsuited for the academic world. But a moment's reflection reveals that this view is unreasonable. If acupuncture indeed demonstrates actual clinical effects, should not the position of empirical science be to investigate the mechanism of how the effects are obtained? Although China accepted Western medicine, she has not repudiated traditional medicine and is today studying and making a modern reevaluation of her traditional cultural legacy under the slogan of unifying Western and Chinese medicine. Eastern medicine has caught the attention of Western doctors since Richard Nixon's visit to China, and is currently studied globally.

A handful of researchers, however, have preserved the tradition of Eastern Medicine even in Japan. Much research has been accumulated since the end of the war through the efforts of many researchers. Owing to this research we can expect that the enigma of this mysterious phenomenon, *ki,* will be solved in due time. In the following then, I shall first delineate for the general reader the essential points of Eastern medicine's theory of the body along with its Eastern characteristics. Afterwards, I shall comment on the results of recent research.

II. FUNDAMENTAL CHARACTERISTICS OF EASTERN MEDICINE'S THEORY OF THE BODY

Foundational to Eastern medicine's theory of the body are the so-called meridians.[1] There are twelve regular meridians called "*seikei*" [Chin. *zhèngjīng*], which form circuits while connecting the distal, limbic system with the head and the various visceral organs. The characteristics of this system differ completely from the circulatory and nervous systems known by today's anatomy. And since the meridians have no anatomically recognizable vessel system, their existence has been questioned from the standpoint of modern medicine. In addition to twelve regular meridians, there are eight irregular meridians called "*kikei*" [Chin. *qíjīng*]. These irregular meridians are often compared to a reservoir of *ki*-energy and have been regarded as important in Chinese martial arts. Among the irregular meridians, the *toku*-dorsal and *nin*-ventral meridians are employed in meditation methods. The *shōshūten* breathing method mentioned earlier uses these two meridians.

The twelve major meridians (and also the eight irregular ones) are broadly divided into *yīn* and *yáng* groups. The meridians traveling in the dorsal and lateral regions are considered *yáng*, and those running in the ventral region and on the inner side of the limbs are considered *yīn*. Each meridian is given the name of a specific solid viscus and hollow viscus [*zōfu;* Chin. *zàngfŭ*].[2] The function of each viscus pertains to itself and, to a greater or lesser degree, to the other viscera as well. This point is the first characteristic of the theory of the body based on the meridians. Modern medicine assumes the localization of function such that a specific viscus is assigned a role with a specific physiological function, but it is noteworthy that Eastern medicine takes an integrative way of looking at the functions of the whole body from a holographic standpoint.

Since the term "holography" has recently come into use, I shall briefly explain the concept. It originally derived from a special technique of photography in which no lens is used. Unlike regular film, the dry-plate of a hologram contains information about the whole of its object in each of its parts, and so the whole can be reproduced from part of the dry-plate. Furthermore, when a laser beam is applied to this plate, the original object appears as a three-dimensional figure. Therefore, in the holographic model each part invariably contains information about the whole, and holds the relationship of an interconnected web where the part is equal to a whole. This holographic model has become well-known since Karl Pribram, a neurophysiologist, used it in order to overcome the theory of cerebral localization. In short, the theory of the body held by Eastern medicine attempts to grasp the whole of the bodily functions from a holographic viewpoint, which is in principle different from the theory of the body held by modern medicine, where the whole is construed by gathering the sum of its parts.[3] Noting this point, Joseph Needham points out that whereas Western medicine is analytic and reductionistic, Chinese medicine is organistic and psychosomatic.[4] This is the first characteristic point of the Eastern theory of the body.

Ki in Eastern medicine is an energy, unique to the living body, that flows through the meridians with the above-mentioned characteristics.[5] Now, I shall give a concrete explanation of the system of the twelve major meridians to show how *ki* flows in them.

As noted in the beginning of this chapter, the meridians form circuits connecting the distal points of the limbs with the head or with the solid and hollow vicera, depending on where the center of each meridian is identified. There are both centrifugal (efferent) and centripetal (afferent) circuits in the meridians just like in the nervous system. This relationship is shown in Figure 4.1. The flow of *ki* circulates through the whole body in the order designated by the numbers assigned to each meridian in the figure. More specifically, it starts with (1) the lung meridian [*haikei*], located in the left column in the figure, and moves to (2) the large-intestine meridian [*dai-chōkei*] in the right column, and then to (3) the stomach meridian [*ikei*]. It terminates in (12) the liver meridian [*kankei*] after going through (4), (5), and so forth. And again it connects back to (1) the lung meridian. The meridians in the left column (designated by the odd numbers) are centrifugal, and begin in either the head or in a solid or hollow viscera, and are directed to the distal points of the limbs. The meridians on the right column (designated by the even numbers) are centripetal, originating in the distal points of the limbs and moving to the head and viscera.

As far as the division between *yīn* and *yáng* is concerned, the meridians located in the dorsal and lateral sides of the body are *yáng*, in which *ki* flows downward; those meridians located in the ventral area are *yīn*, in which *ki* flows upward. In an ordinary

FIGURE 4.1
FLOW OF THE MERIDIANS AND *ZŌFU:* FRONT AND BACK

Yīn, Back, Zō					Yáng, Front, Fū		
Greatest in yīn	Hand	Lung meridian	(1)······▷	(2) ▽	Large-intestine meridian	Hand	Bright yáng
	Foot	Spleen-pancreas meridian	(4) ◁······ ▽	(3)	Stomach meridian	Foot	
Smallest in yīn	Hand	Heart meridian	(5)······▷	(6) ▽	Small-intestine meridian	Hand	Greatest in yáng
	Foot	Kidney meridian	(8) ◁······ ▽	(7)	Urinary-bladder meridian	Foot	
Lack of yīn	Hand	Heart-constrictor meridian	(9)······▷	(10) ▽	Triple-Heater meridian	Hand	Smallest in yáng
	Foot	Liver meridian	(12) ◁······	(11)	Gall-bladder meridian	Foot	

Meridians are connected throughout the body vis-à-vis the fingers, feet, chest, face, and shoulders. The arrow indicates the direction of interfusing flow.

posture where the arms hang down from the shoulders, the *yáng* meridians in the hands can have an upward flow. But when both hands are raised, *ki* in all the *yáng* meridians flows downward whereas *ki* in all the *yīn* meridians flows upward. There are terms to designate the degree of *yīn-yáng* qualities such as "greatest *yáng*" [*taiyō*], "smallest *yáng*" [*shōyō*], "bright *yáng*" [*yōmei*], "greatest *yīn*" [*taiin*], "smallest *yīn*" [*shōin*], and "lack of *yīn*" [*ketsuin*]. These terms reveal that the *yīn-yáng* polarity is not of a rigid demarcation; it admits of ambiguous phases or degrees. Along the twelve major meridians are distributed numerous acu-points (approximately 350), which are therapeutic points. They are points where *ki*-energy is concentrated, and if the flow of *ki* becomes stagnant, a pathological condition follows. Fundamental to acupuncture therapy is allowing the flow of *ki* to run smoothly by inserting acupuncture needles. An old medical text says "there is no pain if *ki* is allowed to flow through."

A few more points may be added concerning the acu-points. There are special acu-points called "*yu*" along the bladder meridian at the dorsal region, and they are collectively called "transporting acu-points" [*yuketsu;* Chin. *yúxuè*].[6] Abnormalities in the various solid and hollow viscera appear most distinctly at these points, and so they are the important therapeutic points to address pathological change. Corresponding to each transporting acu-point is the distribution of "gathering acu-points" [*boketsu;* Chin. *mùxué*][7] in the various solid viscera in the ventral area where *ki* for each of these viscera is gathered. This suggests that according to acupuncture theory, *ki* flows into the gathering acu-points on the surface of the abdomen, passing through the interior of the body from the transporting acu-points located in the back. (Although the meridians are usually thought to flow through the area close to the surface of the skin, this indicates that some meridians pass through the interior of the body.) Moreover, there are twelve specific acu-points, called "primary acu-points" [*genketsu;* Chin. *yuánxué*[8]] along the twelve major meridians, which serve as important therapeutic points to address pathological change in the solid and hollow viscera.

As has been seen, in the theory of the body based on the meridians all the physiological functions of the viscera are resolved into functions of the meridians on the surface of the body. They are arranged as an integrative system, which NAGAHAMA Yoshio prefers to call the "viscera-meridian system" [*naizō keiraku kei*]—a circulatory system of *ki*-energy. This way of understanding the bodily functions is radically different from the theory of the body espoused by modern Western medicine. What then are the fundamental characteristics of this theory?

First, I would like to point out the relationship between the body and the *external world*. As previously mentioned, the terminating points for each meridian are the distal points in the limbs, and there is an exchange in the flow of *ki* with the external world through these distal points. (The acu-points at the distal points in the limbs are referred to as "well acu-points" [*seiketsu;* Chin. *jǐngxuè*].[9] I think this point is the fundamental characteristic of the Eastern theory of the body. Modern medicine has first separated the body from the external world, taking it as a closed, self-contained system, and then by dissecting its structure into various organs has attempted to understand their respective functions. In contrast, Eastern medicine has from the outset understood the body as an open system connected to the external world. In so doing it has conceived that, although undetectable by sensory per-

FIGURE 4.2
TWELVE MERIDIANS AS THE MAJOR CIRCUITS OF *KI*

Centrifugal Circuits

Name	Major point	Relative yīn/yáng
1. Lung meridian	Hand	Greatest yīn

Stomach/intestines ——▸ Lung ——▸ Inside of hand and arms ——▸ Thumb

Centripetal Circuits

Name	Major point	Relative yīn/yáng
2. Large intestine	Hand	Bright yáng

Index finger ——▸ Outer side of hand and arm ——▸ Lung ——▸ Large intestine

Name	Major point	Relative yīn/yáng
3. Stomach meridian	Leg	Bright yáng

Nose ——▸ Carotid artery ——▸ Stomach/spleen ——▸ Second toe

Name	Major point	Relative yīn/yáng
4. Spleen-Pancreas meridiann	leg	Smallest yīn

Big toe ——▸ Inside of leg ——▸ Spleen/stomach ——▸ Throat

FIGURE 4.2
continued

Name	Major point	Relative yīn/yáng
5. Heart meridian	Hand	Smallest yīn

Heart ▸ Small-intestine
▸ Eye
▸ Lung ——▸ Inside of hand and arm ——▸ Little finger

Name	Major point	Relative yīn/yáng
6. Small-intestine meridian	Hand	Bringht yáng

Little finger ——▸ Outer edge of hand —▸ Shoulder and chest ——▸ Stomach and intestines

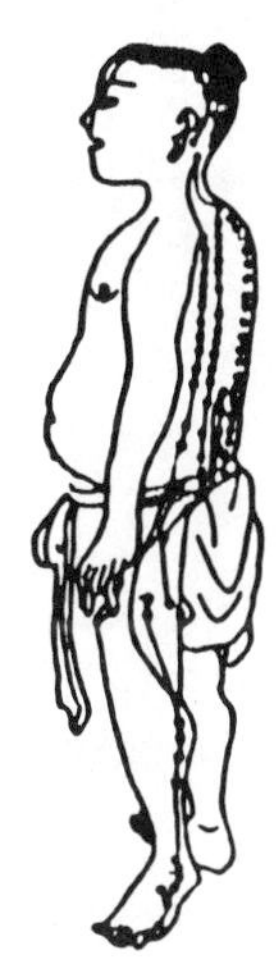

Name	Major point	Relative yīn/yáng
7. Urinary/bladder meridian	Leg	Greatest yáng

Eye ——▸ Head ——▸ Back ——▸ Kidney/bladder ——▸ Outer edge of Little toe

Name	Major point	Relative yīn/yáng
8. Kidney meridian	Leg	Smallest yīn

Little toe —▸ Sole of foot ——▸ Inside of leg ——▸ Kidney/bladder ——▸ Liver ——▸ Lung

FIGURE 4.2
continued

Name	Major point	Relative yīn/yáng
9. **Heart constrictor meridian**	leg	Lack of yīn

Chest ──┬─► Heart constrictor ──► Triple heater
└─► Inside of arm Heart ──► Middle finger of hand

Name	Major point	Relative yīn/yáng
10. Triple heater meridian	Hand	Smallest yīn

Middle finger ──► Outer edge of hand and arm ─► Shoulder
──► Heart constrictor ──► Triple heater

Name	Major point	Relative yīn/yáng
11. Gall bladder meridian	Leg	Smallest yīn

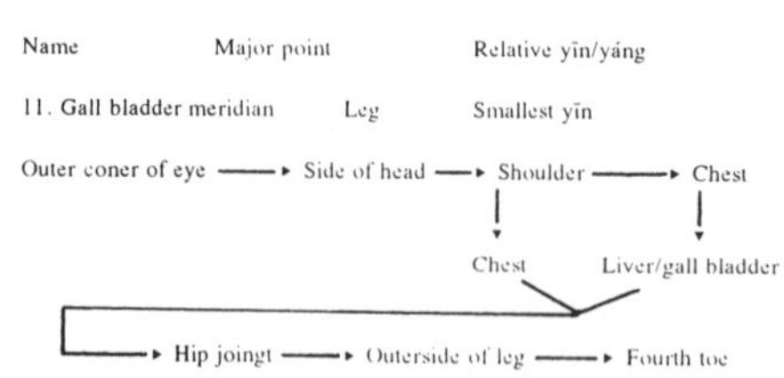

Outer coner of eye ──► Side of head ──► Shoulder ──► Chest
↓ Chest
↓ Liver/gall bladder
──► Hip joingt ──► Outerside of leg ──► Fourth toe

Name	Major point	Relative yīn/yáng
12. Liver meridian	Leg	Lack of yīn

Big toe ──► Inside the center of leg ──► Liver/gall bladder
┬─► Lung ──► Stomach
└─► Side of Chest ──► Bronchia ─► Eyeball
──► Crown of head
↓ Cheek/lip

ception, there is an exchange of life-energy of some sort between the body and the external world, that is, there is an absorption and release of *ki* between them. Here we see a view of the human being as a microcosm corresponding to the universe as a macrocosm, and of the human body as a vessel for the flow of *ki* in the universe. (An historical origin for these views of the human being and the universe can be traced back to the *Yìjīng*.)

From a modern medical standpoint, Eastern medicine's theory of the body has the shortcoming of not giving a sufficient anatomical analysis of the *interior* mechanisms of the body. We must admit that this is indeed an important detrimental point, but this shortcoming is derived from the fact that Eastern medicine has been a *medicine of the somatic surface*. That is, the foundation for its clinical therapy has been treatment on the skin surface. Methodologically, I find it very interesting to view the body with the skin as its foundation, for the skin forms a boundary wall between the body and the external world. It is *a boundary demarcating one's interior and exterior,* as it were.[10] An issue that emerges here, when seen from the mind-body theory, is how to understand the relationship between the ego (or "I") and the world.

When viewed somatically and physiologically, inside the skin is what clearly belongs to one's own self, and outside of it is the external world. However, looked at spiritually and psychologically, the distinction between "inner" and "outer" is not all that precise. Although we use such terms as "inner world" and "outer world," or "introverted" and "extroverted," we must recognize that the "inner" and "outer" in these instances are *metaphoric* or symbolic expressions. To say that the mind exists within the body is a metaphorical expression, because the mind itself is a being that cannot be located spatially. To be more accurate, the "inner" and "outer" referred to here mean respectively the world of mind and the world of matter. Since in this case the body belongs to the order of matter, as long as we hold to the Cartesian dichotomy, we must think that for one's self (ego-consciousness) the body belongs to the "outer" world. For this reason, modern theory has altogether excluded the problem of mind from the investigation of the body. Taking the body as an objective (material) substance, it has relegated the problem of consciousness to philosophy. Consequently, the physiological and the psychological issues have been rendered completely unrelated in theory.

However, it is contrary to common sense to regard one's own body as matter existing outside of oneself. Consequently, according to modern science, there is a discrepancy between common sense and scientific knowledge which leaves psychological problems and physiological (and physical) problems totally unrelated. In short, the logic of modern science started with a methodology which disregards the fact of mind-body union that common sense recognizes in our everyday experience. This suggests that the logic of science is divorced from our human life, and proceeds independent of us. In a broad perspective, this would seem to bear on where contemporary science and technology are situated. Contemporary scholarship should search for a position that unifies the logic of science and common sense in daily life.

The concept of *ki* has a characteristic which can dissolve this methodological difficulty. *Ki,* as I will explain later in detail, is by nature an energy unique to the living body with both psychological and physical characteristics. It therefore has a bearing on *both* mind and body. As mentioned earlier, the flow of *ki* is closely connected to meditative training, and in this respect is *psychological in nature*. But when seen in light of the therapeutic effect which acupuncture demonstrates, it has the effect of *activating physiological functions*. In other words, one's body is a psychological being when it is felt as within the skin (the sensation of one's own body), whereas the body observed from outside, wrapped in skin, is a field on which the inner physiological functions issue forth. The flow of *ki* is a passage mediating this interior and exterior.

Furthermore, *ki*-energy, while circulating in the interior of the body, is connected through the distal points of the limbs to the flow of *ki* in the outer world. We take the sensation of our own bodies, or whole state of coenesthesis, individually as "I," but this "I" intermingles with the outer world through the boundary of the skin. In short, the skin is a field making unique contact with the material world, within which an interchange takes place through the flow of *ki* between psychological and physiological functions, that is, between the mind and the body.

Methodologically, this theory of the body leads us to a view of the human being and the world which is different in principle from the modern mind-matter dichotomy. In the history of philosophy, the human being has been regarded since ancient times as a microcosm, as a being spiritually connected to the macrocosm. In the West, we can find examples of this view in ancient Greece and, in modern times, in Leibniz. Modern science has rejected this view of human beings and the world, but the meditation method and the Eastern theory of the body seem to provide us with a starting point to reevaluate this old view from a contemporary perspective. "My self" is for now understood as "the body *qua* the interior of the skin" ("my self" as a microcosm) and the macrocosm as "the world outside of the skin." The concept of *ki* connects these two orders. *Ki*-energy suggests that there latently exists a reciprocal relation of exchange between these two orders transcending the mind-matter dichotomy.[11]

The macrocosm is the world of nature. Therefore, if the life-energy called *ki* exists in some form, there is an (unconscious and psychic) exchange between macrocosm and microcosm vis-à-vis *ki*-energy. The world of nature, filled with *ki,* is not simply a world of matter, but becomes understood as a living order of vital nature. To use a contemporary term, the East, since ancient times, has understood the relationship between human beings and the world from an *ecological* perspective, and the body has been taken as the field [*ba*] where this relationship is actually lived and positivistically known. To characterize this in another way, a human being is not a "*homo faber*" reigning over the world as in the modern conception, but is a being incapable of living in isolation. A human being is a passive-active being which is made to live by nature. *Ki* is a key concept for empirically and scientifically verifying this view of human beings and nature.

III. THE RELATIONSHIP BETWEEN *KI* AND EMOTION IN THE MERIDIANS

Next, I shall deal with some contemporary research in Eastern medicine, but first I would like to briefly explain some important problematic points.

The problem of emotion is regarded as extremely important in the etiology of Eastern medicine. Three etiological factors are traditionally considered major: the "internal cause," the "external cause," and the "cause which is neither internal nor external." The internal cause refers to the seven emotions: joy, anger, anxiety, longing, sorrow, fear, and surprise (in some cases, it counts only the first five).[12] These are usually thought to stagnate initially in the viscera, and subsequently to show their symptoms throughout the body. If we reinterpret the internal cause from a contemporary perspective, it clearly pertains to the function of emotion. Since the functions of these emotions are taken to be major etiological factors, Eastern medicine originally has a character analogous to today's psychosomatic medicine. In noting this point, Needham says that the fundamental idea in Chinese medicine is its psychosomatic orientation. Yet the major difference between the present therapeutic method of psychosomatic medicine and that of Eastern medicine is that while the former mainly employs a psychotherapy suggested by meditation methods, the latter relies mainly on the insertion of acu-needles, which as a therapeutic method seems at first glance to be more physiological in nature. Therefore, the point of the problem is to examine the *psychophysiological correlation between the skin and emotion.* (The "external cause" refers to "five excessive factors" including cold and hot temperature, aridity, humidity, wind, and heat. It covers environmental factors. The last, the "cause that is neither internal nor external," refers to an irregular life-style, a careless attitude toward one's health, and exhaustion, all of which go counter to the order of nature. Since these factors are pertinent ones even from the standpoint of modern medicine, no special treatment is needed here.)

When meditation is viewed from the standpoint of depth psychology, it means training to control the emotional complexes that spring forth from the unconscious, while the etiology of Eastern medicine, as was mentioned in the foregoing, considers distortions in emotion to be extremely important. The concept of *ki* is concerned with both the meditation method and acupuncture therapy. Meditative training attempts to control distortions of the emotions by psychologically activating *ki*-energy, while therapy by insertion of acu-needles tries to accomplish the same goal by means of stimuli from outside the skin. Seen in this light, *ki* seems to be potential energy in the unconscious holding a close connection with emotion. Moreover, the meridians represent the circuits in which this potential energy circulates.

In chapter 2, I examined the functions of the body by distinguishing three circuits. The first circuit is the external sensory-motor circuit concerned with the environment or the external world. The second is the circuit of coenesthesis which is concerned mainly with motor and splanchnic sensations. It designates the *self-apprehending of internal sensation* in one's own body *qua* the *interior of the skin*. The third and the last circuit is the emotion-instinct circuit which is connected with the activity of the autonomic nerves. Here we must reinterpret the function of the body comprehensively by introducing the fourth potential circuit of the meridian system, or the circuit of *ki*—that which NAGAHAMA Yoshio calls the "visceral-meridian system" [*keiraku naizōkei*].

Both the first and second circuit, when seen psychologically, belong to "consciousness," and the third circuit occupies a position which mediates between consciousness and the unconscious. Take the example of meditation training. It has a goal of bringing the activity of the third emotion-instinct circuit to awareness by arresting the activity of the first external sensory-motor circuit. To meditate by sitting quietly is to shut off the sensory stimuli from the external world and to arrest the muscular movements of the limbs. It brings the activity of the external sensory-motor circuit to a standstill. When we meditate, we assume a posture looking into the interior of the body (the abdominal cavity inside the skin). However, nothing is seen in the interior of the body because it is dark. The active state of the various visceral organs are for the most part buried in the unconscious, except for what appears as a vague awareness, though only in small part, of the whole of the internal organs. What is felt in this instance is the activity of the circuit of coenesthesis as the *self-apprehending sensation of one's own body*, that is, as an awareness [*kizuki*] of the somatic sensation of the whole body.

However, as meditation deepens emotional complexes, which take the form of wandering thoughts and delusions, gradually appear out of or against this self-apprehending sensation of one's own body. To use the terminology of Gestalt psychology, meditation is a training method through which an emotional complex surfaces as a figure (image) against the background of the self-apprehending sensation of one's body. Eastern medicine's theory of the body takes *emotion as the flow of ki*. Here, the relationship between the meridian and the dermal sensation becomes important.

Research in Eastern medicine from a contemporary standpoint has been actively pursued more in Japan than in China. Japanese researchers have had to clarify the value of Eastern medicine from a contemporary standpoint because Western medicine has long been dominant, whereas in China the authority of traditional theories is recognized even today. There are many forerunners in this area, but since I cannot deal with the achievements of all the Japanese researchers, I shall introduce a few of the cases that I deem to be most important.[13]

The results of contemporary research in Eastern medicine are relevant to the preceding problematic points. I would like to mention at the outset that cases of "meridian sensitive persons" [*keiraku binkanjin*] have been discovered one after another. Drs. Nagahama Yoshio and Maruyama Masao of the medical school at Chiba University discovered the first case of a "meridian sensitive person" in 1949, soon after the war. They came across a patient who had an abnormality in his optical nerve after being struck by lightning when he was young, and showed a sensitive receptivity to acu-needle insertion. He could feel, upon the insertion of an acu-needle, the direction of a flowing vibration along his skin. The "vibration" [*hibiki*] here is an abnormal, yet special sensation which the insertion of an acu-needle generates—a sensation of something being dispersed. When Nagahama and Maruyama traced the direction of this vibration, it was found to coincide with the traditionally recognized paths of the twelve meridians. In the course of treating this patient, who was suffering from atrophy of the optical nerves, they discovered that the patient could accurately sense the speed and direction of the flow of the vibration. They examined the path it ran by inserting acu-needles, and discovered that the path coincided, to a surprising degree, with a meridian path which has been recognized since ancient times.[14] On this occasion, they also learned that since the dispersion speed is considerably slower than a nerve impulse, the nerves and muscles have nothing directly to do with this flow (of *ki*). Its speed is close, among those so far known, to that of lymph. (The transmission speed of a nerve impulse is approximately five to eighty meters per second, and according to Nagahama's measurement, the transmission speed of *ki* in the meridians is approximately fifteen to twenty centimeters per second, which is considerably slower.)

This discovery was reported in China and generated a considerable response. Similar cases were already recorded in the works of Lǐ Shízhēng (sixteenth century) in the Ming dynasty period, but had been forgotten in contemporary China. A person with this kind of sensitivity is referred to in China as a "meridian sensitive person" [*jīngluòmǐnggǎnrěn*],[15] and Chinese researchers are conducting systematic investigations of such people.

The findings in this case were discovered by an accidental abnormality incurred in a bodily function, and there seems to be a fair number of people with this kind of disposition toward a specially developed sensation. The case of the "meridian sensitive person" seems to suggest that a potential circuit, that is, the system of *ki* meridians, which is invisible to anatomical recognition, latently exists at the base of the circuit of kinesthesis *qua* the self-apprehending sensation of one's own body [*karada*]. This circuit is distributed through the whole body within the immediate interior of the skin.

The case of the "meridian sensitive person" enables us to infer the existence of the meridian system from an inner, psychological aspect. However, from the empirical scientific standpoint, a method is needed here to prove the existence of the meridian system from an outer, physiological aspect. What has been most studied in response to this problem is a method of measuring the electric current of the skin.

The phenomenon of electric current in the skin was originally studied in psychology and physiology, quite independently of Eastern medicine. When a weak electric current is applied to a point on the skin that is circuited, a change in the electric potential occurs and is transmitted through the circuit, and its wave is recorded on a graph. This is the so-called "galvanic skin response" (GSR). It is alternatively called "*psycho*galvanic reflex" (PGR). Since GSR has a close connection with emotive functions, it is used in psychological tests. The lie detector is an application of this principle: when a question strongly stirs a subject's emotion, a strong response is displayed in GSR. This phenomenon was discovered in the beginning of this century, and when Jung saw the experiment in its initial phase, he apparently remarked that the skin is a window to look into the unconscious.

The physiological mechanism of GSR is usually explained in terms of viscero-cutaneous reflex (VCR). This is a reflexive circuit connecting the autonomic nerves and the skin. Autonomic nerves branching out from each section of the spinal cord spread into the visceral organs and then reach the skin; and reversing again into the interior, they return back to the spinal cord. The pathway of the autonomic nerves connecting the spinal cord, visceral organs, and skin may be regarded as a centripetal circuit, while the pathway running from the skin through the visceral organs to the spinal cord may be taken as a centrifugal circuit. Because of these circuits, what are called Head's zones of hyperalgesia are distributed on the surface of the skin. By examining the condition of the skin, it is possible to diagnose, to a certain degree, abnormalities in the visceral functions. In short, the viscero-cutaneous reflex plays the role of an information circuit conveying to the surface abnormalities in the autonomic nervous system and visceral functions.

In view of this information circuit, researchers in Eastern medicine wondered if they might not be able to prove the existence of the meridian system by relying on the measurements of electric current on the skin. The "positive conductive meridians" [*ryōdōraku*], which Dr. Nakaya Yoshio of Kyoto University has proposed, is representative of these experiments. He closely examined electric resistance on the skin and discovered points where the resistance is low (points where electric conductivity is easy). He also found that these points corresponded well with the routes of the twelve meridians, which he named the "positive conductive meridians." Nakaya's discovery aroused great interest among researchers, and consequently the electrophysiological method has been widely used for the study of meridians. Although his interpretation is that this phenomenon occurs through the mechanism of viscero-cutaneous reflex (VCR), this interpretation remains questionable, because as was already mentioned, the flow of *ki* which a meridian sensitive person feels has nothing to do with the nervous system.

Dr. Motoyama Hiroshi's research is focused on this problem.[16] Henry Head's (1861–1940) zones of hyperalgesia on the skin surface are divided into sections called "dermatomes." According to this concept, all the surface skin of the body is understood as a collection of dermatomes. Each dermatome section is linked to the spinal cord via the system of viscero-cutaneous reflex, that is, using the autonomic nerves as a connecting path. Therefore, it is possible to know anatomically which part of the dermatome is linked via the nerve to which section of the spinal cord (Fig. 4.3).

Motoyama's idea was that it would be possible to detect the flow of *ki*, mediated in the meridian system, by measuring and making use of this mechanism, which would be different in nature

FIGURE 4.3a
DERMATOMES OF SYMPATHETIC NERVES

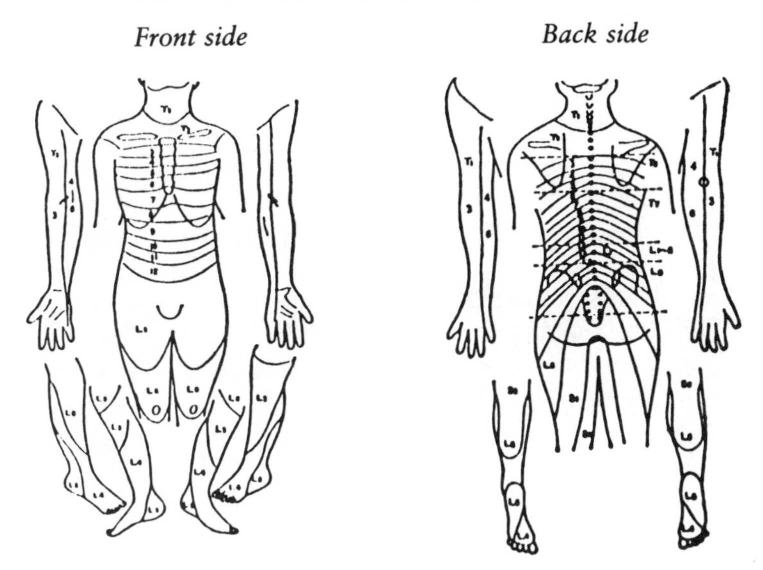

From Motoyama Hiroshi, *Kieraku: zōkinō sokutei ni tsuite.*

from the galvanic skin response (the viscero-cutaneous reflex) mediated by the autonomic nervous system. Motoyama's experimental data requires specialized knowledge to understand its details, so I shall just summarize the results. If a relatively strong electric current, of the degree to which a subject feels a light pain, is applied to the circuits formed on the surface of the skin, which are selected from certain meridians, waves admitting no repeatability are detected along the points (acu-points) of these meridians (see Fig. 4.4a). This is clearly a galvanic skin response, that is, it is generated through the nerves. However, when the electric stimulus is lowered, the above response does not occur, but instead a different response is generated on these specified points which is appropriate for the theory of meridians (see Fig. 4.4b). Judging from the distribution of dermatomes, there is clearly no connecting pathway by means of the nerves. The fact that a different response is generated in spite of this cannot be explained unless we assume the existence of a potential circuit (the meridian system) which is different from the system of viscero-cutaneous reflex.

FIGURE 4.3b
DERMATOMES OF SPINAL NERVES

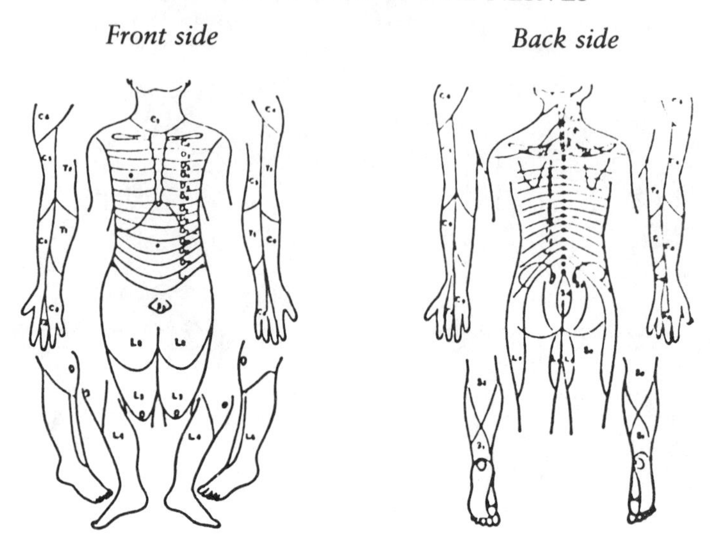

From Motoyama Hiroshi, *Kieraku: zōkinō sokutei ni tsuite.*

Motoyama's measurements present us with an interesting issue. Both the nerves and blood vessels are vessel systems which are anatomically recognizable, and therefore, they can be found in a corpse. However, the meridian system is a potential circuit unique to a living body, and insofar as it is examined anatomically, no such vessel system exists for the paths of the meridians. In other words, even though there is no anatomical substance to the meridian, its physiological function can be detected by means of electrophysiological measurements. To put it simply, only its function exists and without a supporting substance. Metaphorically speaking, the meridian system is like hearing a voice without seeing the person producing it. What is detected is nothing other than an electric potential in the electric current of the skin. For this reason, it is possible to regard it as another form of galvanic skin response, but it is not a function generated through the nerves like the usual galvanic skin response. In short, a characteristic of the meridian system which is unique to the living body is that *we can understand its function without grasping its substance.*

To summarize the conclusion for the present, the substance of *ki*-energy is not yet known. *Ki* is the flow of a certain energy cir-

FIGURE 4.4a
RESPONSE VIA THE NERVE

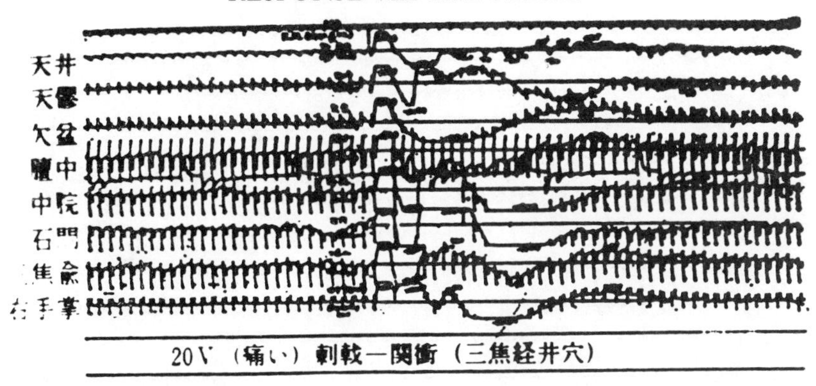

An example of Motoyama's experiment: when a stimulus is applied to the *kanshō* acu-point (the tip of the fourth finger), which is a "well acu-point" on the triple heater meridian, the subject feels pain with a 20-volt current (see Fig. 4.4a). The points measured are *tensei, tenryō* (belonging to the triple heater meridian), *ketsubon* (in the stomach meridian), *danchū, chūkan, sekimon* (in the *nin* ventral meridian), *sanshōyu* (the bladder meridian) and the palm of the right hand. Among them, *sekimon* is a *boketsu* acu-point belonging to the triple heater meridian, and *sanshōyu* is a *yuketsu* in the triple heater meridian. (*Yuketsu* refers to a specific acu-point on the dorsal *toku* meridian while *boketsu* designates a specific acu-point on the *nin* ventral meridian. They are each thought to have an intimate connection with these meridians. *Yīn* and *yáng* are said to travel between these two acu-points).

culating in the living body, unique to living organisms, and its physiological function can empirically be detected. However, what is causing such a function is beyond our current understanding. To be more precise, the flow of *ki,* when it is seen psychologically, is perceived in the circuit of coenesthesis as an abnormal sensation, as a self-apprehending sensation of one's own body under special circumstances. (This is exemplified by the case of the "meridian sensitive person.") When it is viewed physiologically, it is detected on the skin, which is the boundary wall between the body and the outer world. Therefore, *ki*-energy is both psychological and physiological: its substance lies in the region of the psychologically unconscious and the physiologically invisible. In other words, the meridian system is intimately connected with the mind and body as a whole, that is, with spirit and matter as a

FIGURE 4.4b
RESPONSE VIA THE MERIDIAN

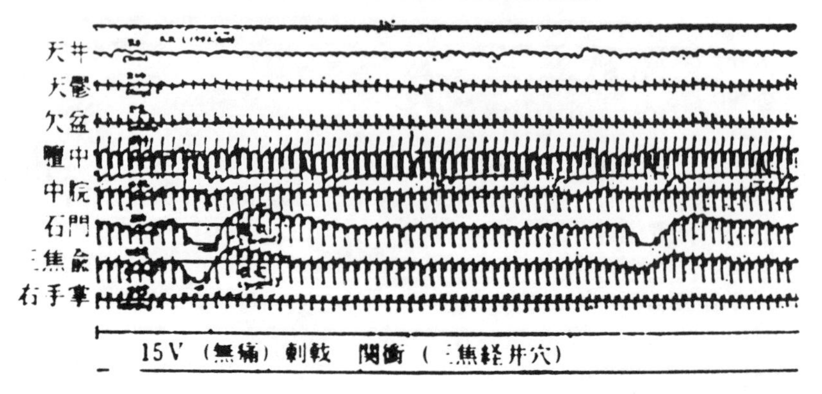

In 4.4a, we can see an unrepeatable response at all of the points measured (GSR). In 4.4b, the stimulus is lowered (15 volts) but is applied to the same *kanshō* as in 4.4a. In this case, responses are found only in *sanshōyu* and *sekimon,* which are *yuketsu* and *boketsu* on the triple heater meridian. The distribution of dermatomes for *kanshō* is C_8, T_1–T_4, for *sekimon* is T_{11}–T_{12}, and for *sanshōyu* is L_1–L_2. Among them there is no connecting link via the nerves.

whole, and it is a middle system influencing their functions. Consequently, it is a third term which cannot be explained in terms of Descartes' mind-matter dichotomy, and yet it is a mediating system connecting mind and matter. A breakthrough point seems to lie here that is capable of transforming the paradigm of empirical science established since Descartes.

IV. THE UNCONSCIOUS QUASI-BODY'S FUNCTION DIRECTED TOWARD THE EXTERNAL WORLD

To recapitulate, there are now four circuits which organize the body. The first is the sensory-motor system which deals with the external world. The second is the circuit of coenesthesis which is the system of self-apprehending sensation of one's own body. The third is the emotion-instinct circuit of the autonomic nervous system, which is connected with the unconscious. And the fourth is the circuit of the meridian system which is connected to the external world while circulating in the skin, which is the boundary wall between the external world and the body. This fourth circuit, insofar as it is examined anatomically, is an *invisible* circuit which cannot be perceived from outside by external sensory perception. Moreover, when it is examined psychologically, it is *a potential circuit in the unconscious* which ordinary consciousness cannot detect. For this reason, I would like to call the meridian system the "unconscious quasi-body" [*muishikiteki junshintai*]. It designates a pathway of emotional energy flowing in the unconscious, and is a quasi-body system which activates physiological functions together with the objective body. As previously mentioned, *ki*-energy flowing in the meridian system has been conceived of as exchanging *ki* with the external world through the well acu-points in the distal points of the limbs. The next subject for research here becomes the question of how *ki* functions in its interaction between the body and the external world.

Some philosophers, from a perspective quite different than the research in Eastern medicine, have to a degree already anticipated that the living body is endowed with an "unconscious quasi-body" system similar to the meridian system. We can find this idea in the theories of the body proposed by Henri Bergson and Maurice Merleau-Ponty, which we dealt with in chapter 2. Starting primarily from the study of external perception, they developed the idea that an invisible system differing from the system of the object-body exists latently in the living body. In view of this, I would now like to examine Eastern medicine's theory of the body while comparing and contrasting it with those of Bergson and Merleau-Ponty.

Bergson calls the centripetal-centrifugal system, consisting of the sensory nerves and motor nerves, the "sensory-motor apparatus" (*les appareils sensori-moteurs*), while Merleau-Ponty refers to it as the "sensory-motor circuit" (*un circuit sensori-moteur*). Borrowing Merleau-Ponty's term, I have called it the "external sensory-motor circuit," which is the first information circuit that organizes the body. This "external sensory-motor circuit" is a circuit which connects the body with the thing-events of the external world. It changes a sensory stimulus into the information of a nerve impulse and carries it to a center in the brain by means of the sensory nerves (centripetal circuit). The center in the brain in turn sends its command, via information through the motor nerves (centrifugal circuit), to the limbs, which are the distal motor organs. Since the mechanism of this circuit is anatomically and physiologically clear, Merleau-Ponty refers to it through such phrases as "the physiological body" (*le corps physiologique*), "the objective body" (*le corps objectif*), and "the actual body" (*le corps actuel*).

Both Bergson and Merleau-Ponty postulate in this connection what they call respectively the "motor scheme" (*un schéma moteur*) and the "body scheme" (*un schéma chorporel*), which they think activates the "objective body." Generally speaking, this is a mechanism which *habitualizes* the various capacities of the body, especially motor skills. First, Merleau-Ponty's "body scheme" is a concept taking into consideration the second circuit of what I have called the circuit of coenesthesis, that is, the self-apprehending (internal) sensation of one's own body, and particularly the circuit of kinesthesis. Physiologically, the circuit of kinesthesis consists of the centrifugal sensory-motor nerves and the centripetal motor-sensory nerves, and has the function of bringing into consciousness the motor-sensation of the limbs as they relate themselves to the external world. It was Husserl who initially took note of this circuit of kinesthesis. It is the self-apprehending sensation of "one's own body" [*karada*] which is found at the periphery of the consciousness of the Cartesian cognitive subject (the clear and distinct *cogito*) when the latter directs itself toward the external world. Merleau-Ponty has incorporated within this circuit of kinesthesis the idea of the "body scheme" of which Henry Head, a neurologist, speaks.[17] Head, who discovered the aforementioned "Head's zones of hyperalgesia" on the skin, thought that in the interior of a living body there exists the system of the body scheme which integrates all of the somatic sensations, such as motor sensation, sensation of balance, and dermal sensation. Head's "body scheme" is limited to the *interior* of the body, however. Merleau-Ponty, going one step further, maintains that the system of the body scheme has a built-in potential function which directs itself toward the thing-events of the external world. He calls it "the lived body" (*le corps vécu*) or "the habit body" (*le corps habituel*).

According to Merleau-Ponty, the system of the lived body with this built-in body scheme exists at the base of kinesthesis, which self-apprehends one's own body, and has the function of preparing and directing the first external sensory-motor circuit toward behavior (action). To put it simply, it refers to the "body" [*karada*] about which we say "the body learns" when we learn or master a certain skill. This "body" instantly apprehends through feeling and intuition subtle changes in kinesthesis without waiting for conscious judgment. It is thus the lived body playing the role of guiding in advance the physiological body to adjust itself appropriately to situations of the external world. In short, Merleau-Ponty contends that at the base of the physiologically recognized "objective body" there latently exists the system of the "habit body" which may be referred to as the "lived body." According to him, this lived "habit body" casts threads of potential intentional functions toward the external world. He calls this casting activity "an existential arc" (*l'arc existentiel*). By means of this "existential arc," the body unconsciously illuminates the region of possible actions and grasps its goal in advance.

In Merleau-Ponty's body scheme we can recognize an idea commensurate with the meridian system *qua* the unconscious quasi-body. The meridian system cannot be recognized by anatomy, and in this sense it does not belong to the "object body." It is a circuit in which *ki*-energy, unique to the living body, circulates. Accordingly, it is appropriate to call the system of meridians the "lived body." Moreover, the flow of *ki*-energy in the meridian system is thought to exchange *ki* with the external world through the distal points in the limbs which are motor organs. Since Merleau-Ponty's "lived body" is a system that casts threads of potential intentional functions, it is also commensurate with the concept of the meridian system. Needless to say, however, Merleau-Ponty's concept of the body-scheme is not influenced by the Eastern theory of the body. He did not pay attention to somesthesis (for example, splanchnic sensation), which forms another pillar of coenesthesis, nor to the third emotion-instinct circuit. The Eastern theory of the body places importance on these two circuits. Merleau-Ponty was led to postulate the body-scheme through the investigation of epistemology, an area which has interested philosophers greatly, that is, through the investigation of cognitive functions. Husserl's phenomenological concept of intentional function is originally conceived to be an activity of understanding, and in light of its relationship to consciousness, is the *meaning* of the object of experience found in the external world. That is, the function of intentionality is that act directed to the *cognition of meaning* found in objects of the external world. Seen in this light, Merleau-Ponty's idea started from a point of interest quite different from the Eastern theory of the body. Nevertheless, the meridian system and the *ki* flowing in it are related to a kind of *intuitive cognitive function* in an extraordinary experience, and they seem somehow connected to the issue of the cognition of the inner world.

The existence of Merleau-Ponty's mechanism of the "lived body," as elucidated in the foregoing, cannot be recognized by previously held physiological methods of verification. Merleau-Ponty himself confessed that "the notion of body scheme is ambiguous, as are all notions which make their appearance at turning points in scientific advance."[18] But he has a reason for it. The "lived body" is "a third term between the psychological and the physiological, between the in-itself and the for-itself."[19] In other words, Merleau-Ponty's concept of the "body scheme" contains content which the mind-matter dichotomy since Descartes is incapable of explaining. To put it in still another way, the verification method of the hitherto accepted physiology analyzes the mechanism of the body after excluding all that is psychological from its consideration, but Merleau-Ponty's concept of "body scheme" is apparently a third system in the lived body that is both psychological and physiological, both spiritual and physical.

Merleau-Ponty's concept is extremely interesting to philosophers, and yet it is difficult to find a method that will connect empirical scientific verification with his philosophical investigation. In contrast, it would seem that the meridian system as the unconscious quasi-body, as found in the Eastern theory of the body, will enable us to bridge them. This theory contends that the potential circuit of *ki*-energy, unique to the living body, and circulating in the boundary wall (the skin) between the body and the external world, exchanges *ki* with the external world through the distal points of the limbs. Moreover, the activity which this energy has in the living body, as was shown in the foregoing, is confirmed experimentally by physiological measurement and clinical therapeutic effect.

V. MEMORY AND THE LIVED BODY

Merleau-Ponty's concept of the "body-scheme" shows an influence from Bergson's concept of the "motor scheme" (*un schéma moteur*). However, since Merleau-Ponty was strongly influenced by Husserl's phenomenology, he did not take into consideration the unconscious. This is because Husserl's phenomenology originally started with *a philosophical investigation of consciousness,* which rejects the value of empirical sciences, such as depth psychology, as adhering to the empirical (natural) standpoint. In this respect, Bergson's concept is more suggestive to us.

Bergson postulates the system of the habituated body, which he calls the "motor scheme," at the base of the "sensory-motor circuit" connected with the cerebral cortex. We may consider it as the predecessor to Merleau-Ponty's concept of "body-scheme." The "motor scheme," which is built up in the body, is a system which unconsciously illuminates in advance the possibilities of action. It directs the body to potential actions, prior to the passive activation of perception by means of the sensory organs. (Bergson did not, however, pay sufficient attention to kinesthesis in relation to this system. Taking note of this fact, Merleau-Ponty developed his concept of the body-scheme.) However, Bergson noted the fact that the function of cognition is closely related to the issue of memory, and attempted to investigate the relationship between *memory and the habituation of the body.*

Bergson dealt with rather unusual cases, such as agnosia, apraxia, and aphasia, and realized that they are broadly concerned with *memory disorders.* For example, aphasia is a memory disorder that manifests itself in the use of language. An aphasic patient, when shown a picture of a dog, cannot recall the word "dog," or upon hearing the word "dog," cannot immediately recollect its meaning. With the agnosic patient, a disorder occurs in the cognitive function as is seen in Schneider's case.[20] When patients suffering from mental blindness, a kind of agnosia, look at places or things that they have seen in the past, they cannot recall where or what they are. Apraxia is a memory disorder affecting the motor sensation of one's hands and legs in which one loses the acquired memory of how to move them. It is, in other words, a memory loss regarding movement. (Consequently, an apraxic patient must always relearn how to move his or her hands and legs, as a baby does.) Usually a patient with this disorder has some form of brain dysfunction, which raises the issue of the relation between the brain and mind, especially the unconscious. This is because memory is an image stored in the region of the unconscious.

Sensing that there are numerous cases of motor dysfunction among patients suffering from memory disorders, Bergson thought that the system of the "motor scheme" exists potentially or latently at the base of the sensory motor circuit. According to Bergson, the motor scheme stores what he calls the "learned memory" (*le souvenir appris*). "Learned memory" refers to those memories which we are trained to learn such as the meaning of a letter or word, or how to use the keyboard on a piano or typewriter. Specific techniques acquired in sports or in theatrical performance are also instances of "learned memory." For example, when we see the letter "A" we immediately recall its *meaning*, that it is the shape of the first letter in the alphabet. In other words, a meaning in the memory is recalled for a figure given to visual perception (the letter "A" as a sensory stimulus). In light of this, perceptual cognition is, generally speaking, a *conjunction of perception and memory*. In learned memory, then, meaning is recollected from the unconscious immediately upon a sensory organ perceiving a stimulus connecting it to the perception. Bergson calls this mechanism "automatic recognition" (*le souvenir automatique*) because the unconscious, as soon as a sensory image is perceived, *automatically* recalls (re-cognizes) its meaning. Bergson says that the lived body is endowed with the system of the motor scheme which stores numerous vocabularies acquired through the learned memory, preparing the body in advance for action. When a disorder occurs in this potential system, a perception entering through the sensory organs fail to link itself with memory, and consequently with its meaning. This happens, for example, when on seeing the letter "A" its meaning cannot be recalled.

Since in recent years numerous case studies have been carried out by neurophysiologists, the concrete aspects of memory disorders are known in detail. I will try to examine the meaning of this issue while selecting a case from Yamatori Shigeru's research.[21] Patient C (an American) had difficulty understanding names. When he was asked where the desk was, he could manage to point to the desk by looking around the room, but he was not sure if the desk was really a desk. For the desk in the room was not "the same" as the one he was familiar with in his daily life at work. Or to put it differently, the desk looked like a desk, but was different from "the desk" which he remembered. Moreover, upon seeing a bed, he also paused to wonder if he could still call it a "bed" when the mattress was removed, because without the mattress it was not "the same" bed in which he always slept.

Yamatori says that language function is lived words supported by an *habituated, automatic* ability. Since the habituated, automatic ability was lost in patient C, the language could function only as an individual, *private language*. The word "desk" applied only to *the desk* with which he was familiar in his daily life, and the word "bed" designated *a state of the bed* in which he currently slept. Language can function when it is applied generally to a social, public sphere; otherwise it cannot exercise its effect. Therefore, the word "desk" must be applied to any desk, which Yamatori calls the "categorization function" [*hanchūka kinō*]. An ordinary, healthy person has an unconscious habituated switch (the categorization function) that changes from a private language to public language, and can perform this automatically and smoothly. We store the meaning "desk in general" by abstracting from the memory of a desk which we have experienced in the past, and apply the general category "desk" to a desk which is seen for the first time, recognizing it as *a desk*. What does the mechanism of the habituated memory mean to the system of the body?

In the unconscious region we possess the space of private words (*parole*), or to be more precise, what may be called the system of private meaning space, habitualized by the behavior and experiences of our past. It stores the learned memory images of the past. This is what Bergson called "learned memory." The system of this learned memory is formed by the past habitualization in the mind and body of everyday *behavior*, as is typically seen in patient C. And in virtue of the fact that this system is linked to an objective system of public meaning space (for example, *langue*), perceptual cognition becomes possible.

This may be explained as follows by borrowing Saussure's (1859–1913) theory of language (see Fig. 4.5). The form of a letter (visual image) and sound (auditory image) correspond to Saussure's "signifying" (*signifiant*). It is a *sign* with a certain meaning. In contrast, the meaning of a word recalled from the unconscious (a concept) corresponds to his "signified" (*signifié*). It is the objective aimed at by the sign (image). Since a theory of language is concerned with the general, universal structure of a language, it analyzes the relationship between "signifying" and "signified" in light of a public language (*langue*). In contrast, what is important to the mind-body theory is the mechanism of *switching* from a private meaning space appropriated by each individual body (the

FIGURE 4.5
THE MECHANISM OF HABITUATED MEMORY

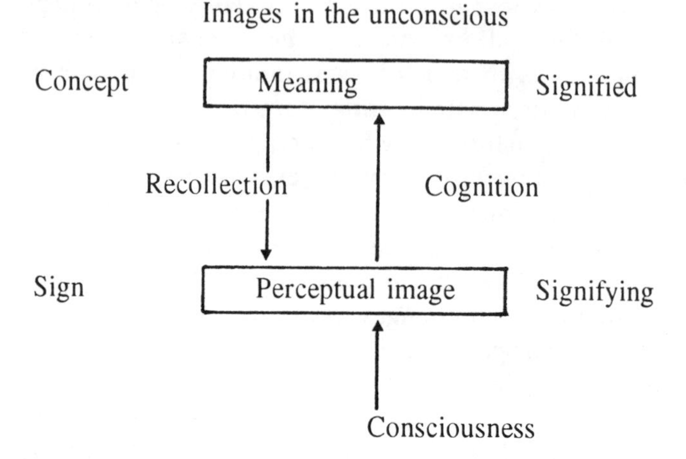

field of individual *parole*) to a public meaning space. We cognize the meaning of *langue* ("signified") through a specific image (perception), and its meaning is selectively recalled from the storage of memory in the unconscious, connecting it to the present perception. The intentional meaning-bestowing function of consciousness searches and picks up the meaning of an image stored in the unconscious (recollection), and comes to cognize its meaning (indicated by the arrow in the circuit). Bergson's "motor scheme" is a system which habituates and directs how this connection takes place in the circuit.

In short, Bergson's "motor scheme" of the body is an integrative system which unconsciously directs the mind-body whole to an external action, while connecting and mediating the *mind's function* of recollecting memory (psychological function) with the *body's function* which receives information from the thing-events of the external world through the sensory organs (perceptual activity *qua* the physiological function). Therefore, it is a *middle-system* of the spirit and body, which is unified through the function of spirit and matter, or through the function of mind and body. This middle system cannot sufficiently be confirmed by the hitherto accepted method of empirical scientific verification in physiology, and yet this system latently exists in the lived body. Bergson reasons that the sensory-motor circuit, which is the first system of information in the body, is activated by receiving the energy of this motor scheme.

What then lies in the depths of the unconscious region which stores the images of meanings? Bergson contends that behind the deep region of learned memory stored in the body's "motor-scheme," exists the region of what he calls "spontaneous recollection" [*le souvenir spontané*]. This is close to Freud's concept of the unconscious in its original sense, and refers to historically dated memory, for example, the recollection of a past broken heart. Memories of this sort are ordinarily stored away deep in the unconscious with an *emotional coloring*. Since learned memory is utilized in everyday life, thus losing its individual emotional overtone, it can be selected at any time as *a memory without a date*. By contrast, a "spontaneous memory" does not have immediate utility for daily life, and if it is constantly recollected, it will cause problems in daily life and behavior. For this reason, it does not surface under normal circumstances.

Bergson calls the region of spontaneous memory "sheer duration" (*durée pure*). "Duration" here designates the flow of time. Spontaneous memory stores images that are connected, as it were, only with *the flow of time in one's life*. "Sheer" in "sheer duration" means that a recollected image is unrelated to the body, that is, to spatiality. Since learned memory is contained in the motor scheme of the body, preparing the body's action toward the external world, it is a region of interchange with the space in which the body is placed. By contrast, spontaneous memory does not have any spatial determination.

To put this in simple terms, space is the world of matter. The body lives in relation to things in space, and it itself exists spatially. In contrast, time is originally found only in the world of the mind. Historical (spontaneous) memory, which is a footprint in the flow of time in one's life, is found only in one's mind. Although we say "two hours have gone by," this means that the mind has measured the passage of time in reference to its perception of the state of a thing (for example, a clock). It is time measured (note the past tense) by means of the thing, but *the state itself* in which time flows (sheer duration) is an inner, immediate experience which cannot be measured from outside. Bergson reasons that the body connects the order of mind, which lacks spatial determination, with the order of matter which in itself has no temporal determination.

However, Bergson did not consider how spontaneous memory is related to the body. He seemed to have thought that the region of spontaneous memory has nothing whatsoever to do with the body's mechanism, although he was cognizant of the fact that learned memory is stored as the "motor scheme" at the base of the external sensory-motor circuit. Since he knew almost nothing about Freud's work, and since the cerebral function below the cortex and the mechanism of the autonomic nervous system were not known in Bergson's time, he seems not to have understood the relationship between the brain and emotion. Merleau-Ponty is no exception in this case. Neither of them gave any thought to the circuit of somesthesis, which deals primarily with splanchnic sensation, nor to the third emotion-instinct circuit of the body. In contrast, the Eastern theory of the body has focused on the function of the emotion-instinct circuit centered on the autonomic nervous system, and has devised technical methods for controlling it. Today we have considerable knowledge of the mechanism of the third circuit thanks to developments in depth psychology and psychosomatic medicine. It is, then, necessary to investigate what role and meaning the system of the fourth unconscious quasi-body circuit possesses.

Bergson's study and recent research in neurophysiology inform us that the functions of perception and memory (and consequently the unconscious) are closely connected to each other. When we use "perception" we usually think of the perception of thing-events in the external world. This is the standpoint of modern epistemology and empirical science. However, the tradition of Eastern thought has emphasized not only perception of the external world (the world of matter) but even more so cognition of the depths of the world of mind (the inner world). Meditation is cognition of states in the unconscious region. And based on the deepening cognition of the world of mind, Eastern thought has aimed at thinking afresh the meaning of understanding the world of matter.

PART III

The Present and Future of the Science of Ki

CHAPTER 5

The Science of Ki *and Its View of Human Being*

I. INTRODUCTION

Eastern medicine's view of the body maintains that the flow of *ki* is interchanged with the external world through the well acupoints at the tips of the fingers and toes. This idea has been well known since ancient times, but no research has been conducted to verify it from a contemporary perspective until recent years. However, Chinese researchers started experimental research on this idea toward the end of the 1970s, and many facts have so far been discovered. In recent years an exchange between Chinese and Japanese researchers and practitioners has been promoted, and Japan is now pursuing its own new research. In this chapter I should like to examine the relation between the function of *ki*-energy and the environment while introducing some of these research achievements.

The research is called the "science of *qìgōng*" in China and *kikō* in Japan. *Qìgōng,* or *kikō,* is standardized terminology neologized to designate *ki*-training. In the past it has been designated by various terms, such as "*dǎoyǐn*" ("guiding *ki*"), "*tǔnà*" ("incoming and outgoing *ki* through breathing"), and "*xínggì*" ("moving *ki*"). Meditation training is included as part of the broad sense of *ki*-training. In China it is referred to as "*jìnggōng*" ("quiet training," that is, *ki*-training in a stationary position). In contrast, *ki*-training involving bodily movement is called "*dònggōng*" ("*ki*-training through movement"). *Tàijíquán* is an example. *Ki*-training in its narrow sense designates *ki*-training through movement.

The historical origin of *ki*-training is as old as Eastern medicine, and goes back to the ancient period prior to the Christian era. We find several descriptions of "*dònggōng*" already recorded in the *Zhuāngzǐ*. It is a health promotion method which has been historically developed in close association with the medicinal arts, the martial arts, and the fine arts. Although Chinese researchers say that *qìgōng* has a bearing on the six fields of Confucianism, Daoism, Buddhism, the medicinal arts, the martial arts, and the fine arts, it would be appropriate to classify the first three as either religion or philosophy. *Jìnggōng*, quiet *ki*-training, with an emphasis on meditation may be regarded as philosophical *ki*-training.

Ki-training through movement [*dònggōng*] is further divided into "internal *ki*-training" [*nèiqìgōng*] and "external *ki*-training" [*wàiqìgōng*]. Internal *ki*-training involves individual performance. By activating immanent natural healing powers, one makes an effort to cure oneself, or to maintain and promote one's health. Medical practice is not regarded as a unilateral performance by a doctor, but as a cooperative task also involving the patient. In contrast, external *ki*-training refers to cases in which a *ki*-therapist or *qìgōng* master with many years of *ki*-training, treats a patient by means of the function of *ki*-energy emitted from the therapist's body. In China, this form of treatment is officially recognized as part of institutionalized medical practice.

One of the major reasons that *kikō* has attracted the attention of researchers is that the *ki*-energy utilized in external *ki*-training has become known through scientific measurements. There are many points that have not been clarified regarding its mechanism and effects, and the present situation is such that many disputes occur in scholarly circles in China. What is noteworthy from a theoretical point of view is that scientific, experimental methods have enabled us to measure and detect the energy activity emitted from the human body. This has been made possible through recent developments in the technique of biophysical measurement.

It is a well-known fact that the human body and living organisms are endowed with energy activities such as bioelectricity. Broadly speaking, the measurements of brain waves and the electro-potential of the skin are a kind of biophysical measurement. Research on the mechanism of the human body through biofeedback can also be included within the scope of biophysical measurement research.

The research which has thus far been performed on the human body, however, is limited to the study of the internal mechanism of the human body, using the skin as a boundary, as it were. Chinese scientists, going one step further, started to study the field of energy activity created outside of the human body. Theoretically, it was probable that if there was an electric phenomenon inside of the human body, then it would have a certain activity outside of the human body. The research which Chinese scientists have inaugurated may be comparable to Columbus' egg. We should recognize their work as a new and important step drawing us into a larger arena of investigation, one which extends the scope of the scientific research on *ki* beyond the interiority of the human body to the relationship between the human body and the environment.

Through this movement the problem of *ki* has received an initial impetus to investigate the function of the living human body in the three fields of psychology, physiology, and physics. A human being, as a synthetic unity of mind and body, is a living being intersecting the environing world formed by "matter." *Ki* research will turn out to be a project for the comprehensive understanding of the correlative relationship of this whole.

II. *KI*-ENERGY AND ITS RELATION TO THE EXTERNAL WORLD

China started its scientific research on *kikō* [Chin. *qìgōng*] in 1977, when the Cultural Revolution was about to end. Dr. Gù Hánsēn, a specialist in the study of microwaves at Shanghai Nuclear Institute of The Chinese Academy of Science, took an interest in *kikō* when she witnessed Mr. Lín Hoùshěng, a *ki*-therapist at Shanghai Institute of Chinese Medicine, perform an external *ki*-emission treatment. On this occasion Mr. Lín emitted *ki* through his hands at approximately twenty centimeters away from the patient, who was suffering from urinary and rectal incontinence, and whose legs were both paralyzed. After thirty seconds, the patient started jerking the lower portion of his body. Mr. Lín then emitted *ki* through his acu-point called *rōkyū* (VA 8),[1] located roughly in the center of the palm, aiming at the patient's acu-point called *yōkan* (GB 33),[2] located on the side of the kneecap. During this time, the patient reportedly felt repeated strong muscular contraction and expansion around the urinary bladder and rectum. The *yōkan* is the acu-point belonging to the gall-bladder meridian which runs on the outer side of the leg. It branches to the ventral and dorsal sides in the lower part of the waist. The tributary branching to the ventral side goes around the pubic hair, merging again with the tributary running in the dorsal region (buttock). The fact that the patient had the repeated sensation of muscular contraction and expansion around the bladder and rectum when he received *ki* on the *yōkan* acu-point, demonstrates that the *ki*-energy emitted from the *ki*-therapist influenced the flow of *ki*-energy in the patient's gall-bladder meridian.

Mr. Lín Hoùshěng is well-known for his ability to perform "*kikō* anesthesia" which stops pain through external *ki*-emission without using anesthetic. In Shanghai in 1989 I saw Mr. Lín perform *kikō* anesthesia on a patient undergoing a thyroid gland operation. Standing less than one meter away from the patient, Mr. Lín slightly opened both of his hands directing them toward the affected area opened through the incision (the pharynx), now and then moving his fingers and arms. Apparently, there are degrees of "*kikō* anesthesia," ranging from a total anesthetic to decreased dosages. The dosage is determined, I was told, in consultation with the patient's wish.

The term "microwave" usually refers to electromagnetic waves with wavelengths shorter than one meter. It includes, in descending order of wavelength, infrared rays, visible rays, ultraviolet rays, X-rays, and gamma rays. Besides these rays, there are inaudible ultrasonic waves, infrasonic waves, and magnetic fields which may also be measured. Dr. Gù first asked Mr. Lín to try an external emission *ki*-treatment on a patient covered by a comforter [*futon*], in order to narrow down what was to be measured. This experiment yielded a positive response. Since ultrasonic waves and particles such as molecules would not penetrate the comforter, the waves that did penetrate may be regarded as a type of electromagnetic wave. Next, she asked Mr. Lín to emit *ki* to the patient located six meters away from him and shielded by a copper screen. In this experiment too, a curative effect was obtained. The magnetic field does not function once an object is moved beyond a distance of six meters radius, and regular electronic waves with longer wavelengths would not penetrate the copper shield. Thus Dr. Gù inferred that *ki*-energy must be a kind of electromagnetic wave with a shorter wavelength, that is, an infrared ray or a shorter length ray. However, since ultraviolet rays and X rays have harmful effects on the human body, they were eliminated for consideration. Reasoning in this manner, Dr. Gù took a measurement of the infrared rays and detected, as she expected, the pulsating

FIGURE 5.1a
MR. LÍN'S EMISSION OF INFRARED RAYS

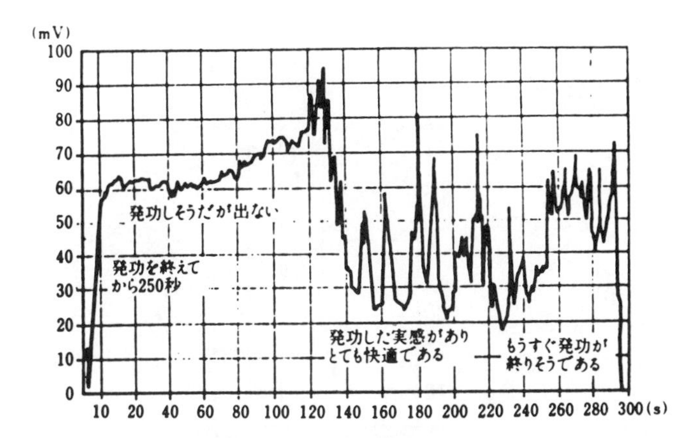

waves of infrared rays with a slow rhythmic change (see Fig. 5.1a). The infrared ray is a type of electromagnetic wave with a longer wave length than visible rays (whose wavelength is about 0.4–0.8 micron) and having a wavelength up to 1000 microns (one millimeter). The results of Dr. Gù's measurements are reported to be a wavelength of 0.3–3 microns, a wave frequency of 0.06–0.9 hertz, and an energy of several microwatts, which were taken at a distance of one centimeter to one meter from the *rōkyū* acu-point.[3]

What we must take special note of in the above experiments is that the detection of infrared rays is itself not important. This point needs to be kept firmly in mind. The emission of infrared rays is in theory detectable from any object above the temperature of absolute zero (−273°C), and so they can be detected from the palm of an ordinary person. What we need to note, is that the *ki*-therapist demonstrates clear and markedly different qualities in regard to the detected data compared to ordinary people. Figure 5.1b is inserted here for comparison. It is taken from a student learning massage. With ordinary people, it is usually the case that the graph has a line without much undulation in it, as shown in figure 5.1c. The data showing Mr. Lín's case was measured at a distance of one to two centimeters away from the *rōkyū* acu-point (VA 8). The explanation given at the left edge of figure 5.1a says that Mr. Lín had emitted *ki* once for a trial, and then the measurements were taken for a period of 250 seconds. The explanation continues that "in the beginning, he felt that he could almost

FIGURE 5.1b
EMISSION OF INFRARED RAYS BY A STUDENT OF MASSAGE

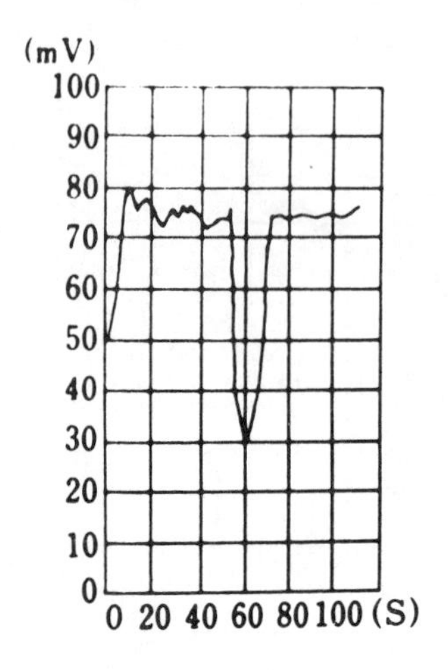

FIGURE 5.1c
EMISSION OF INFRARED RAYS BY AN ORDINARY PERSON

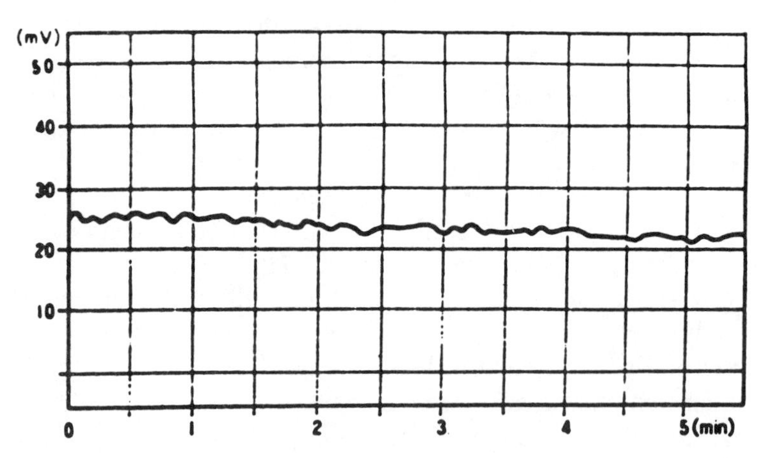

emit *ki,* but could not." But after 140 seconds it was observed in the graph that the apex of the wave was rising. The explanation says that he "felt that he was emitting *ki,*" and further toward the end it continues that "he had a pleasant sensation and terminated the emission." Since the scaling for the graph is divided into small units, the undulation of the wave appears rather violent, but when it is seen in terms of a temporal spread, the graph indicates a relatively slow pulsation of waves.

FIGURE 5.1d
SYNCHRONIZATION OBSERVED IN THE PATIENT'S BODY

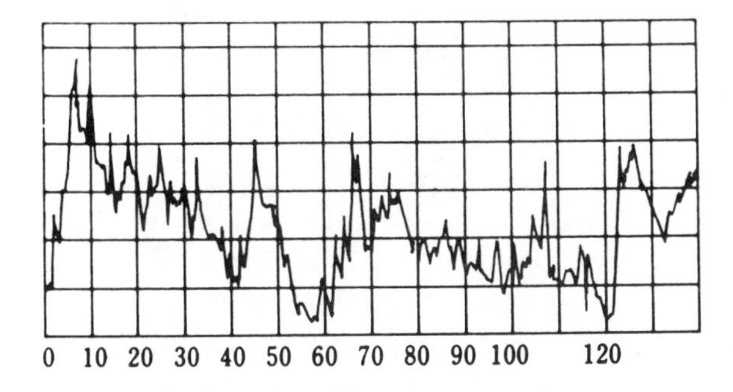

Figure 5.1d indicates the detection of infrared rays at the *yōkan* acu-point (GB 33) of the patient when Mr. Lín emitted *ki* toward the patient. It shows the generation of undulating waves just like those of Mr. Lín. This may be referred to as the "transpersonal synchronization of *ki*-energy." That is, the *ki*-energy emitted from A induces a definite effect on the mind and body of B, who is spatially distanced from A.

The report of Dr. Gù's experiments generated an enthusiastic response, which prompted many Chinese scientists to study *ki*-energy. Dr. Gù's experiments are significant for demonstrating that the phenomenon of *ki* can be investigated through scientific, experimental methods. The physiological ground is not clear yet as to how the curative effect of *ki* occurs. However, it is extremely important theoretically that what has been so far conceived to be the activity of *ki* has proven to have in some form a correlative relationship with the activity of physical energy. This shows that the problem of *ki* has bearing on the three fields of psychology, physiology, and physics (or mind, life, and matter). Moreover, it suggests the necessity of assuming a different perspective from the spirit-matter dualism (dichotomy) established as a fundamental principle in science since Descartes, and also from the division into individualized specializations.

As energy flows in and out of the human body, the magnetic field, ultrasonic waves, infrasonic waves (inaudible sound), and biophotons (a light emitted by living organisms at a micro level) are known to exist, in addition to electrical charges and infrared rays. It is possible that various other functions will be discovered. As for the magnetic field generated in the living human body, there are two cases. One is generated in the visceral organs, such as the brain and heart, through nerve electricity. In the other, particles with a magnetic tendency, inhaled into the lungs along with air, are magnetized by the magnetic field of the earth. Since particles charged with electricity, such as ions and microelectric pulses, are active in the human body, it is natural that a magnetic field is generated in the human body. The magnetic field in the lungs is relatively strong because of the inhalation of air, but it is nonetheless between one ten-thousandth and one ten-millionth gauss; in the heart it is one millionth gauss, and in the brain it is below one hundred-millionth gauss. These could not be detected through previously known methods of measuring the magnetic field. Incidentally, the magnetic field of the earth is about 0.5–0.8 gauss.

The measurement of human magnetic fields was started around 1986 in China. Dr. Gù, previously mentioned, constructed an apparatus for measuring magnetism combining a magnetic sensor and a voltage amplifier, and she measured the magnetic field created by *ki*-therapists.[4] As is shown in figure 5.2a, the output of voltage is in direct proportion to the intensity of the magnetic field. The measurement shown in figure 5.2b using the *ki*-therapist, Mr. Lín, as a subject was taken at a distance of five centimeters from the *hyakue* acu-point (Br 20) located at the crown of the head.[5] The graph shows a sudden increase in the magnetic field as soon as the measurement was taken. The maximum change rate is recorded to be 6.7 gauss/sec and the maximum frequency is 1.67 gauss. In another *ki*-therapist's case (see Fig. 5.2c), the measurement was taken two centimeters away from the *rōkyū* acu-point (VA 8), and a maximum of 1.25 gauss was detected. As in the previous case of measuring infrared rays, the energy emitted from *ki*-therapists frequently reveals pulsating waves.

At present, it is possible to give only a hypothetical explanation of why and how an intense magnetic field is generated in the human body. Where there is a flow of electricity, a magnetic field is naturally created. Bioelectricity flows most actively in nerves, but in addition there is, though very slightly, a bioelectricity generated in the activities of visceral organs and muscles, which also triggers the generation of a magnetic field. For example, when a person compresses the motor nerves and diaphragm through abdominal breathing, a relatively large amount of muscle electricity is generated. In view of these observations, we might say that the

FIGURE 5.2a

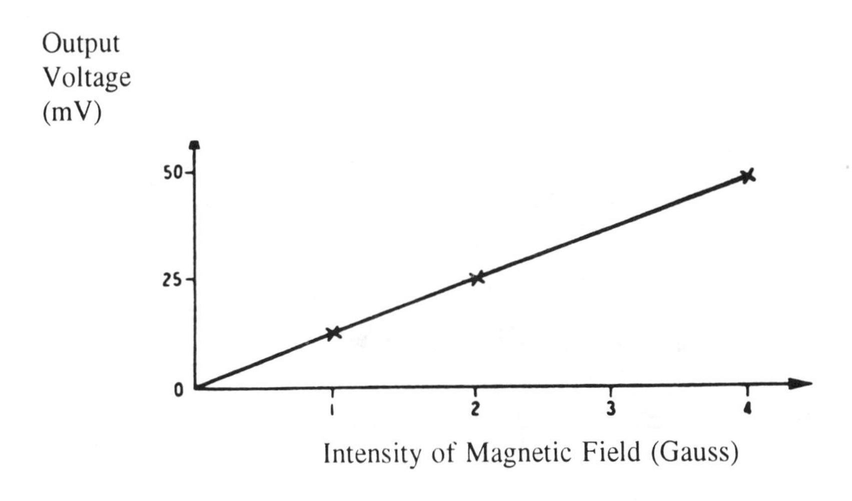

FIGURE 5.2b

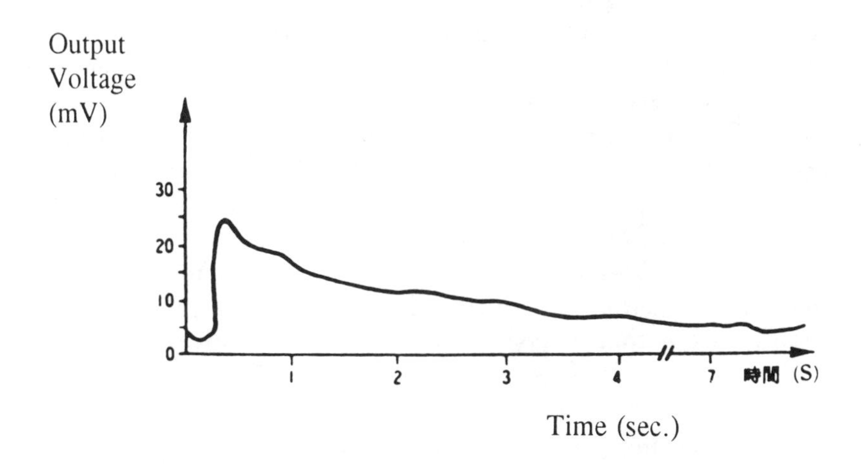

human body has a capability somewhat analogous to a generator. This principle itself has been well known, but that an intense magnetic field, several times stronger than the magnetic field of the earth, could be generated in the human body, was beyond expec-

FIGURE 5.2c

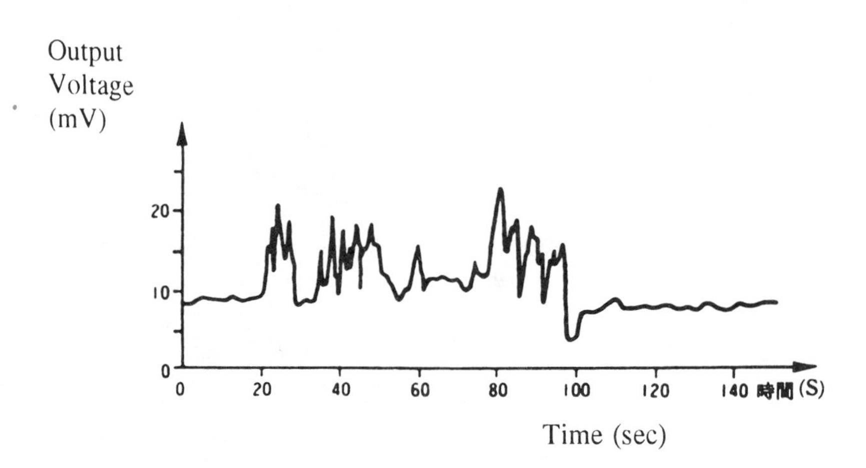

tation. This is why the measurement of the magnetic fields of the *ki*-therapists surprised people. The cells of the human body can be regarded as a biological dipole that is polarized into an N-pole and S-pole. When they are randomly arranged, they only generate a weak magnetic field as a whole, because they cancel out each other. We can postulate that the arrangement of the biological dipole in a *ki*-therapist's body is reconfigured in an orderly arrangement through conscious concentration, and as a result an intense magnetic field is generated like an electric magnet.

At any rate, what is important here is not the fact that the human body generates a magnetic field. Rather, what is of extreme significance is that its generation holds a correlative relationship with *the function of human consciousness,* and that it is detectable most strongly in the meridians (the acu-points). We can postulate that there is, in some sense, a corresponding or correlative relationship between the function of consciousness and physical energy, that is, between psychological phenomena and physical phenomena when it is examined in light of the meridian system, that is, in light of the circuit of the unconscious quasi-body.

The preceding illustration is concerned with electromagnetic waves and magnetic fields, but in addition to these, the generation of static electricity and infrasonic waves can be detected in and around the human body. Moreover, Japanese researchers have detected the generation of biophotons.[6] Since my present concern is not to introduce individual experimental cases, here I shall limit myself to making a general conclusion about their results.

There is no discernible difference between the *ki*-therapist and an ordinary person when measurements are taken in a normal state. However, when the *ki*-therapist concentrates his or her consciousness and emits *ki*-energy, various kinds of intense physical energy functions are detected, as has been observed in the foregoing. Moreover, the functions are invariably detected at the acu-points. Detections are often made in the hand (through the well acu-point), but in other cases they are observed in the forehead. These energy functions are detected in the form of a pulsating wave. Moreover, an activity synchronized to the emitted energy is observed in places on the patient who receives it. When the above points are taken together, it is clear that *ki*-energy flowing in the meridians, which is an interior bodily system, is emitted outside of the body with a definite effect on the surroundings. Therefore, we can tentatively define *ki* as an energy unique to the living human body that becomes manifest, while being transformed, at psychological, physiological, and physical levels. (In this case, it is important to keep in mind that the psychological includes the unconscious region.)

Does this mean then that *ki* is the totality of the physical energies which have been thus detected? Although Chinese scientists seem inclined toward this view, it is, in my judgment, questionable. As discussed in previous chapters, the meridians, which are a system of *ki*-energy in the interior of the human body, are not the same as the organs whose existence can be recognized anatomically (through sensory perception). The existence of the meridians and the effect of *ki*-energy flowing in them are perceived psychologically in an altered state of consciousness, that is, in the unconscious dimension. And they are indirectly detected physiologically through their curative effects and through electrophysiological methods. Nonetheless, they simply indicate the quality of *ki*-energy as it is *expressed* in conscious and physical dimensions; the essence of *ki* itself remains a "third term" mediating between the psychological and the physiological-physical. The existence of *ki* is only *inferred* based on manifest functions in consciousness and the physical dimension, and therefore it cannot be reduced to the functions recognized through sensory perception. Here we encounter a fact which cannot be explained by the Cartesian spirit-matter dichotomy.

III. TRANSPERSONAL SYNCHRONIZATION OF *KI* AND THE PROBLEM OF TELEOLOGY

According to Chinese research, *ki*-energy functions between human beings and has a definite effect on other people. In order to confirm this observation, our Japanese study group with Prof. SHINAGAWA Yoshiya of Japan Medical College as our leader, conducted an experiment using the electroencephalograph (EEG). In the following I would like to present certain segments of this experiment.[7]

The subjects included four Chinese *ki*-therapists, four Japanese *ki*-therapists and martial artists, and a group of ten other Japanese, comprised of beginners in *ki*-training and ordinary people, who served as recipients of *ki*-energy. Altogether there was a total of eighteen people. It is noteworthy in these experimental results that the EEG of *ki*-therapists, taken in a restful state with eyes closed, showed a very low power of α wave[8] compared to that of ordinary people. The EEG shown in figures 5.3a and 5.3b demonstrates a typical difference between *ki*-therapists and ordinary people. The *ki*-therapists display small α and β waves,[9] which appear to resemble so-called flat waves. In the case of ordinary people flat waves are observed in the state of brain death. Skillful *ki*-therapists and masters of the martial arts instantly fall into this sort of state through meditation by concentrating their consciousness. The EEG in figures 5.3c and 5.3d represent examples of *ki*-therapists emitting *ki*-energy. The pattern of this EEG differs from *ki*-therapist to *ki*-therapist, but common to them all was the occurrence of violent discharge and spike waves, which are observed in the paroxysms of epileptics. If this occurs in an ordinary person, he or she would be in convulsions and fall into an unconscious state. Commenting on these phenomena, Professor Shinagawa revealed his feeling that they are "puzzling beyond reason." What this suggests is that the conscious-unconscious struc-

FIGURE 5.3a
ORDINARY PEOPLE IN A RESTFUL STATE WITH EYES CLOSED
(ONE DIMENSIONAL EEG WAVES)

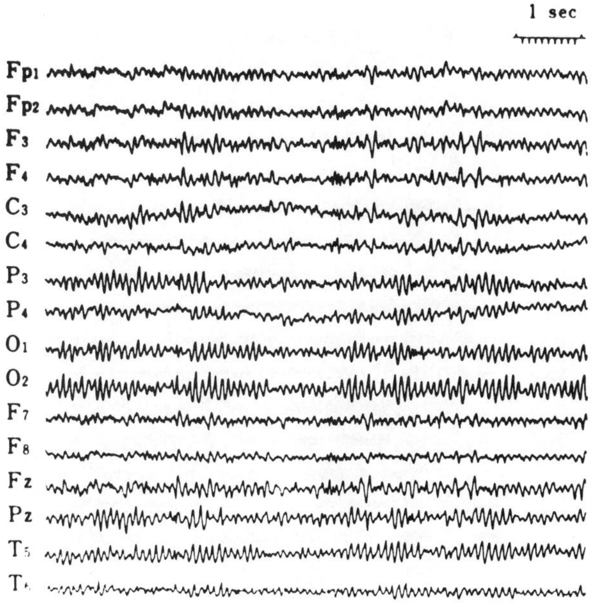

FIGURE 5.3b
EEG OF *KI*-THERAPIST (YK) IN A RESTFUL STATE WITH
EYES CLOSED

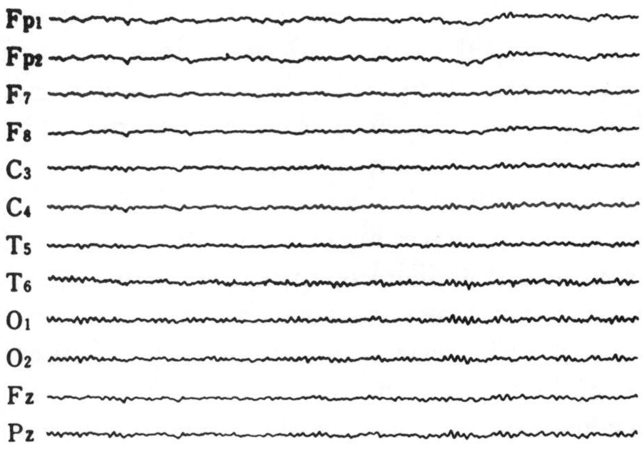

FIGURE 5.3c
EEG OF *KI*-THERAPIST EMITTING *KI*-ENERGY. (I) *KI* GATHERED AT THE *TANDEN,* (II) EMISSION OF *KI* FROM HAND, (III) *KI* BEING EMITTED

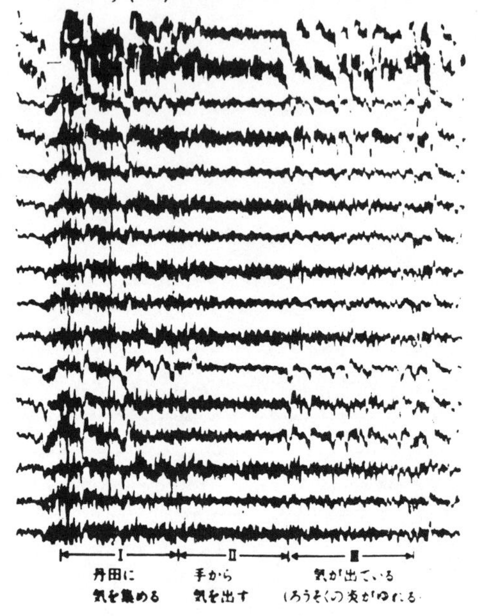

ture of these masters has come to assume, through training, a quality quite different from that of ordinary people.

Next we examined the state into which the recipients of *ki*-energy were put. Figure 5.4 is an instance of an EEG taken from a female subject who received *ki*-energy in her head for the first time. We can clearly see that the α waves and β waves are cyclically repeated with the same periodicity in all channels. The α wave appears in the rear part of the brain under normal circumstances, but when *ki* is received from the therapist, it appeared in the frontal part of the brain where it should not have appeared. Figure 5.5, taken when this occurred, shows topographically the contrast of the brain waves between a *ki*-therapist (R), the sender, and the recipient (SA). The recipient when this was happening spontaneously started to raise her hand. Figure 5.5a was taken in a restful state with her eyes closed, figure 5.5b when her hand began to rise, and figure 5.5c displays β_2 waves[10] when her hand was raised over her stomach. We can observe here a gradual synchronization of the brain waves between the sender and the recipient.

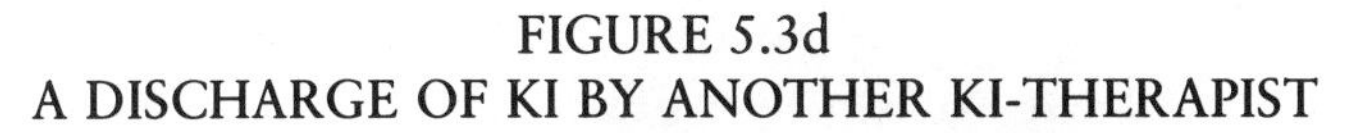

FIGURE 5.3d
A DISCHARGE OF KI BY ANOTHER KI-THERAPIST

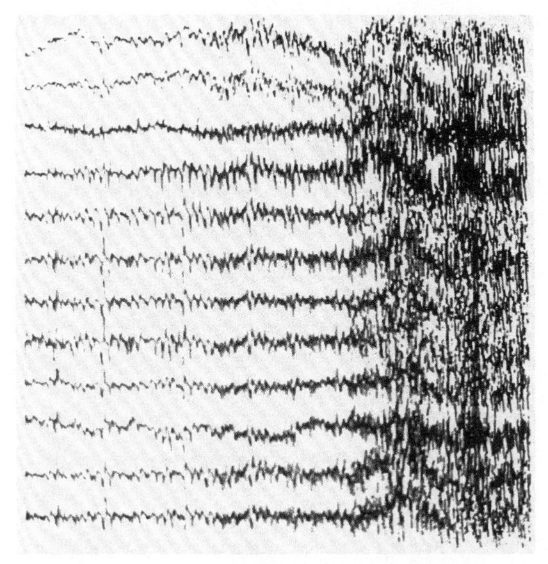

The β wave that appears on the topograph usually takes a convex shape forming toward the frontal part of the brain, but it is very rare to manifest a symmetrically bow-shaped distribution, as seen in Figure 5.5c.

Shinagawa refers to the above phenomenon as the "transpersonal synchronization of *ki* or brain waves." This terminology is suggested by Jung's concept of synchronicity. If we were to explain this phenomenon of synchronization simply by relying on the EEG data obtained through our experiment, it would turn into a causal explanation; that is, some physical energy emitted from the body of the sender caused an effect to be produced in the body of the recipient. This explanation would revert us to the reductionist standpoint of existing science, which ignores the problem of mind. However, what is important here is that the function of *ki*-energy is connected with the region of "mind" which includes the unconscious. Keeping this point in mind, it is possible to offer the interpretation that the interpersonal synchronization of the brain waves bring about what Jung calls "meaningful coincidence" through the function of *ki* as the invisible "third term" mediating the psychological and the physiological.

FIGURE 5.4
AN ORDINARY PERSON'S EEG (IN A RESTFUL STATE WITH HER EYES CLOSED, TAKEN WHEN RECEIVING *KI* ON THE HEAD)

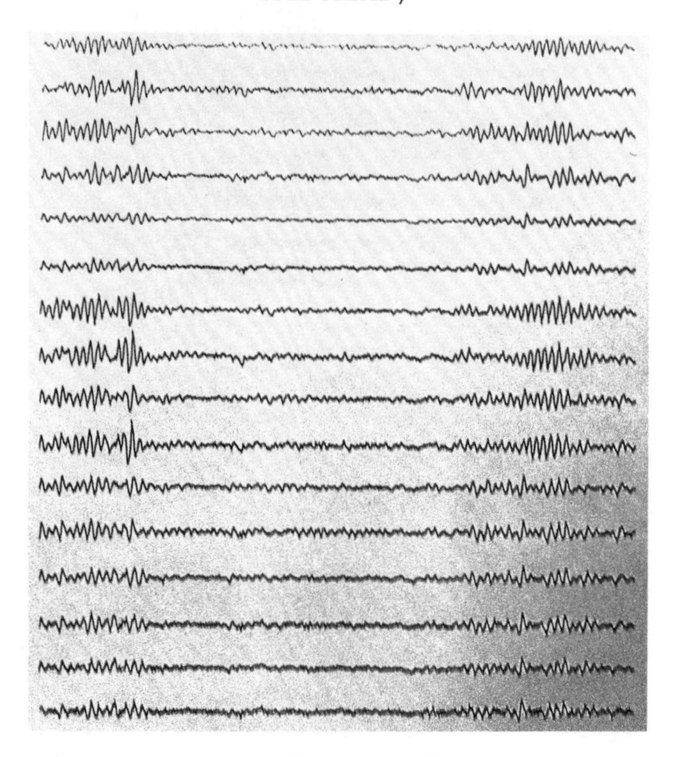

Contemporary psychosomatic medicine and new ideas about the mind-brain relation take the standpoint of correlative dualism, as was observed in previous chapters. In other words, in this correlative dualism there is not only a unilateral causal relationship moving from the various physical processes in the brain to the mind, but also a reverse causal relationship functioning from the mind to the brain. This view simply extends the concept of causality, the principle of existing scientific research, to cover the relationship between mind and matter. However, the concept of *ki* seems to lead us to a standpoint different in principle from that which has hitherto been accepted. This is because from our own perspective we can interpret the various clinical facts, which the knowledge of psychosomatic medicine gives us, to display a

FIG. 5.5
SYNCHRONIZATION OF BRAIN WAVES
(TAKEN AT THE EXTERNAL *KI* EMISSION)

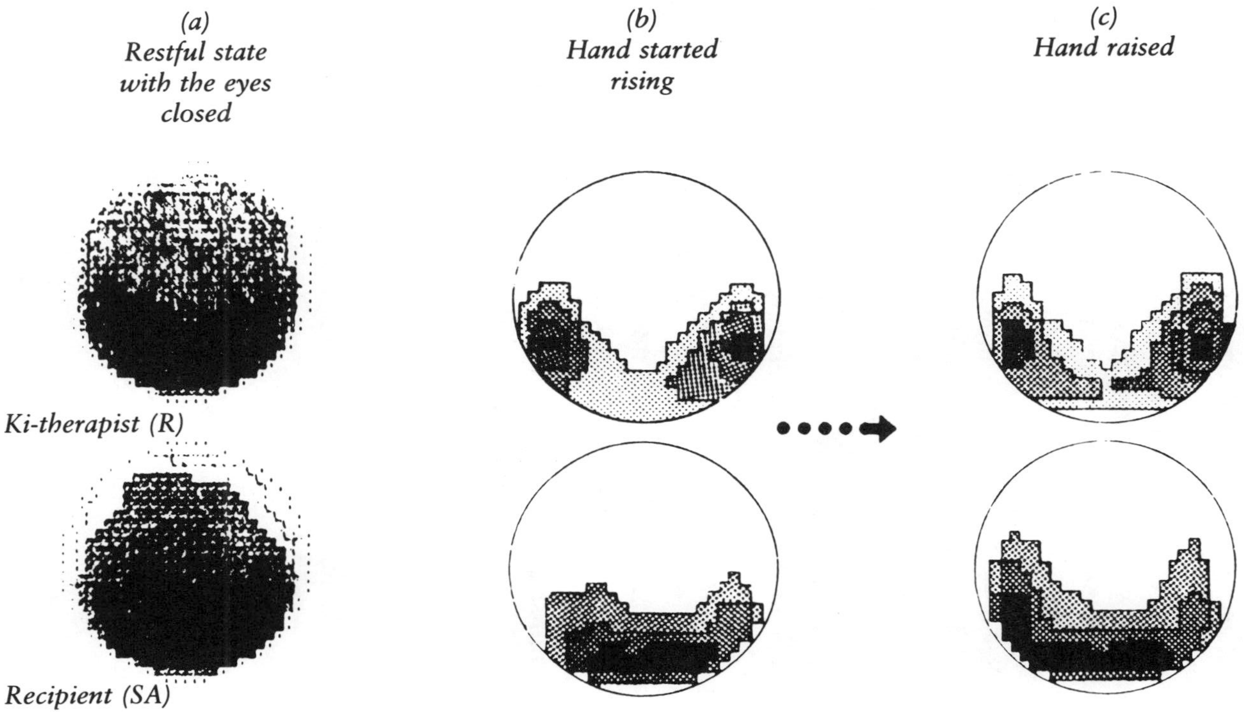

(a)
Restful state with the eyes closed

(b)
Hand started rising

(c)
Hand raised

Ki-therapist (R)

Recipient (SA)

"meaningful coincidence" between psychological facts and physiological (and physical) facts.

Jung thought that the mechanism of the mind in the unconscious region follows a teleological principle rather than a causal principle.[11] When consciousness displays a distorted, pathological tendency, the unconscious acts so as to compensate for the tendency by sending a warning message. However, since the message is sent through symbolic expressions, such as dreams, the ordinary person remains unaware of it. Jung calls this function the "automatic transformation of libido." The concept of *ki* in Eastern medicine teaches us that the human body is endowed with a teleological mechanism as exemplified in the above concept of Jung. *Ki*-energy functions in the interior of the human body at the physiological level as a natural healing power. *Ki*-training means the activation of this power. Moreover, it forms a field of energy that functions outside of the body in the environment.

Teleology has been expelled from modern science. As long as we retain a model of thinking based on consciousness and perception, we will not be able to recognize the principle of teleology existing in the thing-events of the world. However, if we recognize that a domain of experience, not depending on consciousness and perception, exists latently—that is, the unconscious—we will be able to take a new perspective on the relationship between teleology and science.

CHAPTER 6

Ki *and the Problem of Paranormal Phenomena*

I. INTRODUCTION

Professors Qián Xuésēn and Chén Xìn, both considered leaders in *gìgōng* [*kikō*] research, recently stated the following.

> The National Committee for Science and Technology has acknowledged the establishment of the Chinese Association for Somatic Science on 3 May 1987. It has been eight long years since the boy named Tanyu, who has the ability to "read with the ears," was discovered in Sìchuān province in 1979. This period, filled with obstacles and detours, has been truly difficult for those of us engaged in establishing this association devoted to somatic science.[1]

The ability "to read with the ears" refers to a psi ability[2] in parapsychology. In Chinese, it is called "*tèyìgōngnéng*" (extraordinary ability). It was in March 1979 that the case in Sìchuān province was discovered. In the following year in Shànghăi, a symposium with the theme of "Inquiry into the Mystery of Life Science" was held to "scientifically discuss extraordinary ability in the human body." Mr. Hè Chóngyín, who delivered the opening speech for this conference, reported the situation at the time.[3] Initially it was reported that over ten cases of extraordinary ability had been discovered, but later it grew to several times the initial count. Reports gradually poured in from over ten provinces, such as Sìchuān province, Ānhúi province, Hébéi province, Húnán province, Guăngxí province, Gúangdōng province, Níngxià province, Qīnghăi province, Jiāngsū province, Zhéjiāng province, Nèiménggŭ province, and Hēilóngjiāng province, as well as the city of Bĕijīng. The majority of those with extraordinary ability were school children ranging from the ages of eight to fifteen. The distribution peaked between the ages of twelve and thirteen, although there some were adult cases. For example, a woman named Mù Fēngqín, discovered in Hēilóngjiāng province, was twenty-five years old. Preparatory investigations conducted by research centers in each of these regions confirmed that extraordinary ability does exist. Positive results were obtained, for example, by using experiments in which subjects, while blindfolded, saw the content of a sealed envelope in a dark room. After preliminary examinations, those engaged in the scientific committee, in newspapers, and in publishing in their respective provinces, prefectures, and cities—in addition to the staff of each research center—acted as a selection committee and selected fourteen psychics. These fourteen psychics, accompanied by their family members, participated in discussions and experiments for three days in Shànghǎi with an attendance of over two hundred people from the fields of science, medicine, and education. I summarize below the general content of the symposium as reported by Mr. Hè:

1. In the majority of the cases, the parts of the body which recognized characters included the ears, under the armpits, and the fingertips. But with some school children, the crown of the head, the knee, the back, the sole of the foot, and the buttocks were also used for discernment.

2. This kind of ability is capable not only of recognizing characters, figures, and colors placed in a normal state, but also of discerning them when they are crumpled.

3. The same results are obtained when the figures are placed in a plastic container, an iron vessel, as well as in an aluminum container.

4. Although it takes some time for an initial recognition, it proceeds relatively fast after the initial attempt. It seems necessary to give a stimulus in order to activate this kind of ability.

5. It is found that after examining numerous cases, there is a direct correlation between the speed of recognition and its correctness. When the speed of recognition is high, correctness is also high. Although extremely fast recognition is correlated with a perfect score, when the subject has difficulty in discernment, there is an increased probability of failure, and in some cases the subject does fail.

6. Concerning how the subjects recognize these characters and figures, schoolchildren generally give a correct response. The col-

ors and figures are recognized in the frontal as well as the lateral part of the brain as if they have a television screen embedded in them.

7. Compared to visual perception through the eyes, this kind of extraordinary ability is weak and mild in function, but its function becomes sharper in proportion to training: those who could not initially discern the contents of a sealed envelope learned to recognize it, and those who had taken longer for recognition, on the whole, did it more rapidly. There are cases in which those unable to discern the content of a plastic container learned to do so through the training.

8. At present, among school children there is a small number who possess this kind of extraordinary ability, and the number decreases still further among adults. However, when a group from Běijīng University trained twenty to thirty school children in a retreat, all of them became capable of discerning characters with their fingertips. Judging from this case study, there seems to be a certain universality for this extraordinary ability.

9. The manner of discernment among those who possess this kind of extraordinary ability varies from individual to individual. Some demonstrate their ability through contact and others without it. There are still others who can feel the characters and figures under their armpits.

10. This kind of extraordinary ability is intimately related to one's bodily condition as well as mental state. Generally, when the subject is healthy and his or her spirit is taut, fresh, and invigorated, the speed of discernment is fast, whereas in the reverse condition, the speed is slow and in some cases discernment is impossible.

A brief comment is in order here. As was mentioned earlier, it is interesting that this kind of extraordinary ability is discovered more among schoolchildren. This is, in terms of depth psychology, because receptivity through the unconscious is relatively strong in infancy and childhood compared to intellectual ability, which is still undeveloped. This is why both Freud and Jung were interested in the psychology of infants and primitive people. When ego-consciousness, particularly its rational intellectual ability, is developed, the power from the unconscious tends to be suppressed and thus rendered almost inoperative.

II. PROBLEMATICS OF THE DISPUTE

Mr. Hé and his colleagues disseminated the results of the above experiment to various disciplines. He reports that "as soon as it was published, we received a ferocious challenge from those in contemporary science and technology." This response of rejection seems to be the same everywhere in the world. While I plan to deal with this issue later, the following points were raised in China since they adopted the resolution that the pros and cons should be discussed thoroughly without prejudice:

1. The information is received through parts of the human body (for example, the earlobes or under the armpit) without relying on the eyes, and is discerned in the brain, regardless of whether it is of a character, figure, or material object. How are these parts capable of receiving a signal? Is the reception done passively or is there an active emission from the parts of the human body, whose reflection, in turn, is received? Or is it a mutual function of both? How is this signal emitted? Is it a kind of electromagnetic wave? If so, what frequency does it have? How can the electromagnetic waves pass through shields such as paper, plastic, glass, and metals?

2. Processing the signal and the mechanism of transmission. The human body, after receiving the signal through its parts, cannot transmit it unless it performs an appropriate process on it channeling it through the appropriate circuits. A television set receives a signal through a complicated electronic circuit in order to reproduce a figure from the signal, but how can the human body, made up of flesh and blood, receive a signal and transmit it? Latent paranormal ability in the human body functions in such a way that a figure is clearly memorized after processing the signal. However, since this mechanism is impossible within contemporary technology, this puzzle cannot be solved. This is the reason that many people cannot believe in the existence of paranormal ability.

3. Parts of the body for discernment. Those school children with paranormal ability uniformly state that the parts which discern the figures and colors are either in the forehead or in the brain. But why are these particular parts endowed with this ability?

4. Artificial induction. Xiè Zhāohūi in Wŭhàn city became capable of demonstrating this kind of ability through the guidance

and training of his parents. Chén Shoǔliáng's group at Běijīng University succeeded in inducing the ability in over ten children living in the neighboring area. These cases helped not only to dispell the sense of mystery accompanying paranormal ability, but demonstrated that this ability is widely, though latently, present among people. Is this a case of restoring a regressed ability or is it an evolution? Moreover, if we can artificially induce this kind of ability, how can we make use of it for humankind?

5. Clairvoyance and reception at a distance. This phenomenon can be explained as follows. This kind of signal is related to a certain electromagnetic wave. It resembles a radio wave, and there is a good possibility that it is either a microwave or a super ultrashort wave. If so, the body might be capable of receiving different kinds of signals, other than receiving signals for characters and figures.

Mr. Hé summarizes the scholarly significance of paranormal research and its future possibilities as follows. Today, there are many scientists in the world who acknowledge paranormal phenomena, and those interested in this research anticipate that it will become a new field of study for biology. Investigation of psi ability will have serious implications for the future of life science.

1. Discovery of psi ability indicates that the human body is equipped with a certain kind of electromagnetic sensory system, although its existence must be verified by future scientific research. Nevertheless, the discovery of people with extraordinary ability has opened a breakthrough point for research in life science dealing with the human body.

2. Research of this nature will have a great influence on some aspects of basic science. It will promote research into life phenomena in the field of biology, and it will connect physics and life science by bringing problems from the biological domain into the field of physics. Consequently, it is anticipated that new theories will be constructed through cooperation with such basic sciences as biology, physiology, and biophysics.

3. Cooperation with technology. When we proceed to relate psi research to technology, it will be useful for developing new technologies. For example, technological research in physics and engineering may obtain suggestions from psi research that will be useful for producing new technologies for electronic apparatus and radar.

4. Psi research will have great influence in the field of medicine. Not only will it enhance our knowledge of life phenomena concerning human beings, it will also help to introduce the ideas of electromagnetic waves and information transmission into medical science. This might possibly change the whole of contemporary medical science. Investigation of this from a contemporary perspective will pragmatically clarify traditional theories of Chinese medicine concerning the functions of the meridians, *ki*-blood,[4] and hollow and solid viscera. This kind of research can promote a union between Eastern and Western medical science, and it will be useful not only for modernizing Chinese medicine, but for elevating the level of contemporary science.

5. Psi ability itself promises to have many important practical applications. If a blind person succeeds in inducing psi ability, he or she will learn to discern characters and figures. Moreover, by utilizing a certain signal, it might be possible in a learning context to make the brain memorize things. In addition, it may be possible to use psi ability for other special fields.

6. Furthering psi research will open paths of inquiry into special phenomena such as dreams, hallucinations, the perception of time and space, and precognition.

The foregoing is a rough summary of Mr. Hé's report. In closing, Mr. Hé makes the following observation. Ancient people interpreted everything incomprehensible as the power of gods and demons [*shéngŭi*]. We regard such interpretations as superstitious, and to this no one will object. However, it is not a scientific attitude at all to dismiss every phenomenon we do not understand as "superstition." Rather, such an attitude itself may be considered a kind of superstition. Psi ability itself is not unscientific, and it would be more appropriate to say that contemporary science has not yet reached the level of understanding it. It is difficult for a person to conceive of these phenomena if he or she takes the position that they cannot occur. However, the developments in science are such that as research progresses theories are formulated, and in this new discoveries and inventions, that is, new practical experiences alone, are capable of superseding what is previously held as common sense. We should respect facts while adopting the principle that "*prāxis* is the sole standard for clarifying the truth."

The following three points are noteworthy in Mr. Hé's report. First, paranormal research is approached from the standpoint of *life science* while indicating the necessity of cooperation with physics. The parapsychological research carried out so far primarily in Western countries has ignored in principle, as I will explain later, research into the human body and life science. Second, Mr. Hé thinks that research on paranormal ability is related to the traditional view of the human body espoused in Eastern medicine. Third, Mr. Hé points out that this kind of ability is possibly related to psychological phenomena such as dreams and hallucinations.

When I read Mr. Hé's report ten years ago, I was doing research on the psychology of the unconscious while also studying Eastern medicine. I could not make a clear estimate of how paranormal phenomena and parapsychological research were related to Eastern medicine, although I was already aware of them through Jung's many discussions of paranormal phenomena and through my own personal communication with American researchers in parapsychology. In the ensuing years, I devoted myself to the study of Jung's psychology,[5] the self-cultivation methods of Eastern religions,[6] and psychosomatic medicine. I paid hardly any special attention to parapsychology, although I continued to gather information on it. However, scholarly exchange between Japan and China was inaugurated in the mid-1980s, this time on the new research on *kikō* with the subject of *ki* receiving the spotlight. It was in 1978 that Gù Hánsēn and the others succeeded in detecting electromagnetic waves (the infrared rays). This was followed by the above-mentioned discovery of extraordinary ability in 1979.

What drew my interest in *kikō* research was the contention of Chinese researchers that the three fields of Chinese medicine (Eastern medicine), *kikō,* and extraordinary ability should be studied as one continuum. Qián Xuésēn emphasizes this point. The problem is how to relate Eastern medicine to parapsychology. *Kikō* research is in a position to connect these two domains. This fact suggests, in light of *ki* and the human body, that Eastern medicine studies the function of *ki* in the *interior* of the human body, whereas *kikō* clarifies the function of *ki*-energy as it pertains to both the interior and exterior of the human body. Parapsychological research has a bearing on the relationship between the human body (including its mind/heart) and the environment. Accordingly, if parapsychological research can be reappraised from the viewpoint of *ki*, it will become possible to understand the relationship between the human body and the environment, that is, between a human being and the world from the integrative standpoint of the three fields of psychology, physiology, and physics. This was the reason my interest was drawn to *kikō* research.

Referring to these ten years, Qián Xuésēn and his associates say that, "this period, filled with obstacles and detours, has been truly difficult." Their sentiments are quite understandable, for this kind of research, more often than not, receives criticism and attack in intellectual circles, especially in universities. I shall reserve the examination of this topic for later, and shall for now move on to describe the present situation in China.

The disputes surrounding extraordinary ability caused wide repercussions after its publication, and heated disputes are currently being launched within scholarly circles. Triggering recent disputes was an experiment conducted (on 24 January 1988) at Qīnhuá University in Běijīng, with the *ki*-therapist Yán Xīn, who belongs to the Chongqing Institute of Chinese Medicine, serving as the subject. Mr. Yán Xīn emitted *ki* externally several times for a period of thirty minutes while stationed in the city of Guǎng zhōu, approximately two thousand kilometers away from Běijīng, and researchers measured changes in the dissolution of RNA yeast, placed in the analysis center of Qīnhuá University. When the sample receiving the *ki*-energy and the one without it were measured by the flicker photometer for ultraviolet rays and visible rays, it is reported that there was clear evidence in the former of a decrease in the absorption of ultraviolet rays.[7] As soon as the result of this experiment was published, various objections poured out from *ki* researchers, and a strong consensus developed that this kind of experiment should be excluded from research. (I personally know Mr. Yán Xīn, as well as people for and against the issue. Since this is a delicate issue, I should like to refrain from commenting on it.)

A similar dispute previously occurred in other countries. In the beginning of 1960, when the results of parapsychological research in the USSR were made public, it evoked a global response. I am sure some readers can recall the incident. About this time, Prof. Nikolai Wassilieff in Leningrad, considered a leader in parapsychological research in the USSR, conducted an experiment to see whether or not hypnotic suggestion was possible through telepathy between Leningrad and Sevastopol on the coast of the Black Sea (the distance between them is approximately 1,700 kilometers). The result was reportedly that out of two hundred and sixty attempts, one hundred and ninety runs were successful and twenty-seven failed. This experiment was conducted, while shielding off the influence of electromagnetic waves, by gradually increasing the distances, and finally culminating in an ultra-long distance experiment. Apparently, there was no change in success rate due to the difference in distance.[8] This triggered a parapsychological boom in the USSR, but it later dwindled. This was in part due to a warning issued to the general public by leaders in academic circles, including the world famous neurophysiologist, A. R. Luria, and behind this was apparently a political consideration. Disclosure of information to the public at the time in the USSR was due to the "thawing" of the political situation during Khrushchëv's period, but when Brezhnev came to power, parapsychological research in the USSR was again closed to the public. (Public access to information and investigations by foreigners are at present permitted.) I would like to call the reader's attention to the fact that Luria and the others did not deny the existence of parapsychological phenomena. Rather, their warning was directed to the general tendency to exaggerate them without sufficient ground.

This problem tends to spread into society as a whole without the pros and cons being contained within the circle of professional researchers. It appears necessary to first examine the *social and psychological conditions* of why this kind of response is generated in a wide strata of society. Currently there is no uniform idea of, nor definite direction for, parapsychological research. Consequently, I should like to confine myself to stating my fundamental ideas while analyzing the pros and cons concerning this research and its background.

III. AN ASSESSMENT OF PARAPSYCHOLOGY

In the 1930s an American psychologist, J. B. Rhine (1895–1980), a professor at Duke University, provided a foundation for the research field that is now called parapsychology. About thirty years ago when I was still young, I was asked to translate his work into Japanese. While corresponding with Professor Rhine numerous times, I also received explanations several times from his collaborator, Professor J. G. Pratt of the University of Virginia.

Rhine narrowed the object of his research down to two phenomena, extrasensory perception (ESP) and psychokinesis (PK). ESP refers to the discernment of the state of an object without relying on the usual perceptual means, as in the cases of clairvoyance and telepathy. (The ability to "read with the ears," the case mentioned in the foregoing, is an instance of clairvoyance.) PK refers to the phenomenon in which a certain physical influence is effected on an object without the ordinary physical or energy means. The case of bending a spoon, which became widely known, is regarded as an instance of psychokinesis—although it is effected by touching the spoon—if the power exerted on the spoon is not capable of bending it. These extraordinary phenomena have been reported sporadically in various forms since ancient times, but they have never been regarded as the object of scholarly research. The reason Rhine's research received wide response was because he succeeded in demonstrating its result quantitatively by employing a scientific, experimental, operational method. However, the wide response did not mean that his research was recognized as valid by academic circles. Rather, it met with strong opposition. The operational method of his research was examined by the American Association for Mathematics and Statistics. Moreover, in 1938 it was submitted to a special committee in The American Psychological Association, which acknowledged that insofar as the operational method of his experiment was concerned, there were no grounds for doubt. The objections that were raised were that the phenomena cannot exist (and therefore they involve tricks, or are accidental), or even if they do exist, they should not be studied since they do not fall within the purview of science. However, it is rare that these two objections are clearly distinguished from each other when they are raised.

This situation continued until the beginning of World War II. But after the war it changed, especially in the United States during the 1960s, when the attitude gained ground that parapsychology could be acknowledged as scholarly research. In 1969, The American Association for the Advancement of Science, which may be compared to an alliance of American academic associations, ratified the inclusion of the Association for Parapsychology into its membership. This decision gave, after a fashion, academic recognition to parapsychological research, and promoted its research and teaching in various universities and institutes throughout the United States. Currently, there are over fifty such institutions in the United States. There are a considerable number of universities in Western European countries, and also in Eastern Europe, Central and South America, and South Asia which publicly recognize parapsychological research. Among them, China's participation was the most recent, but many universities and institutes are engaged in its research, owing to their government's official approval. (This is probably comparable to the situation in the United States, at least in terms of numbers.)

Various surveys have been conducted in the United States on the acceptance rate of parapsychological research among academics and the general public.[9] In addition to the surveys conducted by organizations for public opinion polls, such as Gallup, there are some others focusing on university professors. According to the latter's results, approximately seventy percent of the academics showed a positive response. In terms of disciplines, researchers in the humanities, arts, and education showed a high favorable response, whereas those in the natural sciences and social sciences were less receptive, with only slightly more than half responding favorably. Social scientists showed an even stronger rejection than natural scientists. The strongest opposition was found, contrary to expectation, among *psychologists* and those in the philosophy of science, of whom only five percent showed a positive response. Moreover, there was also the unexpected result that, compared to the response of the general public, university professors showed a higher rate of acceptance.

Two British sociologists, H. M. Collins and T. J. Pinch, analyzed from a neutral standpoint the methods of refutation that the critics of parapsychology employ.[10] The main points they found are: (1) a rejection at the emotional level, (2) denial through the use of philosophical rhetoric, (3) parapsychology viewed as an unscientific belief, (4) paranormal phenomena regarded as trivial, (5) parapsychological research involves a sleight of hand and therefore all of it is false, (6) personal attacks on parapsychologists, (7) criticism of using as evidence anecdotal, accidental cases, (8) refusal to publish in professional journals, and (9) a low evaluation of the articles on parapsychology published in journals. The reputable science journals such as *Nature* and *Science* do not at present consider papers on parapsychology for publication but accept only papers that criticize it. Aside from the professional journals on parapsychology, academic journals dealing with psychiatry are favorable to parapsychological research.

The above is a rough picture of the present situation in the United States. Rhine wished parapsychological research to be acknowledged publicly in academic circles as a field of experimental psychology, but his wish was not fulfilled. Ironically, the psychologists' response rejecting parapsychology, as mentioned above, is much higher than for scholars in other disciplines. In the academic world, judgment by the experts of a given field is valued and respected. It is unthinkable for a medical scientist to pass judgment on a problem in physics, and conversely even if a physicist passes judgment on a medical problem, it will not carry an authoritative voice. However, this academic (or scholarly) common sense, as it has been held so far, does not work in the case of parapsychological research. The value and validity of parapsychological research is decided by the response of the general public and by those scholars outside the discipline. This situation has continued since the inception of parapsychology, and it does not seem likely to change in the near future. It is then necessary to examine first why this type of situation is generated. The problem, it appears, belongs not to the scholarship itself but to the domain of social psychology.

The present author has never had a sense of incongruity about paranormal phenomena. The issue for me was what meaning these phenomena would have in thinking about human nature, or in examining the views of what a human being is. The scientific standpoint divides the issue in two directions. One is to deny or doubt the existence of any phenomena whose explanation is not scientifically possible. This attitude is based on modern rationalism, and the majority of Japanese intellectuals probably hold to this view. The other is to recognize a fact of experience as a fact even though it may not be scientifically explainable. This attitude does not deny the possibility of these phenomena so long as the phenomena are not demonstrated to be false. This stance was once held by Dr. YUKAWA Hideki.[11] He apparently thought that it was better to maintain this stance when the existence of the atom was called into question toward the end of the last century through the beginning of this century.

If we were to take the former position of modern rationalism, parapsychological research would be rejected as a project unworthy of scholarly investigation. In this case, however, no new way of thinking will emerge, because it simply follows and recognizes the hitherto held rationalism and scientific theories. My position is rather that we should assume a stance of observing the facts themselves while suspending judgment on them.

Paranormal phenomena for many people apparently trigger an instinctive, almost repulsive, response of being "suspicious." We should then examine why this sort of negative response is generated, for there must be a psychological condition appropriate for it. This reaction might be related to the impression that parapsychological research is linked with occultism. Although I shall not define occultism here, the motive which led Rhine to parapsychological research was his interest in psychic research. William McDougall, his teacher, belonged to the same study group as Freud and Jung when he was young, and had an interest in the then flourishing psychic research in Europe. He also served as president of the Society for Psychic Research. When he returned to the United States he became a professor of psychology at Harvard University and later moved to Duke University, taking Rhine along with him, where he established an institute for parapsychology. In view of this historical linkage, it is true historically that parapsychology was born out of psychic research.

Nevertheless, Rhine held the view that psychic research and parapsychology are distinguishable. He abandoned the project of proving the survival of the soul after death, which was the goal of psychic research. Therefore, the fundamental attitude of parapsychology was to study only the mechanism of paranormal phenomena without making any judgment on the issue of survival of the soul. However, among individual parapsychologists there are not a few who have an interest in psychic issues, and among people supporting occultism who look with anticipation toward parapsychology the situation has not changed. Apart from individual research subjects and the personal views of each researcher, it would seem difficult to separate completely parapsychological research from occultism.

Why then do occultism and psychic research evoke a sense of "suspicion" in people? Although no simple explanation can be given for the cause of this kind of psychological response, since it is after all complex, there does seem to be a psychological resistance to subjects dealing with death and an instinctive aversion to believing in "the world of the spirits and souls." If this is correct, the root of the problem is deep. So long as we maintain the accepted academic standpoint, no intellectual solution will be forthcoming.

If for the time being we confine the problem within an academic and scholarly framework, a question emerges: "Is science capable of discussing death?" I think that it is in principle incapable of making any judgment on death. That is, it cannot answer whether or not there is life after death. In this sense, occultism and psychic research are not scientific but rather belong fundamentally to the domain of faith-experience. In other words, their research should not be endorsed or validated by relying on science, but rather should be erected on their own philosophical ground. Even if these studies take on the air of scientific method, they simply end up being a "quasi-science" so long as science has no power to decide on them. Nevertheless, although they cannot be a science, they can still be a philosophy since science is not an absolute judge on every matter. In this sense, the error of psychic research lies in taking the standpoint of *the absolutism of science* without realizing its close alliance with science. The meaning of death is not a problem on which science can decide, rather each individual decides on it as a human being through ethical resolution.

In this respect, Rhine's judgment was quite correct when he severed parapsychology from psychic research, avoiding the problem of death. In other words, the method he adopted was a necessary procedure in order to make parapsychology scientific. Following Rhine's contention, we may point out then that those who either support or object to parapsychology, without clearly separating parapsychology from psychic research, do not understand the nature of the problem. However, even if the domain of parapsychological research is demarcated in this manner, it hardly seems possible to solve sufficiently the question of whether or not parapsychology research can become a science.

The academic reason for this lies in the repeatability of the phenomena. Modern natural science, which has been developed on the model of physics, maintains the fundamental requirement that an experiment yield the same result of measurement, although it does not stipulate that exactly the "same" result must be obtained as long as the result yields a meaningful probability. It is difficult for parapsychological research to satisfy this condition. For example, there were two experiments yielding extremely significant statistical meaning which are well known among professional researchers. One was on psychokinesis conducted by the physicist H. Schmidt, using radioactive isotopes, and the other was on bending metals conducted by Professor John Hasted, experimental physicist of London University. However, similar results were not obtained when the other researchers followed up their experiments using the same methods. Therefore, it is difficult for parapsychological research to become a "science" insofar as it is assessed in light of natural science's criterion of repeatability of experiment. This does not mean, needless to say, that paranormal phenomena do not exist. But even if these phenomena do exist, their research cannot become a science within the accepted paradigm of science.

IV. THE NEED FOR AN EPISTEMOLOGICAL CRITIQUE OF MODERN SCIENCE

When we look back on the history of parapsychological research since Rhine, the support from psychologists, as previously observed, has declined over time. Instead, a noticeable increase of interest developed among those who are related to physics and engineering. For example, in addition to H. Schmidt and John Hasted mentioned above, we may cite Eugene P. Wigner, a Noble Prize winner, Brian Josephson, and David Bohm. Granted that they are a minority, or "heretics," in the field of physics, we can ask why they are interested in parapsychological issues when their concerns seem, at first glance, to have nothing to do with psychology. Qián Xuésēn was originally an expert in astrophysics, and the researchers engaged in researching extraordinary ability in China are overwhelmingly in the fields of physics and engineering.

One reason that physicists take an interest in the problem is probably that, from a theoretical viewpoint, the laws upon which physics is erected are at present not settled, and there are still mysteries in the domain of material substance. If there are phenomena that are inexplicable by the existing laws of physics, then naturally they are of interest to physicists. A novelty of today's inquiry into paranormal phenomena, however, is that it takes into account the *psychological function* as a ground for explanation. Previously, physics did not attempt, in studying material phenomena, to take into its purview a relationship with psychological phenomena. (Although one might mention here the uncertainty principle, it pertains to the issue of measuring apparatus, and it does not mean that conscious function has a direct bearing on the state of material substance.) Alternatively, the heretical physicists' ideas are based on a hunch that there is an unknown relationship existing between spirit and matter.

This suggests that the dualistic paradigm (intellectual dichotomy) established since Descartes is now being squarely put into question. This is the reason that parapsychology presents a serious problem for science. In other words, it requires us to think anew the fundamental principles of science that have been accepted throughout the modern period. This is, in fact, an intellectual reason that those adhering to modern scientific rationalism are unable to accept parapsychology.

The correlativity between mind and body is acknowledged as a fact in the field of today's medical science. Modern medicine understands all bodily phenomena by a reduction to the mechanism of matter. It suggests that the body can be regarded as the sum of bodily substances, but this does not mean that the body *is* matter *in toto*. The same can be said of the relationship between *ki*-energy externally emitted from the body and the environment, as observed in the previously discussed *kikō* research.

In other words, *ki*-energy *can* be regarded (or is detectable) as a material function, but this does not mean that the substance of *ki* is matter (or is reducible to matter). Rather, what is important is that within the interior of the human body, as well as in the relationship between the body and the environment, there can be a methodological or ontological perspective which goes beyond the hitherto held reductionism and dualism that separate spirit from matter. The investigation of the relation between human being and environment (mind and matter) as an extension of the reexamination of the mind-body problem therefore naturally calls into question anew the unknown relationship between spirit and matter. Qián Xuésēn and his colleagues predict that the future of *kikō* research and research into extraordinary ability will bring about a kind of scientific revolution. Regardless of whether or not their prediction comes true, their hope is not at all groundless if the methodological standpoint itself, which has served as a departure point for modern science, is questioned afresh.

In short, the problem which the future of parapsychological research presents does not stop with the fields of psychology and medical science, but extends to the fundamental principles held by modern science since the scientific revolution. Therefore, although this problem is clothed in scientific garb, it is essentially of an extremely philosophical character. It requires an attempt at an epistemological critique of, or self-reflection on, contemporary science, just as Kant reflected upon the *presuppositions* involved in the science of his time for the possibility of its research.

The first condition in scientific research is to observe the facts correctly and to make them determinate through description. This is not limited to scientific research, but is a necessary procedure in other fields such as history. In other words, being "scholarly" and "scientific" do not mean immediately the same thing. Just because an experimental apparatus and method—the means for scientific research thus far—are employed, it does not mean that the research so conducted immediately becomes "scientific." Researchers in parapsychology have utilized various apparatuses and methods as means of measurement in experimental science. These methods are effective for observing the phenomena correctly and establishing them as objective facts. In this sense, the procedure involved can be "scholarly" but the research cannot become "scientific." It simply means that the phenomena are correctly *described,* but it does not clarify the ground of scientific theory as to why these phenomena occur.

The second condition for establishing scientific research, as observed earlier, is concerned with the repeatability of experiments. Research in history does not belong to science, since it fundamentally lacks this condition. At least, it does not belong to science in the hitherto accepted sense of experimental science.

In the case of parapsychology, there is a dispute concerning the first condition, that is, the observation and determinancy of fact. For example, there is the objection that paranormal phenomena do not exist at all, and hence they occur simply due to tricks. As was stated in the foregoing section, it is difficult to come to a definitive, conclusive position through scholarly debate, because at the foundation of the pros and cons surrounding this kind of dispute lies the operation of social, psychological conditions that are different from scholarly dispute and the surface exchange of opinions.

Occultism and the subject of death are problems possessing a character that goes beyond scientific knowledge. Consequently, it is anticipated that the dispute for and against the existence of paranormal phenomena will continue for a long time in the future. However, this kind of dispute is meaningless insofar as it is framed within the perspective of scholarship, because it is an issue of the social, collective psyche based, as it were, on the spiritual situation of the period. The solution for this problem probably has to be relegated to a future historical process.

The second condition of science, that is, the repeatability of experimental results, cannot be sufficiently satisfied by parapsychology, as has been already noted. Therefore, even if paranormal phenomena exist, their research cannot pass the condition imposed by hitherto accepted "science." I am of the opinion that paranormal phenomena exist, but I doubt whether their research can qualify as science. My doubt lies where both the supporters and objectors of parapsychology dispute the matter by using accepted science as an *absolute standard*. The supporters argue that paranormal phenomena exist objectively, and therefore their research falls within the purview of "science," whereas the objectors contend—for whatever reasons—that their research is "quasi-scientific" and should be expelled to fields outside of science. But I wonder if science is an absolute judge of all human experience. Should not the methodological limitations of modern, scientific cognition be questioned in this matter? This is my position.

As stated in the beginning of this chapter, the Chinese researchers maintain that the mechanism of paranormal phenomena can be solved through the extension of *ki* research. Considering the fact that various material energies are detectable in the function of the so-called external emission of *ki*, it might be possible to explain some dimensions of the facts, regarded thus far as paranormal phenomena, by reducing them to the effects of *ki*-energy. However, the cases which Qián Xuésēn and his colleagues discovered and investigated include many phenomena that resist any hypothesis by means of the activity of existing physical energies. In other words, it is fundamentally unclear whether or not the essence of paranormal phenomena can be completely explained as a product of the material energy function related to *ki*-energy.

My present thought is that there seems to be a fundamenal difference in nature between phenomena related to *ki*-energy and paranormal phenomena. Naturally, among actual individual cases, it often occurs that a *ki* therapist is at the same a psychic, but what I mean here has nothing to do with this issue.

As I explained in previous sections, *ki*-energy functions while being transformed into the three dimensions of psychology, physiology, and physics. Parapsychological research centered in the United States has so far focused on spirit versus matter, that is, on a direct correlative relationship between psychological functions and physical functions, whereas there is a step forward in the attitude of Chinese researchers who have attempted to approach the issue by taking note of the *human body* as an intermediary to both the psychological and the physical. This is progress because there is no concrete clue as to how to explain paranormal phenomena vis-à-vis the energy function by means of the hitherto conducted research focused on the direct relationship between the psychological and the physical. However, the fundamental posture of the Chinese researchers still holds to the absolutism of science in its original sense, and consequently takes the standpoint of material reductionism. Yet the most important point in the dispute concerned with the problems of *ki,* it would seem, is that it involves mental functions which cannot be reduced to material functions.

What should be noted in examining the function of mind is that the concept of "mind" is not restricted to "consciousness" as presupposed by modern scholarship. The scope of "mind" includes the region of the unconscious concealed at the foundation of conscious processes. Moreover, the fundamental characteristic of the unconscious function is that *it cannot be experienced through sensory perception.* For example, when we have a dream, we do not see it through our eyes. As stated in the previous sections, the function of *ki* is related to the activity of the unconscious. What we must investigate, therefore, is the energy activity which is convertible into the three dimensions of psychology, physiology, and physics, while including the potential region of experience whose workings cannot be experienced through sensory means.

According to the reductionism and spirit-matter dualism (dichotomy) presupposed by modern science, physical phenomena (physical function) and the mind have nothing whatsoever in common, and life-phenomena and mental phenomena (the physiological and psychological functions) are reduced to the mechanism of matter within the body. In contrast, according to contemporary research on *ki,* the effect of the psychological function, which includes the unconscious, can be detected objectively at the physiological and physical levels. Nevertheless, *ki* does not show itself, and cannot be perceived by any sensory means, for it includes within itself a function of mind. In other words, what can be detected and cognized through experimental, scientific means is simply the objective *effects* that are disclosed at the physiological and physical levels, and based on these the existence of *ki* itself is simply *inferred.* It is analogous to a criminal investigation in which a detective can obtain circumstantial evidence but not material evidence. This is because *ki* is linked to the function of mind, and the mind itself cannot be perceived by sensory means.

Generally speaking, overcoming dualism does not simply stop at recognizing a correlative relationship between spirit and matter. Of foremost importance is the fact that *their modes of being are completely different.* The mind itself, including both that which is conscious and unconscious, can never be perceived through sensory means. In this respect, Descartes was absolutely right in thinking that spirit and matter differ in their modes of being and have heterogeneous characteristics. Because of this insight, however, he concluded that they are unrelated to each other. However, this conclusion is not acceptable to us. It is *possible,* nevertheless, to regard them as unrelated within a certain limited domain. This is the dualism, that is, the spirit-matter dichotomy, which modern science has actually adopted. We acknowledge that the methodological principle of modern science has validity within a certain limited domain, but this does not mean that since it is possible to regard them as unrelated in a certain domain that they *are* altogether unrelated to each other. The exemplary cases clarified through *ki* research and parapsychological research—if they are established, objective facts—suggest that we are now facing *facts* which have gone beyond the methodological principle of hitherto accepted science.

V. BEYOND CAUSALITY

Jung's question regarding parapsychology concerns this point. He had had various paranormal experiences since he was young, and he was in personal contact with Rhine from the beginning of Rhine's research.[12] Jung was quite familiar, therefore, with the content of Rhine's research, and he had a high evaluation of it. However, he was critical of the fundamental research attitude of parapsychology, or of the ideas that were presupposed by it. The direct reason for Jung's criticism is the following.

In research into paranormal phenomena, one has to take into consideration the influence of the psychological conditions of those conducting the experiments as well as of the subjects, but Rhine did not give sufficient consideration to this problem. Naturally he did not ignore the intervention of psychological functions, but what he thought important was rather the objective fact of whether or not the results had statistical significance. He did not give thought to the qualities of the psychological functions in the subjects and experimenter himself, particularly the latter, at the time of experiment and the influence that they might have on the result. That is, Rhine attempted to understand the existence and characteristics of paranormal phenomena by following fundamentally the same attitude and method as conventional science in dealing with physical phenomena. Researchers in parapsychology since Rhine have not changed in this respect.

A fundamental characteristic of the psychological function, that is the working of the mind, is the fact that it cannot be perfectly reproduced. The movement of a human mind is always historical in its original nature, and insofar as it functions in a situation or in one's lifetime, it has the characteristic of "onceness." Freud's discovery of the unconscious points up this fact. The unconscious has the character of a reservoir of past historical memories, and therefore, the function of "mind" including both the conscious and the unconscious is historical in its essence. Napoleon's psychological state, when he stood on the battlefield at Waterloo, could not be reproduced by Napoleon himself. At best, a master actor's performance can achieve a reproduction of a similar condition. That is, insofar as the human being itself is an historical being with only the "onceness" of life, the repeatability of a person's existence is incompatible with the fundamental principle of modern science. Jung says that a human's experience relating to the unconscious has an historical character which embraces all of one's past and present. (According to the Big Bang theory, the law governing matter also has an historical character, though it is true only with units of time of over one-hundred-million years. In the principle standpoint of modern science, repeatability in material phenomena is presupposed. In contrast, insofar as psychological phenomena, including the unconscious, have an historical character, they invariably achieve repeatability only in approximation.)

Jung's fundamental criticism of research in parapsychology is concerned with the fact that it does not reflectively question the causality which is the fundamental principle of modern science. It simply presupposes this causality. Parapsychology presupposes that a subject possesses a paranormal ability (in Rhine's terminology, a psi ability), and that a paranormal phenomenon (an effect) occurs in virtue of this ability as a cause. Parapsychology probably cannot achieve a new methodological standpoint transcending the limitations of accepted science as long as it applies the cause-effect relationship and draws conclusions on the basis of it.

Jung's position on paranormal phenomena is different in principle from the above. He starts with the more fundamental question of how in principle to demarcate theoretically the necessary from the contingent, or of how the phenomena of parapsychology and of accepted science can be distinguished from each other. The fundamental principle of modern science starts by postulating the existence of a definite causal relationship in all phenomena. All coincidences and exceptions, therefore, must be excluded as much as possible. But does nature not recognize exceptions and coincidences? Objective, natural phenomena discovered by the scientific method *can* be regarded as governed by a definite causal relationship, but are there not meaningful coincidences and exceptions discoverable in the activities of living nature?

Jung's hypothesis of synchronicity concerns this point. Synchronicity for now may be defined as a correspondence or synchronization in meaning discoverable between an event in the world of mind and an event in the world of matter (that is, between the inner world and the outer world). Take, for example, when one senses the death of a person in a dream, and the person actually dies. This is simply a coincidence when seen from the standpoint of science which postulates a material causal relationship in all phenomena. But if there should exist in the world phenomena which cannot be explained by means of the scientific causal relationship, what perspective is needed in order to explain them? This is Jung's point.

Freud's conceives of the unconscious as storage of past experiences closely related to the individual's (or individual body's) life experience (personal unconscious). In contrast, Jung thought that deeper beneath the personal unconscious is the region of the transpersonal collective unconscious. We may call this region the "cosmic unconscious," which temporally goes beyond the birth of the individual body, and spatially spreads beyond the limitation of the personal body. The domain where it functions has no temporal and spatial limitations as is the case with the world of sensible matter. One of the reasons which led Jung to this hypothesis is his thinking about the characteristics of paranormal phenomena. The ordinary energy activity in physical space has limitations, for example, that an effect decreases in proportion to distance, or that it take a certain time for an activity to be completed, but do not paranormal phenomena occur disregarding these limitations? To use the terminology of physics, do they not, Jung thinks, have a "non-local" character? (The "non-local" function means that the limitation of distance becomes in theory zero.) Consequently, Jung thought that it may not be inappropriate to postulate the transpersonal unconscious region in which this function can take place.

Jung's idea remains at present simply a hypothesis. Accordingly, there is no reason for postulating an energy activity over an ultra-long distance by extending the hitherto accepted scientific theories, as is done by Chinese scientists, or for denying an attempt to explain paranormal phenomena by means of existing physical energies. The problem still belongs entirely to the future. But if *ki* research or parapsychological research demand a change in the paradigm of thinking (or to use their language, a "scientific revolution") which corrects or transforms the principle of accepted modern science, it appears that the Chinese researchers' method of thinking might fall into theoretical self-contradiction. This is because they advocate a transformation of science while adhering to the principles hitherto accepted by science.

According to Jung, the concept of the collective unconscious is the region of a "third term" mediating between the function of "mind," that is brought to *expression* at the conscious level, and the function of "matter." At the same time its order spreads beyond the limitation of the human mind-body as an individual. He says that our human ego is a place where the vast external and internal worlds are contiguous. The former refers to the world of matter governed by causality while the latter is a world hidden from consciousness and sensory perception. To use an analogy, our ego is the place where these two vast heterogeneous spheres intersect and overlap. The two orders are divided, as it were, by a thick wall. Synchronistic phenomenon means that the power issuing from this potential dimension functions vis-à-vis some stimulus penetrating through this wall. Paranormal phenomena are an instance of this. Consequently, we should not approach these phenomena by applying the causal relationship governing material phenomena. In other words, the human subject does not originally possess an ability that is paranormal. When we are transformed into a vessel which receives the power issuing from the dimension that is hidden from our consciousness, we then become an object to be acted on rather that a subject acting on, and this kind of exceptional phenomena is naturally experienced.

Carl A. Meier, a Jungian psychologist and a professor at Zürich University who is familiar with both parapsychology and psychosomatic medicine, contends that the introduction of a new perspective on mind-body correlativity into present medical science can be understood in light of the perspective of synchronicity. When we presuppose the principle of causality espoused in modern science, various facts discovered through clinical studies of psychosomatic medicine lead to the view that there is a *mutual* causal relationship between the mind and the body, or between the mind and the brain. That is, there are cases in which there occur certain influences (effects) in the mind caused by the material function in the body, or conversely there are cases in which the function of mind as a cause yields a certain physiological effect. Although this explanation adopts a dualistic separation of the mind and body, it is not a disjunctive Cartesian dualism rendering spirit and matter unrelated; rather, it is a correlative dualism which recognizes a mutual relationship between them. A new movement in psychosomatic medicine and brain-physiology

FIGURE 6.1.
THE OUTER AND INNER WORLD

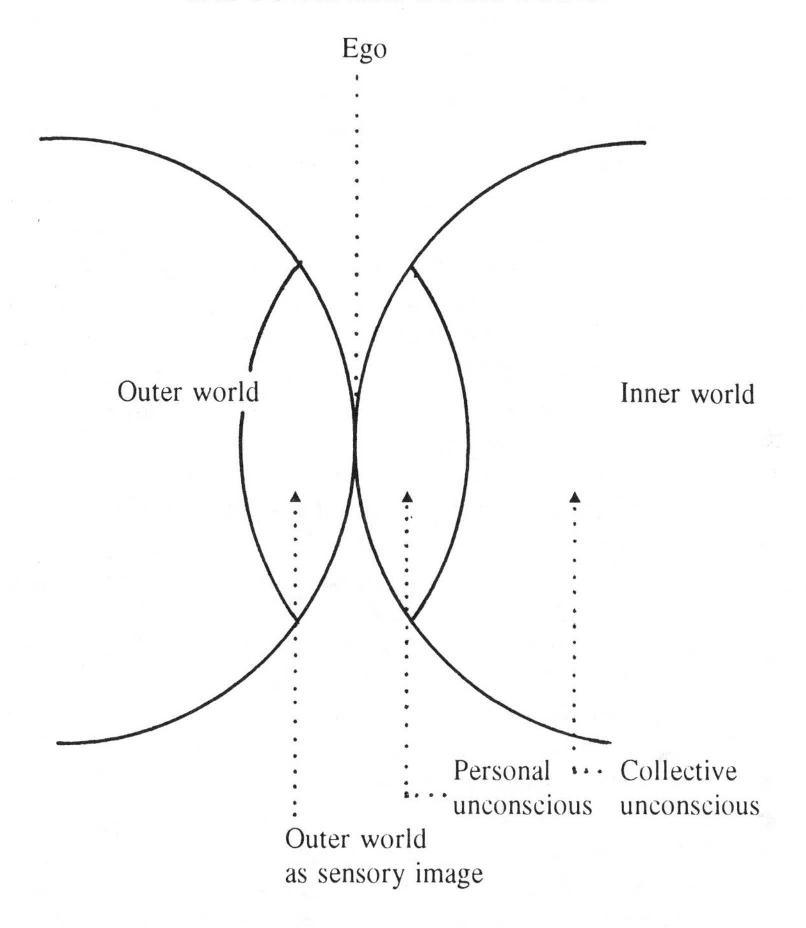

(Roger Sperry, John C. Eccles, and others) at present maintains in principle this correlative dualism. However, it is equally possible to redefine various clinical facts in light of the perspective of synchronicity. Synchronicity is a simultaneous, synchronistic relationship that occurs between the heterogeneous regions of mind and matter (or body). Psychosomatic disease can be reinterpreted from this standpoint.

In short, by assuming the viewpoint of causality, it is to a certain degree possible to study the mind-body relation in an individual, the synchronistic function occurring between one human body and another, and paranormal phenomena occurring between the human body and environment, all of which are found in contemporary research in Eastern medicine, *kikō*, and extraordinary ability. However, these studies will yield only an approximate validity, and cannot reach causality and repeatability with the rigor which the science of material objects has thus far achieved. This is because at the base of the order of causality detectable through the senses there latently exists the mechanism of synchronicity. The order of causality overlaps, but is incompatible with, the mechanism of synchronicity.

Those who are familiar with the history of philosophy will notice that the image of the world proposed by Jung parallels well with the philosophies of Spinoza and Leibniz. Jung thought that behind the order of causality (the world of matter) perceived through consciousness and sensory perception lies latently the region of the collective unconscious which transcends the limitations of the personal body and mind, and within which the mechanism of synchronicity governs. Spinoza thought that the two orders of spirit and matter are linked vis-à-vis the relationship between productive nature (*natura naturans*) and produced nature (*natura naturata*). He characterized this relationship also as "God as Nature" (*Deus sive Natura*). What he meant by "God" is not God which transcends nature, but a pantheistic power immanent in nature. Leibniz, furthermore, philosophized on the mechanism that links these two heterogeneous orders, contending that the order of pre-established harmony latently exists, connecting numerous "windowless monads." Jung says that Leibniz's concept is closest to his image of the world in which there are layers of causality and synchronicity. All the things in nature are "windowless monads," the most representative of which is the human being. Insofar as the human being exists as an embodied individual, it is governed by the law of material nature based on causality. The spirit as consciousness is not equipped with a window which makes it possible to connect itself with the external world. However, when we take into consideration the vast, latent region existing beneath consciousness, one would discover therein a pre-established harmony where monads are mutually connected. This corresponds to Jung's principle of synchronicity.

CHAPTER 7

Toward an East-West Dialogue

I. TELEOLOGY AND SCIENCE

Current scientific research on *ki* assumes the standpoint of causality. The essence of paranormal phenomena, however, must be sought, in terms of its meaning, from a perspective transcending this standpoint. This is Jung's fundamental attitude. His concept of synchronicity takes the standpoint of teleology, which is completely opposite to that of causality. Simply put, teleology states that all phenomena exist for a certain purpose. This idea is often observed in the history of biology prior to modern times, and goes back as far as Aristotle's concept of "final cause" (*telos*). Aristotle was led to this idea because he was knowledgeable in biology, and it is possible to view the character and structure of a living organism as formed to realize a definite purpose. For example, the lungs are a means for the *purpose* of breathing. Generally speaking, that there is purpose means that the phenomenon has a definite *meaning* and *value* for the life of an individual organism. Darwin is said to have initially started from Aristotle's theory of teleology in order to explain the evolution of life.

The above idea is still alive in our commonsensical world. However, teleology has been gradually expelled from the world of science as the latter has progressed. Since the history of modern science started, as in astronomy and physics, with investigating the causal relationships which rule physical phenomena, modern science has excluded from the scope of its investigation the purpose and meaning of life. The issue for science is that a fact *exists* in a certain way. This mode of thinking applied to the phenomena of life arrives at the conclusion that biology and medical science, insofar as they are both sciences, should assume the role and responsibility solely of clarifying causal relationships discernible in perceptively cognizable facts. In nineteenth-century biology there was a vitalism which recognized the existence of a power unique to living organisms, but that has been rejected in this century. It is not the role or responsibility of science to question the purpose, meaning, or value of life. Since modern science presupposes the rejection of teleology, it is quite understandably incapable of recognizing any meaning and value concerning the life of human beings. From the standpoint of science, human life and death are nothing in the final analysis but mere scientific facts. Naturally, individual scientists, perhaps many of them, recognize the meaning and value of human life, but modern science itself can never acknowledge this in virtue of its scientific standpoint.

According to Jung, the teleological function exists latently in the world of the unconscious. It is a power which appears, in clinical situations, as a natural healing power. Analysts and medical doctors simply assist the emergence of this power from within a patient rather then curing him or her by their own power. The art of medicine is different from constructing a machine and enabling it to move.

The phenomenon of synchronicity is felt as a "meaningful coincidence" for the person experiencing it. The unconscious may be compared to a primal reservoir out of which spring forth the various meanings of human life. Accidental incidents which have had a bearing on the meanings of the lives of those persons going through them have quite often triggered and served as the starting points for parapsychological research. An example would be the case of knowing of the death of an intimate friend through a dream. In such incidents we can discern an ethicality in a broad sense. By ethicality I mean that the incident bears on the way a human lives his or her life. It does not designate the moral meaning of good versus evil, rather it pertains here to good and bad luck for the course of a human life: it is "good or bad" insofar as luck is concerned. Among accidental incidents, there are not a few in which paranormal phenomena occur in situations where destiny shapes the course of human lives. When Jung speaks of the "coincidence in meaning" between an inner and outer event, the "meaning" in question has a bearing, in short, on the person's practical way of living. Contrary to this, science as originally conceived stops at research concerning the facts and does not concern itself with the ethical meaning of the issues as they pertain to the course of human life. Since parapsychology has aimed at becoming a science in this sense, it has been scientifically studied, divorcing itself from the issue of meaning and value. Here I discern a fundamental methodological error.

In establishing his hypothesis of synchronicity, Jung sought the opinion of the physicist, Wolfgang Pauli (1900–1958), concerning paranormal phenomena. Pauli recognized the existence of paranormal phenomena and remarked that in dealing with them it is necessary to take within one's purview relationships such as that between the brain and mind.[1] According to him, the psychologist's concept of the unconscious should not be limited simply to the domain of psychotherapy, but should be applied to the general issues of natural science concerning the phenomena of life. In other words, the unconscious function does not remain simply a problem for psychology but should have a bearing on the various fields of natural science which deal with life, such as medical science and biology. Pauli says that physicists are willing to acknowledge that issues centering on the life process are worthy of investigation in physics. He further adds that when this occurs, teleology and teleological intentionality (a function directed toward a purpose), which are essential to the nature uniquely embodied in living organisms, can become issues even for physics.

When Pauli referred to the issue of living organisms and teleology, he probably had in mind the law of entropy. Physics currently takes the law of entropy as a fundamental principle, based on theorization of empirical law, that is, on probability based on experience. Generally speaking, the law of entropy states that over time the cosmos will become chaos. Physical phenomena, for example, the diffusion of heat, generally follow this law. But isn't there a different mechanism functioning in the living organism? The generation of life, or its morphological formation, reveals even at a commonsensical level a process in which the chaotic grows into the ordered. The relation of physics and life has been an important problems for physics since Erwin Schrödinger (1887–1961), providing impetus to the development of today's biophysics. But the issue of teleology has not yet entered its purview. Jung and Pauli thought that in order to examine this problem, it is necessary to enter the dimension of the unconscious.

The teleological function immanent in living organisms appears, at the level of the human body, as a natural healing power operating in conformity with the purpose of living. At the foundation of the theory of *ki*, which has been born out of practical experiences accumulated since ancient times, lies this theory of human being. It would seem that this function occurs, at a level of the unconscious that transcends the individual, in the form of creative, lived experiences which have broadly religious character. Moreover, it seems that the phenomena of synchronicity provide, for now, an entrance into the domain of these lived experiences. This is suggested by the fact that the history of *ki*-training [*kikō*] is closely linked to the traditions of self-cultivation in Daoism and Buddhism.

A look at history reveals that the birth of modern science in the West was ushered in through the confrontation between religion and science.

II. OBJECTIVISTIC SCIENCE AND SUBJECTIVISTIC SCIENCE

At this juncture, I shall again spell out the differences between traditional thinking methods in the East and the West. There was no clear separation between philosophy and empirical science during the time of René Descartes (1596–1650) and Isaac Newton (1643–1727), but philosophy began to slowly move away from science after Immanuel Kant (1724–1804). Kant constructed his epistemology so as to *theoretically* guarantee the validity of the worldview suggested by Newtonian physics. Kant's epistemology dealt only with *a priori* forms in the cognitive subject, for example, the logical form of thinking concerning various conditions prior to empirical cognition. Consequently, philosophy was rendered unrelated to the empirical facts with which science deals. In contrast, Bergson and Merleau-Ponty can be seen as attempting to bring philosophy and empirical science closer again by incorporating clinical accomplishments from contemporary medical psychology. Yet the gap separating them has not been sufficiently bridged.

Jung says that the East did not produce science in the Western sense, but instead produced a unique science in its own sense. According to him, the self-cultivation method of Eastern religions is itself a "science," or alternatively, it is *an empirical scientific investigation* about the world of mind. How should we understand Jung's contention?

Since modern science started with the revolution in astronomy and physics, and with Descartes' dichotomy, it has attempted to understand all phenomena with a model based on the method of studying physical phenomena. Consequently, the mechanism of life phenomena is in principle reduced to the mechanism of physical phenomena, for example, molecular biology. Moreover, in dealing with psychological phenomena, modern science has adhered to the standpoint of observing, from outside, the response and behavior of animals and human beings which react to stimulus, by eliminating as much as possible the subjective factors of mind. This is exemplified in the contentions of behaviorism since John Watson (1878–1958) (for example, the investigation of S-R conditioning). We can call empirical scientific research which assumes this standpoint, "objectivistic science" [*kyakukkanshugi-teki kagaku*].

"Objectivistic science" has two fundamental presuppositions in its research. One presupposition is that objective, scientific cognition is established by reducing the function of subjectivity as near to zero as possible, while separating the epistemological subject from its object, which places them in opposition. In this sense, modern science is "objectivistic." The second presupposition is that all phenomena are reducible to physical phenomena, to the mechanism of "things" which can be objectively observed. Consequently, the essence of life phenomena is understood in light of the mechanism of matter, and psychological phenomena are also reduced to the mechanism of bodily behavior observable in animals and human beings from the outside. In this respect, modern science assumes a "reductionist" attitude, in which life phenomena exist on the basis of physical phenomena, and psychological (spiritual) phenomena on the basis of life phenomena. This is indicated by the ascending arrow in figure 7.1.

It is true that the method of objectivistic science has great validity and has accomplished a great deal, and therefore it has its own appropriateness. However, it starts with the assumption of the mind-body dichotomy which excludes, in advance, the mind or the problem of mind. In contrast, a new movement, starting with depth psychology, developing into psychosomatic medicine and moving to reevaluate Eastern medicine, assumes the standpoint of investigating the mechanism of experiential phenomena

FIGURE 7.1
OPPOSITE DIRECTIONS OF OBJECTIVISTIC SCIENCE AND SUBJECTIVISTIC SCIENCE

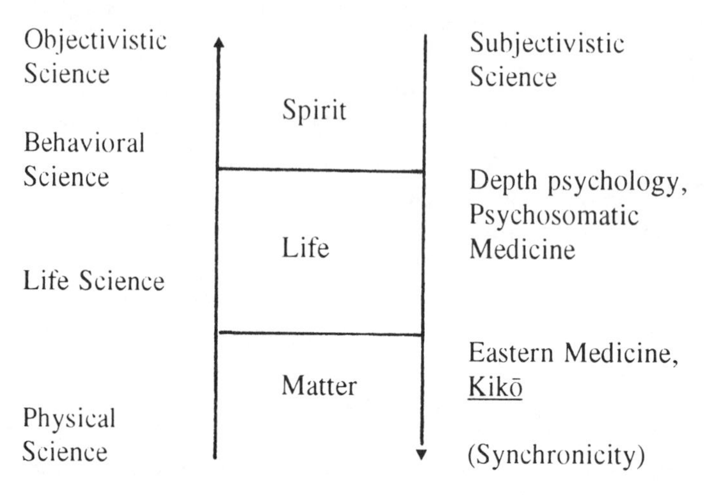

while holding, from the outset, the problem of mind within its purview. In this respect, this movement may be called "subjectivistic science" [*shukanshugiteki kagaku*]. Although it recognizes the validity of objectivistic science, it contends that it is possible to establish, together with objectivistic science, *empirical scientific research while taking into consideration the function of mind.*

The various self-cultivation methods seen in many Eastern religions may be regarded as historical forerunners to subjectivistic science. Jung's remark about the East and the West producing different sciences may be understood from this perspective. Depth psychology, as a subjective science, empirically investigates the structure of the unconscious, the unknown region of psyche latent at the base of consciousness. Psychosomatic medicine attempts to verify empirically the correlative mechanism existing between the function of mind and the mechanism of life phenomena that are the body. This is indicated by the descending arrow in figure 7.1. Therefore, subjectivistic science takes a methodological assumption that is different from the Cartesian mind-matter dichotomy. Our concern for the reevaluation of Eastern medicine and research on *ki*-energy, however, attempts to go one step beyond the standpoint of this subjectivistic science.

Depth psychology and psychosomatic medicine have recognized mind-body correlativity as a clinical fact, but have not yet reached the idea of a third function which mediates the psychological and physiological functions. If the existence of a unique energy in the living body, called *ki*, is granted, it will serve to endorse *positivistically* the inseparable mind-body correlativity. Obviously, if empirical scientific research is possible with a methodological assumption different from the mind-body dichotomy of objectivistic science, research into the problem of mind will in principle cover life phenomena, and even their relationship with *physical phenomena.*[2]

It is noteworthy at this point that methodologically the relation between the cognitive subject and the object is in principle changed in our investigation. Modern objectivistic science has held to its ideal of bringing the cognitive subject to a status of zero in relation to the observable object, as is represented by Newton's words that "I do not make the hypothesis." (Although this presupposition has come into question in microphysics since Heisenberg's uncertainty principle, I shall not go into this issue here.) However, in depth psychology, the empirical phenomena themselves (for example, dreams) cannot be separated from the conditions of one's own mind as the cognitive subject. To use Freud's characterization, dreams are projections by a subject. Consequently, the state in which the subject is placed invariably changes correlative with the objective state that it encounters.

Objectivistic science observes the state of an object from outside by using various apparatuses for measurement, and in these the condition of the subject is considered unrelated to the condition of the observed object. The epistemology of modern philosophy, as is represented by Kant, has had the purpose of guaranteeing theoretically the contentions of objectivistic science and thereby of giving it a foundation. Consequently, epistemology has focused on the *a priori,* formal conditions for knowledge (for example, logical forms of thinking and causality) without dealing with the empirical contents of knowledge. In this manner, philosophy and science have drifted apart. In contrast, the tradition of Eastern philosophy, which is an historical forerunner to subjectivistic science, has held that our mind, which is the cognitive subject, is not merely an observer of phenomena, but is a participant in them. Furthermore, the cognitive subject changes into *an incarnate subject [shutai] enabling the phenomena to appear.*[3] This is because cognition cannot be deepened according to this tradition unless it is accompanied by practice or by a spiritual transformation of the subject.

An act of knowing, when seen physiologically, is a kind of energy phenomenon in a living body. Stimuli such as light and sound entering the sensory organs from the external world are clearly a transmission of energy, and when they are converted into information, the process of cognition is established. In this sense, cognition is *an energy phenomenon unique to the living body.* And if a potential intentional function exists with mind-body inseparability, it must be detectable in some form as an energy phenomenon. In virtue of this detectability, Eastern medicine's theory of the body will be suggestive for uniting the philosophical mind-body theory and empirical scientific research.

III. CONCLUDING REMARKS: MIND, LIFE, AND MATTER

Ki has been a key concept in Chinese philosophy's views of the human being, world, and cosmos. The areas which this concept covers are so vast that they go beyond the scope of the present investigation. Therefore, I would like to conclude by stating my opinion on the relationship between space and the unconscious.

Freud's concept of "unconscious" designates, in principle, the domain of mind where experiences since birth (or since conception) are accumulated and stored. In contrast, Jung contended that there latently exists the region of the collective or transpersonal unconscious going beyond individual experiences. Freud's "unconscious" is the "personal unconscious." The unconscious layer, which is deeper than the personal unconscious, is a transpersonal unconscious region where the legacy of experiences, dating back to our ancestors, is accumulated and stored. It has its foundation in the evolution of life, and includes in principle the ancient animal unconscious. Jung's concept of this collective unconscious is, at least for now, a hypothesis that is impossible to verify empirically. Jung explains it as a kind of image pattern (the form of experience), but his explanation has been criticized because it is based on Lamarck's (1744–1829) theory.

However, it does not seem to me to be meaningful to approach the issue from a biological viewpoint. If we follow common sense, humans have evolved from animals, and there are many mechanisms which are similar in humans and animals. For this reason, it is unquestionable that mechanisms phylogenetically evolved from animals are genetically inherent and active in some form even now in the mechanism of the individual human body. On the other hand, it is also an undeniable fact that the evolution of life has brought development and progress in spiritual capacity, and has given birth to the human species. For this reason, it is possible in principle to think that traces of past evolution (development) are still alive and active in some form in the depths of the mind, by *metaphorically* applying a genetic viewpoint to the problem of mind. Since there is at present no clarification of the principle of the relationship between mind and body (and therefore, between psychology and biology), it would be futile to criticize the above idea from a biological viewpoint. For the present, it is enough for depth psychology to investigate the genetic structure of the unconscious from its own standpoint.

The above explanation is, at any rate, an attempt to think out the structure of the collective unconscious by tracing the history of the mind back to the past. In other words, when we investigate the depths of the unconscious in light of the *temporal axis*, we go from an individual's past experience since birth back to the dimension of the past that in some form transcends the individual delimitation of being. In contrast, Jung in his later years started to probe into the structure of the collective unconscious *in light of space*. In other words, he thought that the collective unconscious is also a common domain spreading through the depths of many individual minds. In this respect, the collective unconscious is a transpersonal unconscious region that both temporally and spatially transcends the delimitation of an individual being. Two individuals, "I" and "the other," are spatially separated beings. However, within the depths of their minds, they are connected to each other by an invisible thread in virtue of a potential, unconscious order. To broaden this perspective, we can think of a potential dimension of what we may call the "cosmic unconscious." If we can think in this manner, we will be able to discover an entrance into the potential experiential dimension beyond the opposition between "I" and "the other."

Jung's ideas on this are stated in his theory of synchronicity.[4] His theory of synchronicity was advanced in his later years and is not theoretically refined. Many points in the theory do not neatly fit into the theoretical system of Jung's psychology, and consequently there has been a tendency among Jungian scholars to ignore it. However, Jung connects his idea of synchronicity with the worldview advanced in the ancient Chinese book, the *Yìjīng,* and this I cannot ignore.[5] There has been an increase in recent years in the number of American and European Jungian scholars who have taken a positive attitude of dealing with the problem of synchronicity.[6] For the present author, the issue of synchronicity is currently a research topic. I have already dealt with this elsewhere. To delve into this issue in detail here would depart from our investigation of the problem of *ki,* so I will just summarize my tentative conclusion on this issue.[7]

Synchronicity is meaningful coincidence. For example, when I think about a person, this person just happens to show up. There is a coincidence or synchronization between the inner experience and the outer experience in regard to the meaning of the event. (The two events are the experience of the same person. The meaning of "this person" coincides or synchronizes the psychological event and the physical event.) This kind of coincidence is usually regarded as accidental, that is, as a meaningless coincidence, but when a phenomenon of this nature is experienced under unusual circumstances, and cannot be dismissed as a mere coincidence, it is called a "meaningful coincidence." When we experience a strange coincidence, we have a strong emotion, feel surprised or anxious, or say that "this is not ordinary," or that "I don't know what it is but this certainly has a meaning." We might say it is a kind of mysterious feeling. When we encounter an event like this many times, we have the feeling that something or some power issuing from the dimension of potential experience is at work. An example would be the news of a close friend's death after we are stricken by anxiety in a dream about that person. In a situation like this, reason often tends to deny the connection and to regard the coincidence simply as meaningless.

Jung's theory of synchronicity is related to the following three pillars of support. One is parapsychology. Based on many of his own experiences, Jung recognized the existence of parapsychological phenomena such as telepathy and clairvoyance, but he had not particularly studied them. Nevertheless, he gradually started thinking about them through his association with J. B. Rhine. He has, however, roughly the following criticism of prior research performed in parapsychology. Parapsychological research has lacked a consistent theoretical principle, and has carried out experiments while dealing with various ad hoc phenomena. Moreover, the research has followed the experimental method of empirical science, which presupposed the previously accepted methodological paradigm and left its methodological foundation unexamined. However, Jung contends that these phenomena indicate the necessity of changing the methodological paradigm on which accepted science is based. Generally speaking, empirical science dealing with physical phenomena is based on the principle of causality. Since it takes time for information to be spatially transmitted according to the principle of causality, the cause-effect relation is governed by temporal and spatial delimitation. But Jung reasons that the essence of parapsychology transcends temporal and spatial determination, for what is at issue in parapsychology is not simply physical phenomena. Rather it is the coincidence in meaning, or the relation of synchronization, between psychological and physical events. Consequently, Jung thinks that latently existing behind the order of causality observed under temporal and spatial determination is the order of the cosmic, collective unconscious, within which the principle of *teleological synchronicity,* totally different from causality, is dominant. Spatial distance and temporal flow do not, in principle, play any role in the order of synchronicity. In this order, the localization of *where* an event occurs cannot be determined, and moreover, the distinction between past, present, and future loses its meaning. For example, precognition is an act of knowing what will happen in the future, but what has not yet happened cannot be observed as an energy process. Jung's position is that supranormal phenomena occur when under certain circumstances the synchronistic dimension and the observable causal dimension make contact with each other.

On this point, Jung criticizes the method of parapsychological research. It has focused only on the physical event in an observable situation, and has paid no attention to the psychological condition which is the moment triggering these phenomena; that is, it has neglected in toto the subjective aspect of the event. Jung contends that although parapsychologists have shown an interest in the observed physical event, what is more important here is the psychological condition within *the interior* of a subject participating in the event. For without the psychological condition, the physical event cannot take place. This is an important point. One of the fundamental conditions demarcating supranormal phenomena from ordinary physical phenomena is that there is invariably participation by a definite living body (for example, a psychic). Therefore, when we try to take the supranormal phenomena as a kind of energy phenomena, it is necessary to analyze first the functional process of the unknown energy, unique to the living body, in view of both the psychological and physiological function of this body. In this regard, research in *ki*-energy and parapsychology might be connected.

The second pillar for the hypothesis of synchronicity is an internal change taking place in the field of contemporary physics. In advancing the theory of synchronicity, Jung sought cooperation from the well-known physicist, Wolfgang Pauli. Noting that the relationship between consciousness and the unconscious in depth psychology parallels in theory the problem of measurement (observation) in quantum physics (since Heisenberg), Pauli maintains that physics must take into account the issue of life phenomena (for example, the psychological and physiological processes in the brain), and that it should theoretically be possible to do so. There are some physicists today who are of the opinion that in view of the problem of measurement (observation) and the related function of non-localization, the problem of consciousness or mind should be incorporated in some form within the framework of theoretical physics (for example, Eugene Wigner and David Bohm). Their ideas are as varied as they are different and have not gone beyond philosophical speculation. Yet overall they maintain that ultimately the essence of matter and of spirit coincide with each other at the micro level.

Those physicists, however, discuss only the ultimate relationship between spirit and matter, and ignore the existence of the life-phenomenon between them. Between "mind" and "thing" is the region of the lived human body [*karada*] connected to our life [*inochi*]. The ancient Eastern tradition of philosophy and empirical science started with this primordial point—our individual "life"—and investigated the latent harmony between microcosm and macrocosm. Here lies the centrality of the issue of *ki*.

To pursue the central issue of *ki*, we will need a new perspective for integratively understanding the three dimensions of mind, life, and matter. This means, in light of current scholarship, that depth psychology and psychosomatic medicine would assume the role of mediating philosophy and life science, but would extend their scope as far as physical science. The hitherto accepted method and principle of objectivistic science possess their own validity and scope of application, but its research has been conducted by a prior elimination of the problem of mind. Therefore, when scientific investigation is envisioned as incorporating within itself the problem of mind, we will face a new question regarding what paradigm shift will be needed for this scientific endeavor.

The third pillar supporting Jung's hypothesis of synchronicity is the worldview proposed by the Chinese classic the *Yìjīng*. The *Yìjīng* forms the original foundation of Chinese philosophy. When we trace the historical origins of the views of human being and the world presupposed by Eastern medicine, we return to the worldview articulated in the *Yìjīng*. To put this simply, the *Yìjīng* maintains that there is an invisible pre-established harmony, or a latent synchronized correspondence between the human being as a microcosm and the movements of the macrocosm. The *Yìjīng* deals with techniques for bringing the functional power, operative in this latent order, to possible cognition within the field of our everyday experience. According to Jung, Western science has always shown an interest in investigating the external world, while the East has been interested in investigating the internal world. For this reason, science as developed in the Western world has not been produced in the East, for Eastern science has originally been a science of the mind. Today when modern science and technology seem to have reached their apex, it would appear that we are required to think afresh the meaning of the traditional wisdom of the ancient East.

There is a famous passage which is said to have been added by Confucius to the commentary of the *Yìjīng*. It runs as follows, though I will supplement it with a sinologist's interpretation:

> That which is beyond form [*xíngérshàngzhě*] is called Dao and all that is formed is called a vessel or an instrument [*qì*]. (Dao is a law designating the pattern in the fluid changes of *yīn* and *yáng* energy. When its activity takes on form as a definite phenomenon, it is a vessel and a tool. Hence, everything in the cosmos is a vessel, which receives the activity of Dao and is a tool for its activity. There is no vessel apart from Dao nor is there an activity of Dao apart from the vessel. Both are originally one.

> The function of Dao permeates the vessel. Our human flesh is also a vessel for Dao, wherein dwells the original nature of human being. Therefore, the original nature of human being is the Dao.) Following the ceaseless natural flow of changes, the sage cuts off its flow at an appropriate place and shows it to us. This is called change [*piàn*]. When the sage further presses on the change, and actualizes the activity of Dao, it is called penetration [*kăn*]. It is the task of the sage to make all the activities of Dao practical, making them available to people under Heaven.[8]

What is translated as "that which is beyond form" is "*xíng-érshàng*" in the original Chinese [Jap. *keijijō*], and is used both in Japan and China as the translation for the term "metaphysical." Insofar as "Dao" designates that which is invisible and transcendent, this rendition is not all that inappropriate. However, the concept of "Dao" is not based on the attitude of theoretically observing nature from outside as is the case in Western metaphysics. Nature is understood rather as a practical performing stage on which to actualize the original human nature latent in human beings. For this purpose, we must come to know that our flesh is a "vessel" for the original Dao. Chinese people called this invisible function of Dao "*qì*," which is in Japanese "*ki*."

Western philosophy and science since the modern period have developed while focusing on the physical world as external nature. In contrast, traditional philosophy and science in East Asia developed as a kind of practical anthropology to actualize the original human nature latent in the mind and body. For this reason, this philosophy, when seen from a contemporary standpoint, developed in close connection with the psychology of the unconscious and with medical science, rather than in connection with physics. The view of human being espoused by this philosophy maintains that the human being is not a *homo faber* who conquers nature, but is an ecological, receptive being made alive by the invisible power working from beyond nature, for the human being is originally a being born out of nature.

POSTSCRIPT

About ten years ago I published a book entitled *Shintai: tōyōteki shinshinron no kokoromi,* [*The Body: Toward an Eastern Mind-Body Theory*]. I wrote it with a limited audience in mind, since it dealt with special fields of philosophy and Japanese intellectual history. However, it was favorably received, and an English version even appeared through the efforts of my friends in the United States. What surprised me was that it was read in Japan not only by researchers in philosophy and Japanese intellectual history, but also by people in various disciplines such as physical education, the martial arts, Eastern medicine, and *kikō*. Since its reception exceeded my expectations, I was very thankful. Because of this unexpected readership, I made the acquaintance of people in these disciplines, and they have in turn drawn me into their fields.

The present book is a collection of pieces I wrote and revised after the publication of the above-mentioned book. Although I am aware of many unsolved and insufficiently treated problems, I will leave them as a future task. For now, this book presents the current status of my thought. Compared to the previously mentioned work, I have tried to address it to a more general audience.

Part I, "Eastern Mind-Body Theory and the Contemporary Period," is based on a manuscript I prepared as a guest lecturer for the Fourteenth Conference of the Japanese Association for the Study of the Martial Arts held at Tsukuba University in the fall of 1981. *Part II,* "*Ki* and the Body," is newly written for the present publication. *Part III,* "The Present and Future of the Science of Ki," is added to the English version and it is taken with some editorial revisions from chapters three and four of *Ki towa nanika* [What is *Ki*?] (Tokyo: NHK Books, 1991).[1]

Throughout this book my concern has been directed toward three themes. The first is Eastern spiritual-intellectual history centering on Japan. The second is problems connected to depth psychology and psychiatry, with an emphasis on Jung. And the last is philosophical problems focusing on the mind-body theory.

In light of the specialization and classification of scholarship, these three themes belong to different disciplines. When they are seen from the respective standpoint of these specialized fields, I am afraid that the reader may have difficulty finding relevant connections among these themes of my concern. However, since the value of "interdisciplinary" approaches is currently being acknowledged, I have not felt too restrained in entering various disciplines. It is true that there is an academic attitude maintaining that progress in scholarship lies in deepening a specialized field. If the present work is examined with this attitude in mind, I am aware that many questions and objections may be raised. I will be much obliged if the limitations of my understanding in these diverse studies are corrected by more knowledgeable readers.

As I reflect now, it seems that the concern I have for the above three themes came from the same root within myself. About thirty years ago, there was a period when I devoted myself to self-cultivation because I was spiritually at a dead end. I feel that the experiences I had during that time implicitly gave a direction to my research. As a beginning researcher, I had an interest in Japanese spiritual-intellectual history and in Western philosophy; my interest in psychology was entirely personal. Eager to learn what Zen and Yoga were, I thumbed through the pages of many books on these topics, and this gave a direction, I think, to my scholarship. I never thought that this personal interest would some day have a bearing on my research task.

However, as I studied Japanese intellectual history, I began to feel that what may be called an ethos of "self-cultivation" flowed through the history of Japanese religion and through the tradition of the arts. With this feeling as my guide, I groped into the process of interaction between Shintōism and Buddhism in ancient history. While focusing on the theme of self-cultivation I began to understand the meaning of self-cultivation and meditative experience in Esoteric Buddhism. A product of this concern was realized in an earlier book, *Kodaijin no seishinsekai* (The Spiritual World of the Ancient People), where I focused on Kūkai (774–835). My interest in the theory of body as a philosopher was guided, as I reflect now, by the same concern which shaped, though quite unknowingly, the direction of my thinking. Research and scholarship, which are a matter of public discourse, and which seem at first glance to have no bearing on personal feeling, may after all be related to the life of an individual human being in some form.

Several years ago I promised to Ms. FUJII Aiko of Hirakawa Shuppan Publishing Company to complete the present work, but I left it unfinished for a long time. When I made the promise, I thought I could complete it with ease. However, once I started I realized, quite contrary to my expectations, that the problem of the Eastern theory of the body as it is related, for example, to *ki* and Eastern medicine, contains unfathomable depths. It goes into the most fundamental problems of philosophy and empirical science. There were times when I thought I should abandon the project, but Ms. Fujii encouraged me on many occasions with her patience. With her patient encouragement, I moved on and have barely managed to fulfill my promise. I would like to extend my most sincere appreciation to her. The title of the book has emerged through the wisdom of the editing staff at Hirakawa Shuppan Publishing Company, for which I also feel thankful.

YUASA Yasuo
Summer, 1986

NOTES

TRANSLATOR'S INTRODUCTION

1. American astronauts who have gone into space and had the opportunities to observe the Earth from afar almost unanimously state that our planet is beautiful and yet fragile. See, for example, the reports of these astronauts contained in TACHIBANA Takashi, *Uchū kara no kikan* [Returning from Space] (Tokyo: Chūōkōron Sha, 1988).

2. Consider, for example, how these phenomena will be affected by the present global population explosion, which is expected to peak in the beginning of the twenty-first century. The population explosion will throw off food distribution, both for the supplier and the supplied.

3. See, for example, Robert N. Bellah et al., *Habits of the Heart: Individualism and Commitment in American Life* (New York: Harper & Row, 1985).

4. Those who uphold the idea of rationality as the most sublime faculty of mind should ask themselves how many minutes a day they are rational. Rationality as we know it today was raised high by Descartes and was made decisively so by Kant when he distinguished between *a priori* and *a posteriori* knowledge. It culminated in Hegel who deified human reason vis-à-vis his concept of the absolute spirit. However we might remind ourselves of Aquinas's thought during the medieval period in which human reason (*ratio*) was simply an inferential faculty of mind inferior in status and power to *intellectus*. The concept of *intellectus* goes further back to Plato's *nous*.

5. NISHITANI Keiji in his *Religion and Nothingness* argues that the predicament into which modern man has fallen has led to the abyss of nihilism as a result of accepting materialism, science, and technology along with the idea of progress as the guiding principle for living. He suggests overcoming this predicament by appealing to the experience of *śūnyatā*.

6. Unlike the later Heidegger, who reverted back to the premodern image of the world in which the "earth, sky, man, and gods" are primarily important elements in tackling the problem of modern *techné*, Yuasa's option is to create an interdisciplinary field that he calls "subjectivistic science" in which subjective experience and its scientific veri-

fication are conjoined. See Yuasa's discussion on this point in section II of chapter 7.

7. *Qìgōng,* or *kikō,* is a neologism and means literally *ki*-training. For an extensive treatment of this term, see Yuasa's discussion in Chapter 3.

8. Following the Aristotelian either-or logic, whose commonsensical model assumes metaphorically the image of a pendulum swinging from one extreme to the other, some Western scholars looking at the adverse effects of science and technology, tend to think that the twenty-first century will be a *spiritual* century. Since Yuasa does not accept the model based on the either-or logic, because it presupposes dualism and since he is an Eastern scholar, he opts for a *middle way* judging that science and religion as we understand them today cannot accommodate the upcoming *Zeitgeist.* If science focuses on the analysis of facts without questioning philosophically their meaning, value, and spiritual implication it will be destructive for humanity, which the latter will not tolerate. On the other hand, if religion adheres to traditional dogmas without incorporating scientific discovery it is incapable of satisfying the intellectual and emotional demand of ordinary people. Yuasa advances beyond these positions by proposing a "subjectivistic science" which examines the psychological meaning of inner experience while at the same time investigating such phenomena positivistically. This position is theoretically suggested to Yuasa by his study of *ki*-energy, which he understands as a third term resisting comprehension in terms of either mind or matter.

9. Although the term *ki* (Chin. *qì*) is translated into English in various ways such as "ether," "physical force," "bio-energy," or "vital energy," the present rendition as psychophysical energy is adopted in view of Yuasa's philosophical position.

10. On this point see, for example, MARUYAMA Toshiaki, *Ki: rongo kara nūu saiensumade* [*Ki*-energy: From the Analects to New Age Science] (Tokyo: Tokyo Bijitsusha, 1986). For an historical account of the concept of *ki* as understood within Chinese intellectual history, see *Ki no shisō,* ed. ONOZAWA Seiichi et al. (Tokyo: University of Tokyo Press, 1980).

11. The practical implication of this idea is extremely significant, especially in understanding an interpersonal relationship. For example, it will be useful for studying the unconscious transference between psychoanalyst and patient, and for learning to dissolve conflict situations, although it will require further practical and theoretical investigation of the phenomenon of intercorporeality.

12. I have elsewhere given a detailed account of this position. See Shigenori Nagatomo, *Attunement through the Body* (Albany, N.Y.: SUNY Press, 1992).

13. This suggests that Yuasa is taking the living and lived body as energy phenomena while viewing the human being as a life phenomenon. If a human can read off information from the environment, for example, through perception, Yuasa reasons that, whether the environment is internal or external, there must be a transmission of energy between the living and lived human body and its environment. This concern cannot be brought out clearly as long as we adhere to the Cartesian disjunctive mind-matter dualism, because in this dualism we cannot discern an animating principle in the body that is divorced from spirit.

14. As will be evident later, Yuasa adds to this three-layered body-scheme the fourth circuit of the unconscious quasi-body circuit, incorporating the *ki*-meridians of acupuncture medicine. For this point, see chapter 4, section IV. I have given a little more detailed account of Yuasa's concept of the body-scheme in *Giving the Body its Due,* ed. Maxine Sheets-Johnstone (Albany, N.Y.: SUNY Press, 1992), 48–68.

15. Yuasa, in his *The Body: Toward an Eastern Mind-Body Theory,* ed. T. P. Kasulis (Albany, N.Y.: SUNY Press, 1987), conceived of the body as comprising two layers of surface and base structure. The surface structure is characterized as the "bright cogito," much like the Cartesian *ego cogito,* while the base structure is the "dark cogito," within which original human nature is concealed. See chapter 9 of the above book along with T. P. Kasulis's introduction.

16. The only exception to this is perhaps Edmund Husserl.

17 YUASA Yasuo and SADAKATA Akio, trans., *Ōgon no hana no himitsu* [The Secret of the Golden Flower] (Kyoto: Jinbun Shoin, 1980) provides useful footnotes which correct many of the philological and hermeneutical mistakes committed in the English translation.

18 Compare this, for example, to the achieved ideal of martial arts, which is the idea of harmonizing and accommodating the *ki*-energy shared between "I" and "other." This has the philosophical implication that many disputes concerning the establishment of intersubjectivity are misguided in orientation. Husserl, for example, in his *Cartesian Mediations,* as well as in the *Crisis* attempted to establish the ground of intersubjectivity through empathy, which is quite inadequate and unsatisfactory. On the other hand, Yuasa's study on *ki*-energy suggests that our research on intersubjectivity must first investigate the *ki*-energy field of intercoporeality, because if there is an emission as well as a detection of *ki*-energy both in the interior and the exterior of "one's own body," the field of *ki*-energy is more important and primary than the field of intersubjectivity that may be established within the confines of *ego cogito.*

19. See below, p. 108.

20. Below, p. 116–117.

21. Below, p. 126.

22. Below, p. 169–170.

23. Broadly speaking, philosophy has pursued the *a priori* structure of knowledge, while empirical science has pursued *a posteriori* knowledge, rendering philosophy and science totally unrelated.

24. Below, p. 188.

AUTHOR'S PREFACE

1. YUASA Yasuo, *The Body: Toward an Eastern Mind-Body Theory* (Albany, N.Y.: SUNY Press, 1987).

CHAPTER 1. EASTERN MIND-BODY THEORY

1. The term "*shugyō*" is translated throughout this book as "self-cultivation," or simply "cultivation." It consists of two Chinese characters, "to master" and a "practice." Literally then, it means "to master a practice." As is clear in this literal rendition, the term "self" does not appear in the original phrase. The rendition of "self-cultivation" is adopted because of the individualistic orientation of Western society. Philosophically this rendition is felicitous for initial stages of "self-cultivation," but since its ultimate goal is to achieve the state of "no-mind" or "no-self," it does not do justice to the full meaning of the original phrase. As long as the reader is aware of the fact that a psychological, existential transformation occurs in the course of "self-cultivation," where the self of everyday experience is discarded and transformed, the rendition of "*shugyō*" as "self-cultivation" should not pose any difficulty. Yuasa seems to think that the concept of "no-self" or "no-mind" parallels Jung's concept of "*Selbst,*" although they may not be identical.—TRANS.

2. *Shugendō* literally means "the way of mastering auspicious abilities" and, as Yuasa points out, its origin goes back to ancient Shintōism, which held a belief in mountain-worship. Many mountains such as Mt. Fuji and Mt. Osore are still believed to be "sacred" because of their inherent supernatural powers. Those who practice *shugendō* are called "*yamabushi,*" mountain dwellers in pursuit of the experience of the "sacred." An historical record about the *yamabushi* cites Enno Ozunu, who is said to have lived around the seventh century, as the first practitioner of *shugendō*. He is also credited with various paranormal abilities.—TRANS.

3. *Kaihōgyō* literally means "the practice of going around the mountain tops and ranges." For a brief explanation of this practice, see p. 12ff.—TRANS.

4. Mt. Hiei is located in the northeastern part of Kyoto, and its original temple was founded by Saichō (767–822), who introduced Tendai (Tīantái) Buddhism to Japan in the beginning of the ninth century. Mt. Hiei served as a major religious, cultural, and educational center until the Kamakura period (1185–1333). Almost all the great religious figures during the medieval period were educated at Mt. Hiei.—TRANS.

5. The term that is translated as "spirit" here and throughout this book is a compound phrase "*seishin,*" consisting of two Chinese characters, "*sei*" (Chin. *jīng*) and "*shin*" (Chin. *shén*). "*Sei*" is often associated with sexual or reproductive energy with the connotation that it is materially based. On the other hand, "*shin*" suggests a subtle, spiritual energy devoid of materiality. Unlike the English word, "spirit," which clearly suggests disembodiment, "*seishin*" means both material and spiritual energy. Yuasa's discussion of these terms may be found in chapter 3.—TRANS.

6. HARA Minoru's *Koten indo no kugyō* [*Tapas* in Classical India] (Tokyo: Shunjū Sha) is a detailed philological study of "*tapas.*"

7. The view of human being held by Gnosticism and alchemy, which originated with the former, maintained that the spiritual is stored within the flesh, or in material substance, and could be actualized. Alchemy is usually thought to be a technique for transforming a base metal to a precise metal, but when seen from the standpoint of depth psychology, it involves the transformation of the mind (psyche). In other words, the "base" and "precious" metals are a kind of analogical expression. The purpose of alchemy was to transform the human psyche, which is in an impure state like a base metal, into a luminous state like a precious metal. If we follow this idea, it is possible to bring forth a spiritual transformation and purification of the psyche by changing the functional activity of mind within the flesh. We witness here a view different from the orthodox view of human beings, which is the flesh-spirit dualism, and this view, it seems, is close to the tradition of the Eastern view of the human being. There has been a tendency in Western intellectual history, however, to regard both Gnosticism and alchemy as heretical. For this issue, see C. G. Jung, *Psychology and Alchemy,* and YUASA Yasuo, *Yungu to yōrōppa seishin* [Jung and the European Spirit] (Kyoto: Jinmon Shoin, 1979).

8. The English translation appeared as *The Body: Toward an Eastern Mind-Body Theory,* tr. and ed. T. P. Kasulis and S. Nagatomo (Albany, N.Y.: SUNY Press, 1987). A French version is to be published.

9. Tendai Buddhism was developed by Chigi (538–597), or Chiyi in Chinese, who is called the Master of Tiāntái. The name is derived from the location where Chigi used to live, and designates a "heavenly terrace." Doctrinally, it relies on the *Lotus Sūtra* (*Saddharmapundarika*

Sūtra), and so it is also called the Lotus school. This school of Buddhism was introduced to Japan by Saichō (767–822).—TRANS.

10. "*Samādhi*" generally refers to a state of meditation in which the meditator and the object of his or her concentration become one at a level subtler than the physical dimension.—TRANS.

11. Chigi, *Makashikan* (Tokyo: Iwanami Shoten, 1981), 72ff. Although Chigi divides the cultivation method into four forms, "constant sitting," "constant walking," "half sitting and half walking," and "neither sitting nor walking," its basic forms are "constant sitting" and "constant walking."

12. The phrase translated as "wandering thoughts" is "*zatsunen*" in Japanese and designates thoughts and images that wander off from the object of concentration in the course of meditation.—TRANS.

13. Kōbō Daishi Kūkai (774–835) is the founder of Esoteric Buddhism in Japan. For an extensive treatment of Kūkai and his thought, see Yoshito S. Hakeda, *Kūkai: Major Works* (New York: Columbia University Press, 1972). Also see David E. Shaner, *The Body-Mind Experience in Japanese Buddhism* (Albany, N.Y.: SUNY Press, 1985), chapters 3 and 4, which deal with Kūkai's philosophy from a phenomenological perspective.—TRANS.

14. "*Hanshu Zanmai*" appears originally in *Hanshu Zenmai kyō* or *Pratyutpannasamādhi Sūtra*.—TRANS.

15. Amitābha Buddha is the central Buddha worshipped in Pure Land Buddhism, and means "infinite light." It also has the meaning of "infinite life," in which case it is called Amitāyu Buddha.—TRANS.

16. Shinran (1173–1262) is the founder of Pure Land Buddhism in Japan. For a general introduction to Shinran's thought, see Alfred Bloom, *Shinran's Gospel of Pure Grace* (Tucson, Ariz., University of Arizona Press, 1977), and D. T. Suzuki, *Shin Buddhism* (New York: Harper & Row Publishers, 1970). For Shinran's writings in translation, see the Shin Buddhism Translation Series published by Hongwanji International Center, Kyoto, Japan and the Ryūkoku Translation Series published by Ryūkoku University. For a basic introduction to Shinran's faith, see *Tannishō*, trans. Taitetsu Uno (Honolulu, Hawaii: Buddhist Study Center Press, 1984).—TRANS.

17. "Dancing *nenbutsu*" was initiated by Ippen (1239–1289), a founder of the Jishū school of Buddhism. *Nenbutsu* was originally a visualization practice of Amitābha, or Amitāyu, Buddha in Pure land Buddhism.—TRANS.

18. The five parts of the body mentioned here refer to the head, two knees, and two arms.—TRANS.

19. Great Master Jikaku Ennin (794–864) was a disciple of Saichō. He studied primarily Esoteric Buddhism when he went to China between

838 and 848. After returning to Japan, he endeavored to establish a synthesis of the Tendai school of Buddhism with Esoteric Buddhism, and hence is credited with being the synthesizer of Tendai Esoteric Buddhism. The title, "Great Master," was granted posthumously in 866.—TRANS.

20. For the process of formation of *kaihōgyō,* see the chapter entitled "*Mikkyo to Nihon bunka*" [Esoteric Buddhism and Japanese culture] in YUASA Yasuo, *Nihonjin no shūkyōishiki* [Japanese Religious Consciousness] (Tokyo: Meicho Kankōkai, 1981).

21. For a more detailed explanation of this practice, see for example John Stevens, *The Marathon Monks of Mt. Hiei* (Boston: Shambala Press, 1988).—TRANS.

22. This statement is taken from a well-known passage in Dōgen's "*Genjōkōan*" fascicle which reads, "To learn the Buddha Way is to learn one's own self. To learn one's self is to forget one's self. To forget one's self is to be confirmed by all dharmas. To be confirmed by all dharmas is to effect the casting off of one's own body and mind, and of the bodies and minds of others as well."—TRANS.

23. Heian Buddhism refers to the Buddhism which flourished during the Heian period (794–1185). It arose as a reaction to the preceding Nara Buddhism. The main impetus for the rise of Heian Buddhism was to separate Buddhism from governmental control. The most representative figures in this movement were Saichō, who established the Tendai school of Buddhism at Mt. Hiei, and Kūkai who established Japanese Esoteric Buddhism at Mt. Kōya.—TRANS.

24. The use of Acalanātha for meditation as well as for an object of worship was especially developed in Japan, compared to India and China. *Fudōmyōō* (in Japanese) is believed to protect the cultivator from all the great powers which he or she encounters in the course of meditation. Entrusted with power by the central Buddha of Esoteric Buddhism, Mahāvairocana, it is believed to enable the cultivator to awaken his or her aspiration for unexcelled knowledge, to dispell evils and promote good, and eventually to enable the cultivator to reach satori. *Fudōmyōō* is usually depicted, as the text makes clear, in the state of fire *samādhi.*—TRANS.

25. This belief can be traced back to the Vāc theory during the Vedic period where it is contended that only a quarter of the totality is manifest in the empirical, phenomenal world, while the three other quarters remain hidden. The latter was believed to be the abode of heavenly beings including gods.—TRANS.

26. SEKIGUCHI Shindai, ed., *Makashikan* (Tokyo: Iwanami Shoten, 1981), vol. 1, 77.

27. This statement may sound puzzling, since if a hallucination starts carrying a sense of reality, it is no longer a hallucination. It may be

appropriate here to distinguish between a pathological or delusory hallucination and a "real" hallucination. When a hallucination is "real," it corresponds to an external "thing-event" or reality which can be intersubjectively verified. When this intersubjective verification is absent and there is pain or discomfort, the hallucination may be considered pathological. In fact, reality as we understand it through our senses and intellect is considered "delusory" in Buddhism, or "illusory" in Hinduism. In this sense, one knows in "real" hallucination that what is conventionally accepted as "real" is provisional in character, but one still has not achieved the ultimate sense, to use a Buddhist characterization, of "seeing things as they are." In order for this transition to occur, one must experience a practical, existential transformation of what we ordinarily understand as "reality."—TRANS.

28. The term translated as "mind/heart" is *shin,* or *kokoro,* in Japanese. Unlike the Western concept of "mind" whose central locus is identified with the intellectual, rational capacity of a person, the Japanese term carries in addition the sense of the affective or emotive dimension of a person. To indicate this difference, the term *shin* or *kokoro* is translated as "mind/heart." When Yuasa uses this term in the book, especially in the context where the Eastern mind-body theory is discussed, it is pertinent to keep in mind the above connotation.—TRANS.

29. Recent studies of Japanese history inform us that this Zen master's name was not read as Eisai, but instead as Yōsai. However, the translators have retained the name that he is commonly known by, which is Eisai, for the controversy surrounding how to read this Zen master's name properly has not been completely settled. For example, one of his disciples, according to the Kenniji genealogy of dharma-successors, bore the name of Eichō, inheriting the first character of this Zen master's name.—TRANS.

30. Eisai (1141–1215) is known for having introduced the Rinzai school of Zen Buddhism to Japan. He went to China twice (in 1168 and in 1187) and studied at Mt. Tīantái. In promoting Zen meditation, he encountered pressure from the existing Buddhist schools in Japan. In order to avoid conflict, he established his temple as auxiliary to the order of Tendai Esoteric Buddhism of Enryakuji Temple at Mt. Hiei.—TRANS.

31. Dōgen is the founder of the Sōtō school of Zen Buddhism in Japan. For a comprehensive treatment of Dōgen's life and works, see Hee-Jin Kim, *Dōgen: Mystical Realist* (Tucson, Ariz.: University of Arizona Press, 1973). For a philosophical treatment of Dōgen's works, see T. P. Kasulis, *Zen Action/Zen Person* (Honolulu, Hawaii: University of Hawaii Press, 1981), chapters 6, 7, and 9; and David E. Shaner, *The BodyMind Experience in Japanese Buddhism* (Albany, N.Y.: SUNY

Press, 1985), chapters 5 and 6. For a reliable translation of Dōgen's major work, *Shōbōgenzō,* see the translations by Masao Abe and Norman Waddell which have appeared in *The Eastern Buddhist.*—TRANS.

32. Dōgen, *Shōbōgenzō,* ed. TERADA Tōru (Tokyo: Iwanami Shoten, 1980), 125.

33. Myōe (1173–1232) was a revitalizer of Kegon Buddhism in the beginning of the Kamakura period. He is known to have led his life in strict observance of the Buddhist precepts. His *Record of Dreams* contains valuable accounts of his meditation experiences from about the age of twenty until his death. KAWAI Hayao, a Jungian scholar, has recently given a detailed analysis of Myōe's meditation and dream experience from a Jungian perspective. See KAWAI Hayao, *Myōe: Yume o ikiru* (Kyoto: Hōzōkan, 1987). An English version of this book, translated and edited by Mark Unno, appeared under the title, *The Buddhist Priest Myōe: A Life of Dreams* (Venice, Ca.; The Lapis Press, 1992). See also George Tanabe, *Myōe Shōnin (1173–1232): Tradition and Reform in Early Kamakura Buddhism* (Michigan: University Microfilms International, 1983).—TRANS.

34. *Shinshin gyōnen* may be translated here literally as "body-mind coagulation," but it is rendered as "body-mind crystallization" to suggest the transparency of this experience.—TRANS.

35. The *waka* poem is a traditional Japanese literary genre, contrasted with the Chinese poem. It consists of thirty-one syllables, divided into five, seven, five, seven, and seven syllables. Haiku, which is now known worldwide, is formed by taking the first three lines of the *waka* poem.—TRANS.

36. Nō or *Nōgaku* was systematized by Zeami (1363–1443 or 1445) and KAN'AMI Motokiyo (1338–1384). It is a combination of "field dance" and "monkey (acrobatic) dance," which were popular among the common people, and the court dance formalized for use by the aristocrats. In this theater the actors wear masks, and the themes mainly concern spiritual phenomena. The performance of Nō is characterized by simplicity of props and symbolic acts.—TRANS.

37. *Sadō,* the way of tea, was developed under the influence of Zen Buddhism. Tea was originally brought from China by Saichō, the founder of Tendai Buddhism in Japan, although its use did not spread among the populace. Eisai (1141–1215) reintroduced it again for medicinal purpose. Shūkō (d. 1502) is credited as being the founder of the way of tea, but it was Sen no Rikyū (1521–1591) who perfected the ceremony with the motto that "Zen and tea are one."—TRANS.

38. The term *budō* consists of two characters, *bu* (martial arts, military) and *dō* (the way or Dao). One who practices *bu* is called *bushi,*

and the way to practice it is known as *budō*. The tradition of *budō* may be historically traced back to the ideals of the *bushi* as depicted in such medieval literature as *The Tale of Glory, The Tale of the Heike,* and *Taiheiki,* but the most well-known codification of the *bushi* way is found in the book *Hagakure*. See, for example, the translation of YAMAMOTO Tsunetomo's *Hagakure,* trans. William Scot Wilson (New York: Avon Books, 1979).—TRANS.

39. For the following relationship between self-cultivation methods and artistry, see my *The Body: Toward an Eastern Mind-Body Theory* (Albany, N.Y.: SUNY Press, 1987), chapters 4 and 5.

40. NOSE Asaji, *Zeami jūrokubu shū* [Commentary on Zeami's Sixteen Books] (Tokyo: Iwamani Shoten, 1963), vol. 1, 120.

41. For Yuasa's interpretation of Nishida's concept of "pure experience," "acting intution," and "absolute nothing," see YUASA Yasuo, *The Body: Toward an Eastern Mind-body Theory* (Albany, N.Y.: SUNY Press, 1987), chapter 2.—TRANS.

42. NISHIDA Kitarō, *Zenshū* [Complete works], vol. 10, 36ff.

43. This idea is found, for example, in such familial codes of the samurai warriors as *Chikubashō* and *Imagawajō* written during the Muromachi period.

44. TOKUGAWA Iëmitsu (1604–1651), the third shōgun, firmly established the feudal system. Among the policies he enacted were the persecution of Christians and the policy of isolation (1639).—TRANS.

45. YAGYŪ Munenori (1571–1646) served the first shōgun, TOKUGAWA Iëyasu, in 1594 and was order by the shōgun to transmit his knowledge and techniques of swordsmanship to posterity. The third shōgun, Iëmitsu, reportedly visited Yagyū in order to learn from him the ultimate secret of swordmanship.—TRANS.

46. For the thought of the martial arts, see MINAMOTO Ryōen, *Bunka to ningenkeisei* [Culture and Formation of Personality] (Tokyo: Daiichihōki) and *Kinseishoki jitsugaku shisō no kenkyū* [A Study of Practical Learning in the Beginning of the Modern Period] (Tokyo: Sōbunsha).

47. Takuan, *Fudōchi shinmyōroku,* ed. ICHIKAWA Hakugen (Tokyo: Kōdansha, 1978), 202–203.

48. Ibid., 207.

49. The entire phrase points to a state in which no bifurcation takes place, and as such it designates a non-dual state. The word "original" in "original face" carries a sense not primarily of temporal priority, but rather of existential source or grounding. This existential source or grounding is metaphorically spoken of as "face." Practically, the mediator reaches the "face" through an existential retrogression into his/her psyche.—TRANS.

50. YAGYŪ Munenori, *Heihō kadensho* [The Family Transmission of the Military Method], ed. WATANABE Ichirō (Tokyo: Iwanami Shoten, 1990), 95.

51. Ibid., 97.

CHAPTER 2. BEYOND THE CONTEMPORARY PERIOD

1. See, for example: John C. Eccles, *Facing Reality: Philosophical Adventure by a Brain Scientist* (New York: Springer Verlag, 1970); Wilder Penfield, *The Mystery of the Mind: A Critical Study of Consciousness and the Human Brain* (Princeton: Princeton University Press, 1975); Karl Pribram, *Languages of the Brain: Experimental Paradoxes and Principles of Neurophysiology* (Englewood Cliffs, N.J.: Prentice-Hall, 1971); and Roger Sperry, *Science and Moral Priority: Merging Mind, Brain, and Human Values* (New York: Columbia University Press, 1983).

2. See YUASA Yasuo and KUROKI Mikio, trans., *Tōyōteki meisōhō* [The Eastern Meditation Methods] (Osaka: Sōgensha, 1984). This is a collection of essays which Jung wrote on Eastern religions.

3. For the following explanation, see my *The Body: Toward an Eastern Mind-Body Theory* (Albany, N.Y.: SUNY Press, 1987), especially chapters 8 and 9. In that book I divided the structure of the body into a surface structure (the sensory-motor circuit) and a base structure (the emotion-instinct circuit). However, in the following explanation, the structure of the body is conceived of in terms of the three layers of the information system. This idea is probably more appropriate for investigating the mind-body problem, especially for clarifying the characteristics of the Eastern mind-body theory.

4. See, for example, Edmund Husserl, *Experience and Judgment*, trans. James S. Churchill and Karl Ameriks (Evanston, Ill.: Northwestern University Press, 1973), 84–85, 104, 251.—TRANS.

5. In addition to the emotion-instinct circuit, Yuasa postulates a still deeper circuit (in chapter 4) of what he calls the "unconscious quasi-body." What is referred to as "the deepest" here simply means among the three circuits so far articulated.—TRANS.

6. *Daimoku* is practiced by the followers of the Nichiren school of Buddhism. Its practice is primarily the recitation of the phrase *Manmyōhōnrengekkyō*, meaning that "I entrust myself to the Lotus Sutra" (*Saddharmapundarīka Sūtra*).—TRANS.

7. For the practical procedure of performing "*shōshūten*" (small circulation of light breathing), see MOTOYAMA Hiroshi, *Toward a Superconsciousness* (Berkeley, Ca.: Asian Humanities Press, 1990), appendix two.—TRANS.

8. See, for example, HIRAI Tomio's *Zen Meditation Therapy* (Tokyo: Japan Publishing, Inc., 1975).—TRANS.

9. For a detailed explanation of this point, see, for example, MOTOYAMA Hiroshi, *Mikkyō Yōga* [Tantric Yoga] (Tokyo: Ikedashobō, 1978), particularly 33–71.—Trans.

CHAPTER 3. *KI* AND THE BODY IN THE MARTIAL ARTS

1. The term *riki* (*lǐqì*) is comprised of two characters, *ri* (*lǐ*) and *ki* (*qì*). *Ki* (*qì*) designates an empirical phenomenal order, whereas *ri* (*lǐ*) represents a transcendent order. The latter is usually rendered into English as "principle." The etymological origin of this word indicates the meaning of pattern as is, for example, exemplified in the grain of wood. Since it is not clear that ancient Chinese people (and therefore these Sung philosophers as well) had an idea of universalization as is found in Western intellectual history, it is questionable to translate *ri* (*lǐ*) as "principle." No doubt, the term *ri* (*lǐ*) is a conceptual recapitulation of experience that can be had only through a superconsciousness. It is perhaps better to translate it as "pattern," or more abstractly, "patternment." Two representative *riki* philosophers are Zhūzǐ and Wáng Yángmíng.—TRANS.

2. For Yuasa's interpretation of *riki* philosophy, see Yuasa, *Tōyōbunka no shinsō* [Deep Layers of Eastern Cultures] (Tokyo: Meicho Kankōkai, 1982).—TRANS.

3. "Kneading medicine" is a metaphorical expression for the Daoist meditation in which a meditator develops the inner working of the psychophysical energy called *ki*. As will become evident through Yuasa's explanation, it is also called developing the *tanden*, of which Daoists count three (or five). They are the upper *tanden* (the area between the eyebrows), the middle *tanden* (the area where the heart is located), and the lower *tanden* (the area around the lower abdomen). The other two are located in the back. For Yuasa's discussion of *tanden*, see below, p. 79ff.—TRANS.

4. KAWASE Ken'ichi, *Jūjitsuhiden* [A Secret Transmission of Jūjitsu] (Kyoto: Keiji Kankō Shinbusha, 1973), 19, 35, 50ff.

5. *Kokoro* is the Japanese reading of the Chinese character "*xin*" meaning mind/heart, and the sound "*ko-ko-ro*" is said to be onomatopoeic for the beating of the heart. When the term "mind" appears in the text in connection with the Eastern tradition, the reader may wish to keep in mind that it also embraces the affective dimension of the heart, unless Yuasa specifices otherwise.—TRANS.

6. It is located 5–6 cm below the navel, and is referred to as *svadhisthāna cakra* in Yoga. See Yuasa's discussion of this term on p. 79—TRANS.

7. "Acu-point" is an abbreviation for acupuncture point. In acupucture medicine, an acu-point is a therapeutic, curative point where an acu-needle is inserted. According to the theory of acupuncture medicine, sickness is a result of stagnation in the flow of *ki*-energy, and acu-points are places where the stagnation manifests most clearly. See chapter 4 for a discussion of the acu-points.—TRANS.

8. The Japanese term rendered here as "one's own body" is *karada.* It can also be translated as "human body." Since the Japanese connotation of this term is close in meaning to Merleau-Ponty's concept of "one's own body" (*le corps propre*), the present rendition is adopted. Merleau-Ponty contends that "one's own body" is a third term, neither for-itself nor in-itself. See Maurice Merleau-Ponty, *Phenomenology of Perception,* trans. Colin Smith (London: Routledge & Kegan Paul, 1962), 101, 117.—TRANS.

9. "Object-body" is phenomenologically contrasted with "subject-body" which is lived from within and resists any objectification at the time when it is lived. On the other hand, the "object-body" is the body which is constantly objectified, primarily through our sensory perception.—TRANS.

10. "Our own body" should be understood as a plural form of "one's own body."—TRANS.

11. Eugen Herrigel, *Yumi to Zen* (Tokyo: Fukumura Shuppan, 1980), 75ff. See also, *Zen in the Art of Archery* (New York: Vintage Books, 1971), 22ff.

12. For an explantion of what the meridians are, see "Fundamental Characteristics of Eastern Medicine's Theory of the Body" in chapter 4.—TRANS.

13. For a more extended treatment of *kikō* (Jap.), or *qìgōng* (Chin.), see the section "*Ki*-Energy and Its Relation to the External World" in chapter 5.—TRANS.

14. *Shushi Ōyōmei* (Tokyo: Chūōkōron Sha, 1974), 365.

15. For a depth-psychological interpretation of *riki* theory, see my "Tōyō no ryōshinron no tokushitsu" [Characteristics of Eastern Theory of Conscience] in YUASA Yasuo, *Tōyō Bunka no Shinsō* [The Deep Layers of Eastern Culture] (Tokyo: Meicho Kankōkai, 1985).

16. Erwin Rousselle, "Spiritual Guidance in Contemporary Taoism," in *Spiritual Disciplines: Papers from the ERANOS Yearbooks* 4, Bollingen Series XXX (Princeton: Princeton University Press, 1970). [YUASA Yasuo, trans., "Dōkyō no shugyōho to tōyō igaku," in *Shūkyō to Shinri,* vols. 24, 25, 30 (Tokyo: Shūkyō Shinri Shuppan).]

17. In view of the Yoga theory of *cakras,* the upper *tanden* corresponds to the *ājñā cakra,* the middle *tanden* to the *anahāta cakra,* and the lower *tanden* to the *svādhisthāna cakra.* For the experiential meaning of

these *cakras,* see, for example, MOTOYAMA Hiroshi, *Toward Superconsciousness: Meditational Theory and Practice* (Berkeley Ca.: Asian Humanities Press, 1990).—TRANS.

18. According to Jung, the self as the totality of psychic energy and its center can never become an object of consciousness.—TRANS.

19. *Kishitsu no sei* is here rendered as "nature of *ki* quality." According to Zhūzǐ's understanding, this also contains original human nature, but it is "smeared" by contingent, empirical dispositional characteristics, which are formed by the combination of pure and impure *ki*-energy.—TRANS.

20. This ambiguity results in Jung's thought because he calls the "self" the state of unification between ego-activity and the unconscious activity whose latent center is also referred to as the self. Yuasa's reference here is to the latter sense of the self. Jung calls the unifying activity between consciousness and the unconscious the "transcendent function."—TRANS.

21. Richard Wilhelm, trans., *The Secret of the Golden Flower* (New York: Harcourt Brace Jovanovich, 1962). [YUASA Yasuo and SADATAKA Akio, trans., *Ōgon no hana no himitsu* (Kyoto: Jinmon Shoin, 1980).] (The translation by YUASA Yasuo and SADAKATA Akio is useful because it corrects numerous mistakes found in the English translation of *The Secret.*—TRANS.

22. Genshin (942–1017) wrote this piece when he was forty-four years old. When it was sent to Sung China, it attracted many followers. In Japan, it established a foundation for the development of Pure Land Buddhism during the Kamakura period (1185–1333). The book advocates the *Dhyāni-Amitābha Sūtra* as the main vehicle for salvation. Its realistic depiction of various hells are valuable for studying the depth-psychological structure of the psyche as reflective of the time in which Genshin lived.—TRANS.

23. YUASA Yasuo and SADAKATA Akio, trans., *Ōgon no hana no himitsu* [The Secret of the Golden Flower] (Kyoto: Jinmon Shoin, 1980), 150.

24. The reader might like to take note of Yuasa's qualification that the flow of *Ki* specified in this paragraph pertains to an *ordinary* state. Apparently, there are some people whose "ordinary" flow is the reverse of the majority of the cases.—TRANS.

25. According to MIYUKI Mokusen's interpretation, cited in YUASA Yasuo and SADAKATA Akio, trans., *Ōgun no hanano himitsu* [The Secret of the Golden Flower] (Kyoto: Jinbun Shoin, 1980), 270, the phrase *enchū* [*yuánzhōng*] is conjectured to be an abbreviation for *engichūddō,* that is, relational co-arising is the middle way. Yuasa interprets the phrase "*enchū*" as "the ultimate arrested in the midst of flow-

ing phenomena." See YUASA, *Ōgun no hanano himitsu* [The Secret of the Golden Flower] (Kyoto: Jinbun Shoin, 1980), 174. According to the original, the mind/heart must be connected to both *enchū* [*yuánzhōng*] and *chūkō* [*zhōnghuáng*] during meditation.—TRANS.

26. YUASA Yasuo and SADAKATA Akio, trans., *Ōgon no hana no himitsu* [The Secret of the Golden Flower] (Kyoto: Jinmon Shoin, 1980), 183.

27. Ibid., 182.

28. Ibid., 183.

29. Ibid. 185.

30. This work was written by Vasubandhu (420–500) and is a chief treatise of the Sarvastivadin school which divides the elements of existence into seventy-five categories. This school of Buddhism claims the reality of these elements.—TRANS.

31. This text was edited by Kuichi (632–682), a prominent disciple of Xuánzhuàng, and belongs to the Chinese "Consciousness-Only" school which maintains that the only thing there *is*, or that is real, in the world is "consciousness."—TRANS.

32. YUASA Yasuo and SADAKATA Akio, trans., *Ōgon no hana no himitsu* [The Secret of the Golden Flower] (Kyoto: Jinmon Shoin, 1980), 165. This experience marks a turning point in meditation. "Something" that is referred to in the previous sentence designates a supersensory being. Its existence is experienced outside of what we ordinarily understand by being, which is captured through our external sensory perception and its intellectual abstraction.—TRANS.

33. Ibid.

34. According to Early Buddhism and the Buddhist schools following it, a human being is said to be composed of five aggregates (*skandhas*): matter, sensation, perception, mental formations, and consciousness. The five aggregates, taken together, are the psychosomatic constituents of a human being. In light of this idea, the five demons of the *skandhas* indicate psychosomatic disorders, with their accompanying images and pains designated as "the five demons."—TRANS.

35. The record of Xuánzhuàng is found in the biography of Jion, *Taitō daijionji sanzō hōshiden* [A Biography of Dharma Master Sanzō of Jionji Temple of the Great T'ang]. NAGASAWA Kazutoshi, trans., *Genjō Sanzō* [Xuánzhuàngsānzāng] (Tokyo: Kōfūsha, 1985), 17.

36. For various aspects of hallucinatory experience, see OGINO Kōichi, *Bunka seishiu igaku nyūmon* [An Introduction to Cultural Psychiatry] (Tokyo: Seiwa Shoten, 1979), chap. 5.

37. Eugène Minkowski, *La Schizophrénie: Psychopathologie des Schizoïdes et des Schizophrènes* (Paris: Payot, 1927; 2nd ed., Paris: Desclée de Brouwer, 1953).

38. YUASA Yasuo and SADAKATA Akio, trans., *Ōgun no hana no himsitsu* [The Secret of the Golden Flower] (Kyoto: Jinmon Shoin, 1980), 194.

39. Ibid., 205.

40. Ibid., 206.

41. Ibid., 205.

42. Ibid., 210.

43. Ibid., 219.

44. C. G. Jung, "Psychological Commentary to the Tibetan Book of the Great Liberation," in *Psychology and the East* (Princeton: Princeton University Press, 1978), par. 768.

CHAPTER 4. *KI* AND THE BODY IN EASTERN MEDICINE

1. Concerning the fundamentals of the Eastern medicine, I have relied much on NAGAHAMA Yoshio's *Tōyō igaku gaisetsu* [An Outline of Eastern Medicine] (Osaka: Sōgensha, 1982).

2. *Zō* and *fu* both mean storage. Acupuncture medicine usually counts five solid viscera and six hollow viscera; the former includes the liver, the heart, the spleen-pancreas, the lungs, and the kidneys, whereas the latter includes the gall bladder, the small intestine, the stomach, the large intestine, the urinary bladder, and the triple heater. Although some of these names correspond to the names of viscera given by Western medicine, these organs may be thought of as a functional unit working in connection with the twelve major meridians. See figure 4.1.—TRANS.

3. For a detailed explanation of holography, see Yuasa's commentary included in *Nyū saiensu to ki no kagaku* [New Age Science and the Science of *Ki*], ed. YUASA Yasuo and TAKEMOTO Tadao (Tokyo: Seidosha, 1987). This is the third volume in a five-volume series entitled *Kagaku gijutsu to seishin sekai* [Science, Technology, and the Spiritual World].

4. NAKAYAMA Shigeru, ed., *Jōsefu Niidamu no sekai* [The World of Joseph Needham] (Tokyo: Nihon Chiikishakai Kenkyūjo, 1988), 126.

5. What is rendered here as "living body" can alternately be translated as "living organism," and the corresponding Japanese term is "*seitai*," which consists of two characters, "to live" and "body." In a biological sense, "living organism" is probably a better translation for "*seitai*," since it encompasses a wider range of phenomena than the living body.—TRANS.

6. *Yu* in *yuketsu* means "to transport."—TRANS. See, for example, Lu Gwei-Djen and Joseph Needham, *Celestial Lancets: A History and Rationale of Acupuncture and Moxa* (New York: Columbia University Press, 1980), 12, 62.

7. *Bo* in *boketsu* means "to gather or collect," so the term may be translated as "gathering acu-point." As explained in the text, this acu-point gathers the *ki*-energy of the viscera.—TRANS.

8. A *genketsu* is a primary acu-point and is considered a source of *ki*-energy. Each of the twelve meridians have this acu-point, and so there are twelve *genketsu* or primary acu-points throughout the human body. One half of these primary acu-points are located around the wrist and the other half around the ankle.—TRANS.

9. *Seiketsu* literally means the opening of a well.—TRANS.

10. Yuasa mentions Ernest Mach as a Western philosopher who has held a similar idea. See David E. Shaner, NAGATOMO Shigenori, and YUASA YASUO, *Science and Comparative Philosophy: Introducing YUASA YASUO* (Leiden, Holland: E. J. Brill, 1989), 262–63.—TRANS.

11. For an explanation of the relationship between macrocosm and microcosm using the body as a key concept, while also taking into account mythology and cultivation methods, see my essay "Cosmic Nature of the Body," in *Shintai, kankaku, seishin* [The Body, Sensation, and Spirit], vol. 9 in the series *Shin Iwanami kōza: Tetsugaku* (Tokyo: Iwanami Shoten, 1986).

12. See, for example, *The Yellow Emperor's Inner Book,* a classic on acupuncture medicine written in the Han dynasty period.

13. For a more detailed account, see YUASA Yasuo, *Ki towa nanika* [What is *Ki?*] (Tokyo: NHK Press, 1991).

14. NAGAHAMA Yoshio and MARUYAMA Masao, *Keiryaku no kenkyū* [A study of meridians] (Tokyo: Kyōrin Shoin, 1950); and NAGAHAMA Yoshio, *Harikyū no igaku* [Acupuncture Medicine] (Osaka: Sōgensha, 1983), 159.

15. This was pointed out to me by Dr. MARUYAMA Toshiaki. Translations into Chinese of the joint work of NAGAHAMA Yoshio and MARUYAMA Masao, *Keiraku no kenkyū* [A Study of Meridians], as well as of Nagahama's *Harikyū no igaku* [Acupuncture Medicine], have facilitated contemporary research in traditional medicine in China under the slogan of "the unification of Chinese and Western medicine."

16. See MOTOYAMA Hiroshi, *Keiraku: zōkinō sokutei ni tsuite* [Measurement of the Function of the Meridians and Visceral Organs] (Tokyo: Shūkyō Shinri Shuppan, 1974), and *Kino nagare no sokutei: shindan to chiryō* [Measurement of *Ki* Flow: Its Diagnosis and Therapy] (Tokyo: Shūkyō Shinri Shuppan, 1985).

17. For a detailed explanation of Henry Head's "body scheme," see SEIGANJI Hiromichi, "*Shintai imeiji*" [Body Image] and DAITŌ Shōkō, "*Shintai zushiki*" [Body Scheme], both contained in Iwanami kōza 4—*Shintai to seishin: seishin no kagaku* [Iwanami kōza 4—The Body and the Spirit: Science of Spirit] (Tokyo: Iwanami shoten).

18. Maurice Merleau-Ponty, *Phénoménologie de la Perception* (Paris: Librairie Gallimard, 1945), 114.

19. Ibid., 142.

20. This is a case Merleau-Ponty deals with in his *Phenomenology of Perception* to contend that motile intentionality is more primary than visual perception. The patient Schneider was suffering from damage in the occipital region of his neoencephalon. He had difficulty in recognizing the shape of a thing through visual perception, but once he was allowed to trace the figure with his finger, he could recognize it. See Merleau-Ponty, *Phenomenology of Perception* (London: Routledge & Kegan Paul, 1962), 103.—TRANS.

21. YAMATORI Shigeru, *Nō kara mita kokoro* [The Mind Seen From the Brain] (Tokyo: NHK Books, 1985), 22ff.

CHAPTER 5. THE SCIENCE OF *KI*

1. VA in VA 8 stands for the vascular meridian and the number 8 specifies the acupoint on this meridian. It is called "*láogōng*" in Chinese and is located "between the second and the third metacarpal bones, where the tip of the middle finger touches when the fist is clenched, perpendicularly." See Louise Oftedal Wensel, *Acupuncture for Americans* (Reston, Va.: Reston Publishing Company, 1980), 36–37.—TRANS.

2. GB 33 is an abbreviation for the gall bladder meridian and the number 33 indicates the location of an acu-point. It is called "*yángguān*" in Chinese and is located in "the depression above the lateral condyle of the femur." See ibid., 40–41.—TRANS.

3. Gù Hánsēn and Lín Hoùshěng, [The Results of Initial Experiments in the Physical Foundation for Investigating the Transmission of *Ki* External Emission Treatment] in Qián Xuésēn et al., *Chuangjian rentikexue* [Establishing Somatic Science] (Szechwan: Szechwan Educational Press, 1989), 393ff.

4. Gù Hánsēn, "Dī Pín Peng Xìn xī shí yàn" [Experiment on magnetic information in low frequency] in Qián Xuésēn et al., *Chuàngjiàn réntikēxué* [Establishing Somatic Science] (Sìchuān: Sìchuān Educational Press, 1989), 393ff.

5. Br 20 is an abbreviation for the brain meridian, and the number 20 indicates the location of an acu-point. It is called in Chinese "*bǎihùi*" and is located "at the middle of the occipital scalp." See Louise Oftedal Wensel, *Acupuncture for Americans* (Reston, Va.: Reston Publishing Company, 1980), 46–47.

6. Concerning the details of this research performed in China and Japan, see YUASA Yasuo, *Ki towa nanika* [What is *Ki*?] (Tokyo: NHK Books, 1991).

7. SHINAGAWA Yoshiya, "Ki to imēji" [*Ki* and Image] in *Ki to ningen kagaku* [*Ki* and Human Science], ed. YUASA Yasuo (Tokyo: Hirakawa Shuppan, 1990).

8. The brain waves are divided into the α wave, β wave, δ wave, and Θ wave depending on the frequency of waves per second. Their frequency is as follows: the α wave is 8–13 hertz/sec, the β wave is 14–30 hertz/sec, the δ wave is 1–4 hertz/sec, and the Θ wave is 4–8 hertz/sec. The β wave is further divided into β_1 (14–20 hertz/sec) and β_2 (over 20 hertz/sec). The α wave often appears in a restful state when the eyes are closed and also is most easily detectable in seated meditation. The β wave is often obtained in a waking state when the eyes are open. The δ wave is often associated with a deep sleep state, but can also be observed when there is a dysfunction in consciousness. The Θ wave usually accompanies a sleep state as well as a special state of meditation. See YUASA Yasuo, *Ki towa nanika* [What is *Ki*?] (Tokyo: NHK Books, 1991), 21.—TRANS.

9. See note 8.—TRANS.

10. See note 8.—TRANS.

11. YUASA Yasuo, *Yungu to tōyō* [Jung and the East] (Kyoto: Jinmon Shoin, 1989), vol. 1, chap. 1.

CHAPTER 6. *KI* AND PARANORMAL PHENOMENA

1. Qián Xuésēn and Chén Xìn, "Jintai kagaku no teishō: jintai kagaku wa gendai kagakugijitsu no ichidaibumon dearu" [A proposal for Somatic Science: One Great Field in Contemporary Science and Technology], in YUASA Yasuo, ed., *Ki to ningen kagaku* [*Ki* and Human Science] (Tokyo: Hirakawa Shuppan, 1990).

2. For the psychophysiological relationship between psi-energy and *ki*-energy as they relate to *cakras,* meridians, and psychokinesis, see MOTOYAMA Hiroshi, *The Correlation between Psi Energy and Ki* (Tokyo: Human Science Press, 1991).—TRANS.

3. Hè Chóngyín, "Seimei kagaku o tankyūsuru" [Inquiry into Life science] in *Shūkyō to chōshinri* [Religion and Parapsychology], (Tokyo: Shn̄kyō Shinri Suppan, 198) vol. 23.

4. Blood in the compound "*ki*-blood" includes in Chinese medicine the bodily fluid. —TRANS.

5. The "studies of Jung's psychology" which Yuasa mentions here are seen in the two volumes of *Yungu to kiristokyō* [Jung and Christianity] and *Yungu to yōrōpaseishin* [Jung and European Spirituality], both printed through Jinmon Shoin, respectively in 1978 and 1979. His studies of Jung's psychology, however, culminate in the two volumes of *Yungu to Tōyō* [Jung and the East] published by Jinmon Shoin in 1989.—TRANS.

6. In addition to *Shintai: Tōtōteki shinshin ron no kokoromi* [The Body: Toward an Eastern Body-Mind Theory], Yuasa wrote during this time: *Kodaijin no seishin sekai* (The Spiritual World of the Ancient People] (Kyoto: Minerva Shobō, 1980); *Nihonjin no shūkyōishiki* [Japanese Religious Consciousness] (Tokyo: Meicho Kankōkai, 1981); and *Tōyōbunka no shinsō* [The Deep Layers of Eastern Culture] (Tokyo: Meicho Kankōkai, 1982).—TRANS.

7. Sūn Mèngyín et al., "2000 km hanareta kōbo RNA yōeki ni taisuru kikō gaiki no sayō" [The Function of External Emission of *Ki*-energy on RNA Yeast Dissolvant from the Distance of 2,000 Kilometers], in SHINAGAWA Yoshiya, ed., *Kino chōsen* [The Challenge of *Ki*] (Tokyo: Midori Shobō, 1990).

8. See the translator's introduction to J. B. Rhine and J. G. Pratt's *Parapsychology* [*Chōshinrigaku gaisetsu*], YUASA Yasuo and MOTOYAMA Hiroshi, trans. (Tokyo: Shūkyō Shinri Shuppan, 1964).

9. KASAHARA Toshio, *Chōshinrigaku hando bukku* [A handBook for Parapsychology] (Tokyo: Burēn Shuppan, 1989).

10. H. M. Collins and T. J. Pinch, *Frames of Meaning: The Social Construction of Extraordinary Science* (Boston: Routledge & Kegan Paul, 1982).

11. YUKAWA Hideki (1907–81) was a Japanese physicist who won a Nobel Prize in 1949.—TRANS.

12. Concerning the personal contacts between Jung and Rhine, see YUASA Yasuo, *Yungu to Tōyō* [Jung and the East] (Kyoto: Jinmon Shoin, 1989), vol. 2, chap. 6.

CHAPTER 7. TOWARD AN EAST-WEST DIALOGUE

1. W. Pauli, "Muishiki no kannenno shizenkagakutei ninshikironteki sokumen" [The concept of the Unconscious in its Natural-scientific, Epistemological Aspect] in *Butsuri to ninshiki* [Physics and Epistemology] (Tokyo: Kōdansha, 1975).

2. For a theoretical investigation of this issue, see my paper "Contemporary Science and an Eastern Mind-Body Theory" in *Science and Comparative Philosophy: Introducing* YUASA YASUO, edited by David E. Shaner, S. Nagatomo, and YUASA Yasuo (Leiden: J. E. Brill, 1989), part IV.

3. Yuasa seems to suggest here more than what phenomenologists claim in respect to the active meaning-bestowing function of intentionality. An example would be the Kegon concept of "non-obstruction between thing-events," or more positively, "interfusion between thing-events." This idea presupposes an intentional generation of synchronistic phenomena by de-intentionalizing conscious activities.—TRANS.

4. See Jung's "Synchronicity: An Acausal Connecting Principle," in C. G. Jung and W. Pauli, *The Interpretation of Nature and the Psyche* (New York: Bollingen Series, 1955).

5. C. G. Jung, foreword to *Abegg: Osten Denkt Anders,* CW, vol. 18, para. 1483. For Jung's idea concerning the *Yìjīng,* see "Eki to gendai" [The *Yìjīng* and the contemporary Period] in YUASA Yasuo, *Tōyōteki meisōh no shinrigaku* [A Psychology of Eastern Meditation] (Tokyo: Sōgensha, 1984).

6. For example, M. L. von Franz, *Zahl und Zeit: Psychologische Überlegungen zu einer Annährung von Tiefenpsychologie u. Physik* (Stuttgart, 1970; J. S. Bolen, *The Tao of Psychology* (New York: Harper & Row, 1979); "Synchronicité: Correspondance du psychique et du physique," and "Synchronicité: un order acausal," *Cahier de psychologie Jungienne,* 28 and 29 (1981).

7. See my monograph, "Kyōjisei towa nanika" [What is Synchronicity?] (Tokyo: Sanō Shuppan, 1987).

8. SUZUKI Yūjirō, *Ekikiyō,* vol. 2 (Tokyo: Shūeisha, 1974), 368.

POSTSCRIPT

1. An insertion by the translators.—TRANS.

GLOSSARY

Japanese Reading	Characters	Chinese Reading
ABE Masao	阿部 正雄	Abù Zhèngxióng
aikidō	合気道	héqìdào
ajikan	阿字観	azìguāng
Amidabutsu	阿弥陀仏	Amítuófó
AWA Kenzō	阿波 研造	Abō Yánzào
ba	場	chăng
basho	場所	chángsuŏ
bo	募	mù
boketsu	募穴	mùxué
bōkōkei	膀胱経	pángguāngjīng
bu	武	wŭ
budō	武道	wŭdào
bunburyōdō	文武両道	wénwūliăngdào
Bunka seishinigaku nyūmon	文化精神医学入門	*Wénhuàjīngshéng yīxué rùmén*
Bunka to ningenkeisei	文化と人間形成	*Wēnhuà hé rénjiāndēxíngchéng*
bunkan	文官	wénguān
bushi	武士	wŭshì
bushidō	武士道	wŭshìdào
busshō	仏性	fóxìng
Butsuri to ninshiki	物理と認識	*Wŭli hè rènshí*
buttai	物体	wùtǐ
byakugō	白毫	baíháo
byakugōkan	白毫 観	báiháoguān
chi	血	xuĕ
Chigi	智顗	Zhì Yì
Chikubashō	竹馬抄	Zhúmăchāo
CHIN Shin	陳 信	Chén Xìn
CHIN Shuryō	陳 守良	Chén Shoŭliáng
chōki	調気	tiăoqì
Chōshinrigaku gaisetsu	超心理学概説	*Chāoxīnglĭxué gàishuō*
Chōshinrigaku handobukku	超心理学 ハンドブック	*Chāoxīnglíxué shoucè*
chūin	中院	zhōngyuàn
chūkan	中関	zhōngguān
chūō	中黄	zhōnghuáng
daichōkei	大腸経	dàchángjīng
daimoku	題目	tímù
Daitō daijionji sanzōhōshiden	大唐大慈恩寺三蔵法師伝	*Dàtáng dàcíēnsì sānzuàn fashītán*
Daitōseiikiki	大唐西域記	*Dàtáng xīyùjì*

DAITŌ Shōkō	大東　祥孝	Dàdōng Xiángxiào
danchū	壇中	tánzhōng
darani	陀羅尼	tuóluóní
Denshūroku	伝習録	*Duànxílù*
dō	道	dào
Dōgen (1200-1253)	道元	Dàoyuán
dōin	導引	dàoyǐn
dōkō	動功	dònggōng
dokusho zanmai	読書三昧	dúshūsānweì
Dōtokugakusha	道徳学社	Dàodéxuéshè
Dōtokukyō	道徳経	*Dàodéjīng*
Edo jidai	江戸時代	Jiānghù shídài
Eigamonogatari	栄華物語	*Rónghuáwùyǔ*
Eisai (1141-1215)	栄西	Róngxī
Ekikyō	易経	*Yìjīng*
Emyōkyō	慧命経	*Huìmìngjīng*
enchū	縁中	yuánzhōng
engichūdō	縁起中道	yuánqǐzhōngdào
Enno Ozunu	役　小角	Yì Xiǎojiǎo
Enryakuji	延暦寺	Yánlìsī
fu	腑	fǔ
fudō	不動	búdòng
Fudōchishinmyōroku	不動智神妙録	*Búdòngzhìshénmiàolù*
fudōmyōō	不動明王	búdòngmíngwáng
FUJII Aiko	藤井　愛子	Téngjǐng Azi
Fujisan	富士山	Fùshìshān
FUJIWARA Shunzei (1114-1204)	藤原　俊成	Téngyuán Jùnchéng
fukuki	服気	fúqì
futon	布団	bù tuán
gachirinkan	月輪観	yuèlúnguān
gaikai kankakuundō kairo	外界感覚運動回路	wàijiègánjuéyùndònghuílù
gaiki	外気	wàiqì
gaikikō	外気功	wàiqìgōng
gaku	学	xué
GA Sūin	賀　崇寅	Hè Chóngyín
genketsu	原穴	yuánxué
Genjō	玄奘	Xuánzhuàng
genjōkōan	現成公案	xiànchénggōngàn
Genjōsanzō	玄奘　三蔵	Xuánzhuàngsānzàng
Genshin	源信	Yuánxìn
genshin	元神	yuánshén
GEN Shin	厳　新	Yán Xīn
gotaitōchirei	五体投地礼	wǔtǐtoúdìlǐ
gyō	行	xíng
Hagakure	葉隠	*Yèyǐn*
hakkikei	八奇経	bāqíjīng
haikei	肺経	fèijīng
haiku	俳句	páijù
HAKEDA Yoshito	ハケダ　ヨシト	
haku	魄	pō
hana	華	huá
hanchūkakinō	範疇化機能	fànchóuhuàjīnéng

hanshū zanmai	般舟三昧	Bānzhōusānwèi
hanshū zanmaikyō	般舟三昧経	*Bānzhōusānwèijĭng*
HARA Minoru	原　実	Yuán Shí
Harikyūno igaku	針灸の医学	*Zhēnjiūdēyĭxuè*
Harikyūno kenkyū	針灸の研究	*Zhēnjiūdēyánjiù*
Heikemonogatari	平家物語	*Píngjiāwùyŭ*
Heian jidai	平安時代	Píngān shídài
Heian bukkyō	平安仏教	Píngānfójĭào
Heihō kadensho	兵法家伝書	*Pĭngfăjiāzuànshū*
hen	変	piàn
hen shin	偏心	piānxin
hi	非	feĭ
hi	火	huŏ
hibiki	響き	xiăng
Hieizan	比叡山	Bíruìshān
hikei	碑経	pĭjĭng
HIRAI Tomio	平井　富夫	Píngjĭng Fùfū
Hokekyō	法華経	*Făhuájĭng*
honzennosei	本然の性	bĕnrándēxìng
honshin	本心	bĕnxĭn
honraino memboku	本来の面目	bĕnláidĕmiànmù
HOSHINO Minoru	星野　稔	Xĭngyĕ Niàn
Hōzō	法蔵	Făzhàng
hyakue	百会	baihùi
i	意	yì
ICHIKAWA Hakugen	市川　白絃	Shìchuān Báixián
igozanmai	囲碁三昧	weíqísānwèi
ikei	胃経	wèijĭng
Imagawajō	今川状	*Jĭnchuānzhuàng*
i mitsu	意密	yìmì
in	印	yìn
in	陰	yĭn
inki	陰気	yĭnqì
inmasō	陰魔相	yĭnmóxiāng
inyō	陰陽	yĭnyáng
inochi	いのち	mìng
Ippen (1239-89)	一遍	Yibiàn
ittennoshinyō	一点の眞陽	yidiāndezhēnyáng
jibutsu	事物	shìwù
Jikaku Ennin (794-854)	慈覚円仁	Cíjué Dānrén
jinkei	腎経	shènjĭng
Jionden	慈恩伝	*Cíēnzuàn*
jō	静	jìng
jōchū kenbutsu	定中見仏	dìngzhōngjiànfó
jōdō honnō kairo	情動本能回路	qíngdòngbénnénghuílù
Jōyuishikiron	成唯識論	*Chéngwéishìlùn*
jōgyō zanmai	常行三昧	chángxíngsānwèi
jōgyō zanmaidō	常行三昧堂	chángxíngsānwèitáng
jūdō	柔道	roúdào
jūjutsu	柔術	roúshù
Jūjutsuhiden	柔術秘伝	*Roúshùmìzuàn*
jūniseikei	十二正経	shíèrzhèngjĭng
junsui keiken	純粋経験	chúngcuìjĭngyàn
jōzazanmai	常坐三昧	chángzuòsānwèi

junyō 純陽 chúnyáng

kadō 歌道 gēdào
kaihōgyō 回峰行 huífēngxíng
kaikō 回光 huíguāng
kaikōbiken 回光微験 huíguāngweīyàn
kaikōchōsoku 回光調息 huíguāngtiáoxī
kaikōkappō 回光活法 huíguānghuófǎ
kaikōsabyū 回光差繆 huíguāngchāimiù
kaikōshuchū 回光守中 huíguāngshóuzhōng
Kamakura jidai 鎌倉時代 Liáncāngshídài
KAMIYA カミヤ
KAN'AMI Motokiyo 観阿弥 元清 Guānamí Yuánqīng
kan 貫 guàn
kan 欠 kǎn
kankakukairo 感覚回路 gánjuéhuílú
kankei 肝経 gānjīng
kanshō 関衝 guānchōng
kansui 欠水 kǎnshǔi
kantoku 感得 gǎndé
karada からだ shēngtǐ
karate 空手 kōngshǒu
KASAHARA Toshio 笠原 敏雄 Lìyuán Mǐngxiǒng
KASAMATSU Akira 笠松 章 Lisōng Zhāng
katsujinken 活人剣 huórénjiàn
Katsuragawa 葛川 Gěchuān
kawa 河 hé
KAWAI Hayao 河合 隼雄 Héhē Zhǔnxióng
KAWASE Ken'ichi 川瀬 健一 Chuānlài Jiànyī
Kegon bukkyō 華厳仏教 Huàyánfójiào
keijijōgaku 形而上学 xíngérshàngxué
keijijōsha 形而上者 xíngershàngzhě
keiko 稽古 jìgǔ
keirakubinkanjin 経絡敏感人 jīngluòmǐnggǎnrěn
keirakunaizōkei 経絡内臓系 jīngluònèizàngxì
Keirakuno kenkyū 経絡の研究 *Jīngluòdeyánjiū*
Keiraku: Zōkikinōsokutei nitsuite 経洛絡：臓器機能測定について *Jīngluò: Zàngqìjīnēngcèdìng*
kekki 血気 xuěqì
kendō 剣道 jiàndào
kenshō 見性 jiànxìng
ketsubon 欠盆 qiànpén
ketsuin 厥 陰 juéyīn
ki 器 qì
ki 気 qì
kikai 気海 qìhǎi
kikei 奇経 qíjīng
kikō 気功 qìgōng
kikōshi 気功師 qìgōngshī
Kinochōsen 気の挑戦 *Qìdetiǎozhàn*
Kinonagare to sokutei: Shindan to chiryō 気の流れと測定：診断と治療 *Qìliúhécèdìng: Zhenbduànhé zhìliáo*
Kinseishoki jitsugakushiso no kenkyū 近世初期実学思想の研究 *Jìnshìchūqīměixǔesī xiǎngyánjiū*
kinyoku 禁欲 jìnyù
Ki no shisō 気の思想 *Qì de sīxiǎng*

Ki: Rongo kara nyū saiensu made	気：論語からニューサイエンスまで	*Qì: cóng luènyǔdàoxīng shídài kēxué*
kishitsunosei	気質の性	qìzhìdexìng
Ki to ningenkagaku	気と人間科学	*Qì hé rénjiānkēxuè*
Kitowa nanika	気とは何か	*Shéměshìqì*
kizuki	気付き	
kobudō	古武道	gǔwúdào
Kobōdaishi Kūkai	弘法大師空海	Hóngfádàshī Kōnghǎi
Kodai bukkyō	古代仏教	gǔdàifójiào
Kodaijin no seishinsekai	古代人の精神世界	*Gǔdàiréndé jīngshénshìjīè*
kōiteki chokkan	行為的直観	xíngwéidezhíguān
KO Kanshin	顧　涵森	Gù Hánsēn
kōki	行気	xíngqì
kokoro	こころ	xīn
kon	魂	hún
konchin	昏沈	hūnchén
Kōteidaikyō	黄帝内経	*Huángdìnèijīng*
Koten indo no kugyō	古典インドの苦行	*Gǔdiǎnyìndùdekǔxíng*
Kōyasan	高野山	Gāoyeshān
ku	口	kǒu
kū	空	kōng
kugyō	苦行	kǔxíng
kufū	功夫	gōngfū
kumitsu	口密	kǒumì
KUROKI Mikio	黒木　幹夫	Heīmù Gànfū
Kusharon	倶舎論	*Jùshělùn*
kyakkanshugitekikagaku	客観主義的科学	kèguānzhúyìdekēxué
kyakutaitekishintai	客体的身体	kètídeshēnti
Kyōjiseitowa nanika	共時性とは何か	*Shéměshìgòngshìxìng*
Kyōzen gokokuron	興禅護国論	*Xìngchánhùguólùn*
majikyō	魔事境	móshìjìng
Makashikan	摩訶止観	*Móhēzhǐguān*
MARUYAMA Masao	丸山　昌夫	Wánshān Chāngfū
MARUYAMA Toshiaki	丸山　敏秋	Wánshān Mǐngqiū
meisōkikō	瞑想気功	míngxiǎngqìgōng
meisōhō	瞑想法	míngxiǎngfǎ
michi	道	dào
Mikkyō	密教	Mìjiào
Mikkyo to nihonbunka	密教と日本文化	*Mìjiào hé rìbénwénhuà*
MINAMOTO Ryōen	源　了円	Yuán Liǎoyuán
mitsu	密	mì
MIYUKI Mokusen	目幸　黙遷	Mùxìng Mòqiān
mizu	水	shǔi
mono	もの	wù
mōshin	妄心	wàngxīn
MOTOYAMA Hiroshi	本山　博	Bénshān Bó
muga	無我	wúwǒ
muishikitekijunshintai	無意識的準身体	wúyìshīdezhǔnshēntǐ
mujūchibonnō	無住地煩悩	wúzhùdefánnǎo
munen musō	無念無想	wúniànwúxiǎng
MU Fūkin	牟　風芹	Mù Fēngqín
Muromachi jidai	室町時代	Shidīng shídài
mushin	無心	wúxín
mushin munen no kurai	無心無念の位	wúxínwúniàndewèi
Myōe (1173-1232)	明恵	Mínghùi

Myōe: Yume o ikiru	明恵：夢を生きる	*Mínghùi:Mèngrúshēn*
Myōōin	明王院	Míngwángyuàn
naizōkeirakukei	内臓経絡系	nèizàngjīngluòxì
NAGAHAMA Yoshio	長浜　善夫	Chángbāng Shànfū
NAGASAWA Kazutoshi	長澤　知俊	Chángzhé Héjùn
naikikō	内気功	nèiqìgōng
naitan	内丹	nèidān
NAKAYA Yoshio	中谷　義雄	Zhōnggǔ Yìxióng
NAKAYAMA Shigeru	中山　茂	Zhōngshān Mào
namuamidabutsu	南無阿弥陀仏	nānwúamítuófó
nanmyōhōrengekkyō	南無妙法蓮華経	*Nānwúmiàofǎliánhúajīng*
nankikō	軟気功	ruǎnqìgōng
nara bukkyō	奈良　仏教	nàiliángfójiào
nenbutsu	念仏	niànfó
Nihonjinno shūkyōishiki	日本人の宗教意識	*Rìběnréndezhōngjiàoyìshī*
ninmyaku	任脈	rènmài
NISHI Amane	西　周	Xī Zhoū
NISHIDA Kitarō	西田　幾多郎	Xītián Jǐduoláng
NISHIHONGANJI Hiromichi	西本願時　弘道	Xībényuànsì Hóngtōng
NISHITANI Keiji	西谷　啓二	Xīgǔ Qǐ èr
nō	能	néng
nōgaku	能楽	néngyuè
Nyūsaiensu to kinokagaku	ニューサイエンスと気の科学	*Xīnshídàikēxué hé qìkēxuè*
obon	お盆	pén
odori nenbutsu	踊り念仏	yǒng niànfó
OGINO Koichi	荻野　恒一	Díye Héngyī
Ōgonno hananohimitsu	黄金の華の秘密	*Huángjīnzhīhuádèmìmì*
Ōjōyōshū	往生要集	*Wangshēngyàojí*
ONOZAWA Seiichi	小野沢　精一	Xīǎoyězhé Jīngyī
Ō Yōmei	王陽明	Wáng Yángmíng
renga	連歌	liángē
rentan	練丹	liàndān
ri	理	lǐ
ri	離	lí
RI Jichin	李　時珍	Lǐ Shízhēng
rika	離火	líhuǒ
Rinzai	臨済	Línjì
riki	理気	lǐqì
Rikyū	利休	Lìxiū
RIN Kōshō	林　厚省	Lín Hoùshěng
RO Keichin	魯　桂珍	Lu Guìzhēng
rokkō	六候	liùhoù
rokuki	六期	liùqī
rōkyu	労宮	láogōng
rōzan gyō	籠山行	lóngshānxíng
ryōdōkei	良導経	liángdǎoluò
RYŪ Kinshō	劉　錦宗	Liú Jíngzhōng
SADAKATA Akio	定方　昭夫	Dìngfāng Zhāofū
sadō	茶道	cádào
Saichō	m门澄	Zuìchéng

sanka	三河	sānhé
sanmitsu	三密	sānmì
sanran	散乱	sǎnluàn
sanshōkei	三焦経	sānjiāojīng
sanshōyu	三焦兪	sānjiāoyù
satori	悟り	wù
satsujinken	殺人剣	shārénjiàn
sei	精	jīng
sei	性	xìng
seikatanden	臍下丹田	qíxiàdāntián
seikei	正経	zhèngjīng
seiketsu	井穴	jǐngxuè
seiki	精気	jīngqì
seikō	性光	xìngguāng
seikō	静功	jìnggōng
seimei	生命	shēnmìng
seishitekimeisō	静止的瞑想	jìngzhídemǐngxiǎng
seitai	生体	shēntǐ
seiza	静坐	jìngzuò
SEKIGUCHI Shindai	関口　真大	Guānkoǔ Zhēndà
sekimon	石門	shíméng
sekishō	石衝	shíchōng
SEN Gakushin	銭　学森	Qián Xuésēn
Sengoku jidai	戦国時代	Zhànguóshídài
SHA Chōki	謝　朝暉	Xiè Zhāohūi
shikishin	識神	shìshén
shin	心	xīn
shin	神	shén
shin	身	shēn
SHINAGAWA Yoshiya	品川　嘉也	Pǐnchuān Jiāyě
shingon	真言	zhēnyán
shinshin datsuraku	心身脱落	shēnxīn tuōluò
shinjinjutai	真人受胎	zhēnrénshòutai
shinka	神火	shénhuǒ
shinkei	心経	xinjīng
shinki	神鬼	shéngŭi
shinki	神気	shénqì
shinkiicchi	心気一致	xīnqìyízhì
shinmitsu	身密	shēnmì
shinpōkei	心包経	xīnbāojīng
Shinran (1173-1262)	親鸞	Qīnluán
shinshin gyōnen	身心凝念	shēnxīnnínglìan
shinshin ichinyo	身心一如	shēnxìnyīrú
shintaikankaku	身体　感覚	shēntǐ gǎnjué
Shintai kankau seishin	身体　感覚　精神	*Shēntǐ gǎnjué jīngshén*
Shintai to seishin	身体と精神	*Shēntǐ héjīngshén*
Shintai:Tōyōteki shinshinron no kokoromi	身体：東洋的心身論の試み	*Shēntǐ: Dōngyángdexīnshēn shìlùn*
shintaizushiki	身体図式	shēntǐtúshì
shinyō	真陽	zhēnyáng
shitaifu	士太夫	shìdàfū
shizentai	自然体	zìrántǐ
Shōbōgenzō	正法眼蔵	Zhèngfǎyǎnzàng
shobutsufudōchi	諸仏不動智	zhūfóbúdòngzhì
shōchōkei	少腸経	xīǎochángjīng
shōin	少陰	shàoyīn

shōshin	正心	zhèngxīn
shoshūten	少周天	xiǎozhoūtiān
shōyō	少陽	shàoyáng
shugendō	修験道	xiūyàndào
shugyō	修行	xiūxíng
shugyōhō	修行法	xīuxíngfǎ
shukanshugitekikagaku	主観主義的科学	zhǔguānzhǔyìdekéxué
Shūkō	秋江	Qiūjiāng
Shūkyō to chōshinri	宗教と超心理	*Zhōngjiào hé chāoxīnlǐ*
Shūkyō to shinrigaku	宗教と心理学	*Zhōngjiào hé xīnlixué*
Shushi	朱子	Zhūzǐ
shutai	主体	zhǔtǐ
Sōshi	荘子	Zhuāngzǐ
Sōkenjintaikagaku	創建人体科学	*Chuàngjīànréntikēxué*
SON Mōin	孫 孟寅	Sūn Mèngyín
SO Tōba	蘇 東坡	Sū Dōngpō
Sōtōshu	曹洞宗	Cáodòngzhōng
Sōō (836-918)	相応	Xiàyìng
sūbun keibu	崇文軽武	chóngwénqīngwǔ
sui	水	shǔi
sūsokukan	数息観	shǔxīguān
SUZUKI Yūjirō	鈴木 由次朗	Língmù Yoúcìláng
TACHIBANA Takashi	立花 隆	Lìhuá Lóng
taiin	太陰	tàiyīn
Taiheiki	太平記	Tàipíngjì
Taiitsukinkashūshi	太乙金華宗旨	Tàiyǐjīnhuázhōngzhǐ
taikyoku	大極	tàijí
taisei naibu kankaku	体性内部感覚	Tǐxìnnèibùgǎnjué
taisoku	胎息	tāixī
taiyō	太陽	tàiyáng
taikyokuken	太極拳	tàijíquán
TAKEMOTO Tadao	竹本 忠雄	Zhúběn Zhongxióng
Takuan (1573-1645)	沢庵	Zhéān
tamashii	魂	hún
tan	丹	dān
TANABE Jōji	田辺 ジョージ	Tiánbiān
tanden	丹田	dāntián
tankei	胆経	dǎnjīng
Tannishō	歎異抄	*Tànyìchāo*
Tendai bukkyō	天台仏教	Tiāntáifójiào
Tendaishōshikan	天台小止観	*Tiāntáixiǎozhǐguān*
tenkō	天光	tiānguāng
tensei	天井	tiānjǐng
tenshin	天心	tiānxīn
tenryō	天膠	tiānjiāo
TERADA Tōru	寺田 透	Sìtián Toù
tokuikōnō	特異功能	tèyìgōngnéng
TOKUGAWA Iëmitsu	徳川 家光	Déchuān Jiāguāng
tokumyaku	督脈	dúmài
tonō	吐納	tǔnà
Tōyōbunkano shinsō	東洋文化の深層	*Dōngyángwénhuàzhīshencéng*
Tōyōigakugaisetsu	東洋医学概説	*Dōngyángyīxuégàishuō*
Tōyōtekimeisōhō	東洋的瞑想法	dōngyángdēmǐngxiǎngfǎ
Uchū kara no kikan	宇宙からの帰還	*Fǎnhúiyǔzoù*

undōkankakukairo	運動感覚回路	yùndònggǎnjuéhúilù
undōkikō	運動気功	yùndòngqìgōng
undōtekimeisō	運動的瞑想	yùndòngdemǐngxiǎng
UNNO Māku	海野 マーク	Hǎiyě
UNNO Taitetsu	海野 タイテツ	Hǎiyě
ushin	有心	yóuxīn
waka	知歌	hégē
wakadarani	知歌陀羅尼	hégetuóloúní
WATANABE Ichirō	渡辺 一郎	Dùbiān yīláng
waza	技	jì
YAGYŪ Munenori (1571-1646)	柳生 宗矩	Liǔshēng Zhōngjù
yamabushi	山伏	shānfú
YAMAMOTO Tsunetomo	山本 常朝	Shānběn Chángcháo
YAMATORI Shigeru	山鳥 重	Shānniǎo Zhòng
yō	陽	yáng
yōkan	陽関	yángguān
yōki	陽気	yángqì
yōmei	陽明	yángmíng
yōshin	陽神	yángshén
yu	兪	yú
YUASA Yasuo	湯浅 泰雄	Tāngqiǎn Tàixióng
yūgen	幽玄	yoūxuán
YUKAWA Hideki	湯川 秀樹	Tāngchuān Xiùshù
yuketsu	兪穴	yúxuè
Yumitozen	弓と禅	*Gong hé chán*
Yumenoki	夢の記	*Mèngzhījì*
Yungu to tōyō	ユングと東洋	*Róng hé dongyang*
Yungu to yōrōppa seishin	ユングとヨーロッパ精神	*Róng é ōuzhōu jīngshen*
zazen	坐禅	zhuòchán
Zazengi	坐禅儀	*Zhuòchányí*
Zeami (1363-1443)	世阿弥	Shíamí
Zeamijūrokubushū	世阿弥十六部集	*Shíamíshíliùbùjí*
zeitakuzanmai	贅沢三昧	aozhésānwèi
Zen	禅	Chán
zenbyō	禅病	chánbìn
zenshinnaibu kankaku	全身内部感覚	quánshēnnèibùgǎnjué
zettaimu	絶対無	juédùiwú
zō	臓	zàng
zōfu	臓腑	zàngfǔ
zui	随	súi

INDEX

Acalanātha, 15, 16, 199n.24
Acupuncture medicine, xii, 99–109
  acu-points, 102–106, 117, 133–134, 205n.7
  view of body, xxii–xxiii, 100–107, 208n.2
  and Western science, 99
Aikidō, 34
Altered states of consciousness (ASC), xiv, 19
Aristotle, 26–27, 175
Asceticism, 97
Autogenic training, 17
Autonomic nervous system, 48–49, 50, 55–58, 60
AWA Kenzō, 74

Bergson, Henri, xxv–xxvi, 43–44, 52, 119–120
  on memory, 123–124, 125, 126–128
  and Merleau-Ponty, 122–123
  on motor-scheme, 122–124, 126–128
Biofeedback, 59–60
Body,
  and cognition, 182
  control of, 25–26, 53–55
  Eastern theory of, 101, 103, 107, 128, 181–182, 186
  and external world, 103, 107, 195n.13
  habitualization of, xxv, 123–128
  and inner-outer distinction, 107
  one's own (*karada*), xx, 72–73, 111, 113, 120, 186
  skin, 107–109

Body circuits, 43–58, 110–111, 118–119
  of coenesthesis, xvi–xvii, 45–47, 49–51, 53–54, 120
  of emotion-instinct, xvii–xviii, 48–49, 50–51, 53–55
  of external sensory-motor, xvi, 43–44, 49–51, 53–54, 55–58, 119–120
  of unconscious quasi-body. *See* Unconscious quasi-body
Bohm, David, xxxiv, 163, 186
Buddha-nature, 33, 81–82
Buddhism, 98. *See also* Esoteric Buddhism; Zen Buddhism
Bushi way. *See* Martial arts

Chén Xìn, 149
Chigi, 11
Cogito, xvi, 45, 120
  bright and dark, 195n.15
Collins, H. J., 159
Complexes, xiv, 18–19, 51, 57, 110–111
Conditioned reflex, 55–57
Confucianism, 69, 93

Dao, xiv, 79, 96, 187–188
  as original human nature, xx, 81, 83, 187–188
Daoism, 69, 92–93
  cultivation (meditation) method of, 76–80, 83–90, 92–97
Demonic states, xxii, 19
Depth psychology, xiv, xxxii, 51, 80–81, 179–181

Descartes, Rene, 9, 45, 168
Dhāranī, 24
Dōgen, xiv, 21–23
Dualism, xv, 9–10, 164, 168
correlative (provisional), 40–41, 52, 146, 168, 172–173
disjunctive (Cartesian), 37, 41, 172

Eastern medicine, 61–63. *See also* Acupuncture medicine
etiology of, 109–110
and *ki*-energy, 155
and *kikō* research, 155
and paranormal research, 154–155
and psychosomatic medicine, 110
treatment of patient in, 132
Ego-consciousness, 45, 52, 87
and supression of extraordinary ability, 151
Eisai, 21
Electroencephalograph (EEG), 59, 142–146
Emotion, 110
as flow of *ki,* xxiv, 111
physiological psychology of, 50–51, 53–55, 56–58
Esoteric Buddhism, 11–12, 15–16
Extraordinary ability. *See* Paranormal phenomena

Freud, Sigmund, 37–38, 80–81, 92, 151, 171, 182
FUJIWARA Shunzei, 24

Galvanic skin response (GSR), xxiv, 113–118
Genshin, 83
Gù Hánsēn, 133–138, 155

Hasted, John, 163
Hè Chóngyín, 149–155
Head, Henry, 120
zones of hyperalgesia, 114–115
Herrigel, Eugen, xx, 74–76, 88
Human being,
Christian view of, 9–10
Eastern view of, xii, 107, 108–109, 187–188
Gnostic and alchemic views of, 197n.7
historical character of, 169–170
Jung's view of, 174
and nature, xiii, xxxiv, 109, 188
Husserl, Edmund, 45, 120, 121, 122–123

Ippen, 23

Jikaku Ennin, 12
Jung, C. G., xiv, xxii, 17–18, 42, 148, 151, 174
criticism of parapsychological research, 169–171, 184–186
on religion and science, 98, 178
on self-nature (*Selbst*), 80–82
on synchronicity, xxviii, xxxi, xxxiii, 145, 170–171, 174, 175–176, 183–187
on the unconscious, 80, 171–172, 182–183

Kant, I., xxxiii, 178
KAWASE Ken'ichi, 70, 73
Ki research, xxvii–xxix. *See also* *Kikō,* research on
in China, 131–142, 166–167, 171
in Japan, 112–118, 142–147
measurement of external emission, 134–147
and parapsychological research, xxxiii, 155–156, 167, 186
and science, xii, 146, 148, 166–168, 171
Ki-energy (*ki*), xx–xxiv, xxvii, 75, 76, 110, 116–118, 141–142, 148, 186–188, 194n.9

exchange of, with external world, 108–109, 121–122
external emission, xxvii, 131–148
flow of, as emotion, xxiii–xxiv, 111
as function of Dao, 187–188
and *kikō* research, 155–156
and the martial arts, 70, 73–76
and mind, 88–89
and mind-body dualism, x, 69, 108–109, 118, 141–142, 164, 168
and paranormal phenomena, 167, 186
as psychophysical third term, xii, xxiv–xxv, 117–118, 141
synchronization of, xxvii–xxviii, 145–148
and teleology, 177–178
transformation of, xx–xxi, 79–80, 87, 88–89
and the unconscious, 110
unification of mind with, xix–xx, 70–71, 73–76
yīn-yáng polarity of, xx–xxi, 78, 84–87, 93–95
Kikō (*ki*-training), xxvi-xxvii, 76, 77, 131–132, 148. *See also Ki* research
research on, 149, 155–156, 174

Leibniz, G., xxxi, 109, 174
Lín, Hoùshěng, 133–138
Lombroso, Cesare, 62
LSD, 18
Luria, A. R., 157

MacDougall, William, 161
Makashikan, 10–12, 16
Mandala, 15–16
Martial arts, xix, 28–36, 70–76
and the body, 71–73
breathing methods in, 73–76
and emotion, 32–33
and Western sports, 32, 34–35
Medicine, Western, 61–63
the body in, 72, 103
mind-body dualism in, 37
normal-abnormal distinction in, 61–63
as reductionistic, 39–40
view of sickness, 37–38
Meditation, xviii, 17, 20–23, 53–54, 80, 82, 83, 88. *See also* Daoism, cultivation (meditation) in; Self-cultivation; Zen, meditation in
breathing exercise in, xviii, 58, 88
confirmatory experiences in, 93–95
and depth psychology, 16–17, 96
image experiences in, 90–95
and psychotherapy, 17–20
Meier, Carl A., 172
Memory, xxv–xxvi, 47–48, 52, 123–128
Meridians (of *ki*),
flow of *ki* in, xxvii, 76, 101–103
sensitive person, 112–113
system of, 84–87, 100–106, 114–119, 121–122
as unconscious quasi-body, xxvii, 119, 121–122
and Western medicine, 100–101
yīn-yáng grouping, 84, 100, 101–102
Merleau-Ponty, M., xxv–xxvi, 44, 45, 119–123, 128
Mikkyō. See Esoteric Buddhism
Mind, 88–89, 167, 168, 200n.28
historical nature of, 169–170
Mind-body. *See also* Body
correlative (provisional) dualism, xiv, xv, xxxii, 41, 164, 172–173, 179–181
disjunctive (Cartesian) dualism, x, xv–xvi, xxxii, 40–41, 172
Eastern theory of, xix–xx, 62–65
oneness of, x, 21–22, 26–28, 32, 64

in subject-object relation, 28
Western theories of, xvii, 63–65
Minkowski, Eugène, 91
MOTOYAMA, Hiroshi, xxiv, 112, 114–117
Myōe, xiv, 22, 90, 93

NAGAHAMA Yoshio, 103, 111, 112
Nature, Eastern view of, xxxiv, 188
Needham, Joseph, 101
Newton, Isaac, 178, 181
NISHIDA Kitarō, 28
Nō (theater), 25–27
No-mind, xv, 22, 27–28, 31–32, 35

Original mind, 31, 33
Out-of-body experience, 94

Paranormal ability. *See* Paranormal phenomena
Paranormal phenomena, xxviii–xxxi, xxxiv, 149–153
and depth psychology, 151
and the unconscious, 151, 172
Paranormal research, 153–156. *See also Kikō,* research on
Parapsychological research, 156–167
Parapsychology, 177–178
assessment of, xxix–xxxi, 157–163
difference from psychic research, 161–162
and *ki* research, xxx, xxxiii, 155–156
and science, xxix–xxxi, 159–161, 162–163, 164–168, 170
Pauli, Wolfgang, xxxii, 177, 186
Pavlov, Ivan Petrovich, xviii, 56, 64–65
Penfield, Wilder, xvi, 40–41, 44, 52
Pinch, T. J., 159
Pribram, Karl, 40, 52, 101
Psi ability. *See* Paranormal phenomena
Psychophysical energy. *See Ki*-energy
Psychosomatic medicine, xxiii, xxxii, 38–39, 146, 176–181

Qì. See Ki-energy
Qián Xuésēn, 149, 155–156, 163
Qìgōng. See Kikō

Rhine, J. B., xxix, 157–158, 160–162, 169
Rousselle, Erwin, 77–79, 82

Samādhi, 11–14, 198n.10. *See also* Meditation
through continual sitting, 11–12,
through continual walking, 11, 12–14
Saussure, F., 125
Schmidt, H., 163
Schrodinger, Erwin, 177
Science
critique of, x, xii, xxix–xxx, 166, 168, 186–187
and ethical meaning, xxiii, 175–176
and *ki*-energy, 168
and mind-body relation, 108, 168, 179
objectivistic and subjectivistic, xxxii, 178–182, 193n.6, 194n.8
and philosophy, 178, 181
principle of causality, xxxi, 170–171
principle of repeatability, 162–163, 165–166
The Secret of the Golden Flower, xx–xxii, 83–90, 92–96
Self, 35, 80–82
and body, 107–108
Self-cultivation (*shugyō*), xiii–xv, xvii–xviii, 7–8, 10, 19, 190, 196n.1. *See also* Meditation; *Samadhi*
and correlative (provisional) dualism, xiv

Daoist, 76–80, 83–90, 92–97
and physiological psychology, 54–55
Selyé, Hans
stress theory, 38–39
SHINAGAWA Yoshiya, 142, 145
Shinran, 12
Spinoza, B., xxxi, 174
Sports, Western, 34–35
and self-cultivation, xv, 8, 32–33, 60
Sū Dōngpō, 75
Supernormality, xix, 62–64
Synchonicity, xxxi–xxxiv, 183–187
and causality, xii, xxxiii, 173–174, 185
and contemporary physics, 186
teleological, xii–xiii, xxxiii, 185

Takuan, 30–32
Tanden, 70, 79–80, 83, 95
Teleology, xiii, xxxi–xxxii, 175–178
and causality, xxxi, 148
and science, 148, 175–176
and synchronicity, xxviii, 176–178
Tendai Buddhism, 11, 197n.9
Theory and practice, 35, 63–65, 98

Unconscious, 20–21, 52, 81, 111, 167
collective, xxxiii, 87, 171–174, 182–183
historical character of, 169–170
and *ki*-energy, 148
and memory, 125–127
and synchronicity, 177–178
teleological function in, xxxii, 148, 176
Unconscious quasi-body,
circuit of, xxv, 118–119
and *ki*-energy, xxvii, 119
meridian system as, 119, 121–122

Waka, 24–25
Wáng Yángmíng, 77–78
Wassilieff, Nikolai, 156–157
Wigner, Eugene P., xxxiv, 163, 186
Wilhelm, Richard, 83, 87

Xuánzhuàng, 91, 98

YAGYŪ Munenori, 30
YAMATORI Shigeru, 124–125
Yán Xīn, 156
Yìjíng, xxxiv, 94, 107, 187–188
Yoga, 60, 79
Yūgen, 24
YUKAWA Hideki, 160

Zeami, 25, 27
Zen Buddhism, 21–23, 92
meditation in, 14–15, 90
satori, xiv, 22
Zen sickness, xxii, 19, 92
Zhūzǐ, 77, 81